THE NEW ELEMENTS
OF MATHEMATICS

Charles S. Peirce as a young man (about 20 years old).

(From the Charles S. Peirce Collection in the Houghton Library, Harvard University).

THE
NEW ELEMENTS
OF
MATHEMATICS

by

CHARLES S. PEIRCE

Edited by

CAROLYN EISELE

VOLUME I
ARITHMETIC

1976

MOUTON PUBLISHERS
THE HAGUE – PARIS

HUMANITIES PRESS
ATLANTIC HIGHLANDS N. J.

© Copyright 1976
Mouton & Co. B.V., Publishers, The Hague

ISBN 90 279 3174 7

The American edition published in 1976 by Humanities Press Inc.
Atlantic Highlands, N.J. 07716

Library of Congress Cataloging in Publication Data

Peirce, Charles S.
Arithmetic

(His The new elements of mathematics; v. I)
Includes index.
I. Arithmetic – 1961-   I. Title.
QA39.2.P42 vol. I [QA107] 510'.8s [513] 76-10942
ISBN 0 391 00612 6

Printed in the Netherlands

GRATEFUL ACKNOWLEDGMENT

The production of these volumes has been made possible through the partial support of

        The National Science Foundation
        The American Philosophical Society
        The John Dewey Foundation

Tasso: I've struggled day and night against this need;
        I'm worn out with the contest in my breast.
        It's useless! Sing I must or life's not life.
        Forbid the silkworm's spinning industry,
        On pain of death, but he will still go on
        Drawing the costly web from his entrails
        And leave not off until his cerecloth's done.

From a translation by Peirce of a
section of Goethe's *Torquato Tasso* for
William Hirsch's *Genius and
Degeneration* (MS. 1517)

It is not a hankering after applause and success nor a regard for his in-
terests which make the artist of genius work. It is solely hankering to
give shape to the work of art that exists in his mind. The true poet does
not versify because he will but because he must. Goethe has painted
this poetic impulse in Tasso.

(MS. 1118)

PREFACE

It is believed by many scholars that all Peirce materials worthy of further scholarly probing have already appeared in the *Collected Papers of Charles Sanders Peirce*, vols. I-VI, edited by Charles Hartshorne and Paul Weiss, and vols. VII and VIII edited by Arthur W. Burks. There is a belief also that Murray G. Murphey in his *Development of Peirce's Philosophy* has definitively summarized Peirce's mathematical thought in elucidating his own thesis on Peirce, especially in the discussion of Peirce's conception of "multitude" and its application to his philosophical architectonic.

But Peirce's widely diversified researches as a pure mathematician have yet to be understood, yet to be assessed, yet to be related to the developments in the mathematics of his own lifetime. The unpublished manuscripts are to be found, for the most part, in the Charles S. Peirce Collection in the Houghton Library, Harvard University. Unless otherwise indicated, the materials in these volumes are from that Collection.

The editor has attempted in the several introductions to provide in the rough the background against which Peirce's thought may be evaluated. They are not intended to evaluate critically Peirce's mathematical output, a task that competent scholars in diverse fields must face in the coming years. The editor's responsibility has been that of making accessible in some cohesive form the major elements of Peirce's mathematical activity. Peirce's unflagging hope of success in his efforts to ape his father and other mathematical contemporaries in the profitable venture of textbook writing makes it possible at the present time to present the spectrum of his mathematical thought beginning with the simplest elements in arithmetic and ending with his general mathematical philosophy. Despite the fact that some of the material is now clearly dated, although by no means obsolete, one finds refreshment always in Peirce's integrated presentation of the diverse branches of mathematics, arrayed as they often are in the context of the metaphysical problems that crowded in on his thought. But most surprising is the mathematical foresight and openmindedness that impelled him to adopt a teaching stance in the eighteen-nineties that has come to be advocated and officially implemented on the highest academic levels seventy-five years later. A short notice of Peirce's philosophy of education in mathematics by the editor of these papers appears in the Second Series of *Studies in the Philosophy of Charles Sanders Peirce*, edited by E. C. Moore and R. S. Robin.

To avoid unnecessary duplication in dating of manuscripts, etc., the editor assumes that the *Annotated Catalogue of the Papers of Charles S. Peirce* by Richard S. Robin (University of Massachusetts Press, 1967) is accessible to the reader desiring further detail. Manuscript numbers used here correspond to those appearing there. The "s" designation refers to "The Peirce Papers: A Supplementary Catalogue," by Richard S. Robin, in *Transactions of the Charles S. Peirce society* 7:1 (1971). She also reminds the reader that some mathematical studies already appear in the *Collected Papers*. These have not been duplicated. In preparing materials for publication the editor has attempted to minimize footnote commentary. A reading of the entire text will bring Peirce's own answer to many a question. For his writings shimmer with the light of revelation. Peirce's footnotes are incorporated in the body of the text in parentheses. Brackets enclose editorial addenda. Editorial footnotes carry numeral identification in the usual way. References to paragraphs in the *Collected Works* will be made in standard fashion, i.e. 4.212 means paragraph 212 in Volume 4.

In the preparation of manuscript tampering with punctuation and spelling has been minimized. For Peirce observed certain psychological principles underlying punctuation, especially in the use of the comma. "We ought to make it a rule that the burden shall lie upon every mark of punctuation of proving its possible utility" (MS. 1221). As to spelling, Peirce wrote: "I would suggest that every man who thinks that the tyranny of orthography ought to be broken down should regard it as a duty to begin spelling a few words, — not so many as to shock people very badly, — in a rational way; and let every man make his own selection, for the very purpose of disproving the popular prejudice that all educated people spell one way. For instance, I have for some time been asserting my individual liberty so far as to write most words in *ise* by *ize*, to spell *intrinsec*, and to indulge a few other protests against the tyrant. I know very well that I am in consequence of this heroic deed, generally set down as a semi-educated crank and nihilist; but I mean to wear the crown of martyrdom with a smile. C." (MS. 1204). The editor has retained *intrinsec* although there have been other changes, notably in Peirce's *indispensible*.

The editor has been privileged to gather together and coordinate these materials with the aid of so many helping hands that these acknowledgments will surely fail of being complete. Yet specific mention must be made of the continual interest, encouragement, and sponsorship of Carl Boyer and I. Bernard Cohen; of Max Fisch and Victor Lenzen; of the permission of the Philosophy Department at Harvard University to examine and use the Peirce manuscripts under its auspices, and of the confidence of the Department in the worthiness of the end result of such a study; of the particular interest of Donald Williams and Burton Dreben of that Department and of the late Ruth Allen; of the financial support in the early stages of the research on the part of the National Science Foundation and of the American Philosophical Society; of the special help of Carolyn Jakeman and her staff at the Houghton Library of Harvard University where the Peirce manuscripts are preserved; of the very special cooperation of the staffs of the Archives Section and of the Duplicating Office at Widener Library, and of Frank Giella of Duplicating Services at Hunter College; of the staff of Special Collections at Columbia University in making accessible materials in the D. E. Smith Collection; of the sympathetic understanding and appreciation of Dean Kerby-Miller of Harvard University and of Eleanor Ross in making possible for the editor the privilege of special residence as a visiting scholar in Cambridge during the preparation of manuscript; of the encouragement and advice of Joseph D. Elder, former Science Editor of the Harvard University Press; of the interest of Ernest Nagel that has eased the last stages of publication. The editor is most grateful to Peter de Ridder of Mouton Publishers for the vision and enthusiasm that brought at last to the printed page this lengthy chapter in the story of Peirce's intellectual life; and to Joel Kasow, the editor of this material at Mouton, for his meticulous care and dedicated labors towards the completion of this task. Mr. Alexander R. James has graciously given permission for the publication of three letters from the William James Collection at Houghton Library (Peirce to James [18 April 1903 (2) and 25 December 1909]). But the individuals to whom the editor is most deeply indebted are Max and Ruth Fisch whose close association in Peirce researches over many years has been an inspiration always. Their helping hands made negotiable many a rough passage along the road to this presentation of Peirce's thought in mathematics.

Gratitude must be expressed also to Victoria Raymer who undertook the task of transliterating Greek forms into Roman, as they appear in the Appendix. Peirce sprinkles his writings freely with Greek allusion and only rarely does he transliterate. There is today no established universal system of transliteration. The equivalents, as used in this work, are often chosen nowadays because they readily identify Greek words with related English loan words while not removing them two steps from the Greek, as was the case years ago when they were first "Latinized." The reader will occasionally find a Greek word appearing twice, spelled in each of two different ways, e.g. *cae, kai.* The first version is Peirce's own transliteration, which he sometimes supplies in his manuscript, the second a rendering of the word he wrote in Greek letters. Peirce's system of transliteration, the traditional "Latinizing" one, has not been adopted in this edition because it is not in general use today.

Appreciation is expressed at this point, too, of the heroic typing of manuscript undertaken by Nancy Donovan whose early commitment to the Peirce cause carried her through many an endless tedious page in the copying of manuscript.

The early stages of this study were supported by two sets of grants: one, institutional grants from the National Science Foundation to Hunter College with the editor as Director, GS-419 and GS-1276; the other from the American Philosophical Society, Penrose Fund #3618 and the Johnson Fund #668. Without them, the undertaking of the project would have been impossible. A subvention from the John Dewey Foundation has aided substantially in effecting the publication of these volumes.

Should anyone wonder why the editor was willing to devote so many years of labor to the organization of these materials in their present form, she would wish to quote the late Leonard Dickson in the preface to the second volume of his *History of the Theory of Numbers*. For he explained there that he had made this great effort over a period of nine years "because it fitted in with his convictions that every person should aim to perform at some time in his life some serious, useful work for which it is highly improbable that there will be any reward whatever other than his satisfaction therefrom."

Carolyn Eisele

Hunter College of the City University of New York
August 1970

GENERAL INTRODUCTION

Charles S. Peirce was born in 1839 into a Cambridge family that enjoyed the finest academic connections to be found in the United States at that time. His father, Benjamin, came to be the most highly regarded American mathematician of his generation, holding, as he did, the Perkins Chair in Mathematics and Astronomy at Harvard (1842-1880), after having served that institution as University Professor of Mathematics during the previous nine years. He became Superintendent of the Coast and Geodetic Survey for the period 1867-1874, and its Consulting Geometer over a long span of time. He was one of the most influential men of science in the country, being a prime agent in the founding of the National Academy of Sciences. In an American Mathematical Society Semicentennial address in 1938 George Birkhoff quoted A. Lawrence Lowell, former President of Harvard University, in the following words: "Looking back over the space of fifty years when I entered Harvard College, Benjamin Peirce still impresses me as the most massive intellect with which I have ever come into close contact, as being the most profoundly inspiring teacher that I have ever had. His personal appearance, his powerful frame and his majestic head seemed in harmony with his brain."

It is generally conceded that America was afflicted with mathematical sterility during the first three hundred years of its existence, its mathematical needs arising mostly from surveying, map-making, and problems in astronomy. As for native mathematicians there was Nathaniel Bowditch (1773-1838), author of *The New American Practical Navigator* that came to be used the world over. His contribution to mathematical research may be appraised by his 1815 paper entitled "On the motion of a pendulum suspended from two points" and from his English translation (1829-1839) of the first four volumes of Laplace's *Traité de mécanique céleste* (1798-1805) with notes and commentary. Then there was Robert

Adrain (1775-1843), mathematician, physicist, and astronomer, who edited Hutton's *Course in Mathematics* and gave an original proof of the law of least squares, with investigations relating to the figure of the earth and the study of "g" at different latitudes.

But it was not until the 1880s that a flowering of native mathematical talent was to be found on the American scene. In his historical survey of "Fifty Years of Algebra in America (1888-1938)" written for the *American Mathematical Society Semicentennial Publications* (vol. II), E. T. Bell remarked that "Sylvester's enthusiasm for algebra during his professorship at the Johns Hopkins University in 1877-1883 was without doubt the first significant influence the United States had experienced in its attempt to lift itself out of the mathematical barbarism it appears to have enjoyed prior to 1878. Elementary instruction was good enough, perhaps better than it is today; research on the European level, with one or two conspicuous exceptions, was non-existent." Bell notes that the United States had had but one great algebraist. And yet "Benjamin Peirce made only a negligible impression on his American contemporaries in algebra, and his work was not appreciated by their immediate successors until it had received the nod of European condescension." Dirk Struik also deemed Benjamin Peirce's linear associative algebra to be the first major original contribution to mathematical progress in the United States. Indeed, before the time of Benjamin Peirce research was not considered to be one of the basic responsibilities of a mathematics department at a university.

At the beginning of the fifty-year period (1888-1938), linear algebra was still in the tradition of Peirce. Bell speaks of a new American tradition being set up around 1905 in the work of Dickson, Wedderburn, and Albert. More specifically, "the year 1905 is also memorable in the subject for Wedderburn's proof that a Galois field is the only algebra with a finite number of elements that is a linear associative division algebra in the domain of real numbers, the analogue for finite algebras of the theorem of Frobenius and C. S. Peirce." But progress was made quickly and recognition was already being accorded the work of G. W. Hill, Simon Newcomb, G. A. Miller, and E. H. Moore around the turn of the century.

In the earlier days the mathematically talented were attracted to the work of the national scientific organizations in which there was need of applied mathematics. The Coast and Geodetic Survey was such an organization, the first scientific institution to be created by the government of the United States. It was started by act of Congress in 1807 under the superintendency of the Swiss mathematician Ferdinand Rudolph Hassler (1770-1843) whose work on the accuracy of standards led later to the establishment of the Bureau of Standards. Many of these Coast Survey workers, like Charles A. Schott, had mathematical gifts that in a later generation would have insured them high status on college campuses, a status enjoyed, indeed, by a number of them during the 1870s. Since his father was so prominent a figure in the administration of the Survey it was natural for Charles Peirce to enter the ranks of workers there, even as a lowly aide, in 1859, to specialize in a science in order, as he said, to carry out his researches in the logic of science. Further reference will be made in the introductory remarks to Volume III regarding the thirty-year accumulation of his reports in the files of the National Archives in Washington that today tell the story of his inventiveness in applied mathematics, and of his skills in using tools that bespeak talent in pure mathematics as well.

The bureau for the *American Ephemeris and Nautical Almanac* was another institution that attracted the gifted in mathematics, talented men like Chauncey Wright. It was organized in 1849 and Benjamin Peirce was its Consultant in Astronomy from the very beginning until 1867. Charles Henry Davis, an uncle of Charles Peirce, was to become its Superintendent in 1865 as well as the Superintendent of the Naval Observatory. Then, too, Abraham Lincoln founded in 1863 the National Academy of Sciences with A. D. Bache as its first President. The Academy harbored a few mathematicians, and Charles Peirce, who was elected to membership on 18 April 1877, read many papers there. However, an amusing story is told of a meeting at which Benjamin Peirce spent an hour filling the blackboard with equations only to remark: "There is only one member of the Academy who can understand my work and he is in South America."

As has been observed, mathematics in America began to flourish with the advent of Sylvester on the academic scene at the newly established Johns Hopkins University. President Gilman had been given permission to engage the best mathematical talent available for the chairmanship of the mathematics department there and with the appointment of Sylvester, American mathematical horizons widened tremendously. Sylvester's mathematical vitality and his ability to inspire others to great achievement nourished the nucleus of a powerful mathematical group, the equal of its European counterparts. In collaboration with W. E. Story, Sylvester founded in 1878 *The American Journal of Mathematics*, published by the Johns Hopkins University. In an address in 1904, Thomas Fiske, then President of the American Mathematical Society, spoke of the first ten volumes as containing about ninety different writers, thirty from foreign countries and about thirty as being Sylvester's pupils. Among the contributors to the early numbers were such scholars as Sylvester himself, Cayley, Hill, Josiah Gibbs, C. S. Peirce, Benjamin Peirce, Simon Newcomb, Thomas Craig, Emery McClintock, all endeavoring to broaden the frontiers of current mathematical knowledge. Craig and Newcomb were both members of the Coast and Geodetic Survey forces even as the two Peirces were.

Associated with Sylvester as teachers on the staff at the University were Thomas Craig and William E. Story and Fabian Franklin. J. W. Gibbs lectured in the Physics Department. Cayley came from England as a special lecturer for a year in the spring of 1882 and conducted seminars during two semesters. At the April meeting of the Mathematics Seminar in 1882, Cayley spoke on "Associative Imaginaries," and said, "I did not perceive how to identify the system with any of the double algebras of B. Peirce's *Linear Associative Algebra*...; but it has been pointed out to me by Mr. C. S. Peirce, that my system in the general case ad-bc, not equal to zero, is expressible as a mixture of two algebras ...."

Charles Peirce's blossoming into what today would be regarded as a professional mathematician was accelerated by his affiliation in the fall of 1879 with the new Johns Hopkins University. By this time his activities on the European scene as well as on home grounds as Assistant in the Coast and Geodetic Survey had established his reputation as an outstanding scientist. He had managed also to publish in professional journals enough of his researches in logic to warrant an invitation to join the staff at The Johns Hopkins University as Lecturer on Logic, offering other courses in the Mathematics Department as well. Over the ensuing five-year period he was to lecture on medieval logic, advanced logic, probabilities, methods of science including methods of mathematics, and the logic of relatives. During that time his courses attracted more students from the Mathematics Department than from any other Division at the University. He also conducted a mathematics seminar on relative forms of quaternions. Illustrative of his mathematical status is the report of a meeting of the Mathematics Seminar, January 1882, when Sylvester and Cayley and Peirce were the speakers, Peirce speaking on "Relative Forms of Quaternions."

Although Peirce's association with the University was abruptly terminated in 1884, it is apparent from his writings that his thought thereafter was of a mathematical cast not to be found so explicitly in the pre-Johns Hopkins period. Had this association with a professionally oriented group of mathematicians not been denied him, he might have become even more deeply concerned with the discovery and proof of new theory — and not essentially in the examination of the validity of the logical processes involved in proof. But the University contact had brought him very far at that into mathematical foundations: number theory, topology, projective geometry, existential graphs and, above all, speculations on the nature of the continuum.

Another organization that accelerated the pace and depth of mathematical research on the American scene after 1885 was the American Mathematical Society organized originally as the New York Mathematical Society. After Thomas Fiske had returned from post-graduate studies at Cambridge University, England, he joined Edward W. Stabler and Harold Jacoby in establishing a mathematical society in New York that might encourage a stronger feeling of comradeship among those interested in mathematics. Thus was born on Thanksgiving Day (24 November 1888), at ten in the morning, the New York Mathematical Society with six members. Membership was by election and by 1890 the number of members had been increased to twenty-three. Charles S. Peirce, B.Sc., M.A., member of the National Academy of Sciences, was elected at the November meeting in 1891, the year in which the genius Carl Steinmetz became a member. Moreover, by this time Peirce was already a member of the London Mathematical Society.

Thomas Fiske had been influential in attracting Steinmetz to membership in the group and in making the now flourishing Society the reality that had been but his personal dream in 1888. Some of Fiske's reminiscences are in the *American Mathematical Society Semicentennial Publications* (vol. I). He recalls that

conspicuous among those who attended the meetings of the Society in the early nineties was the famous logician Charles S. Peirce. His dramatic manner, his reckless disregard of accuracy in "unimportant" details, his clever newspaper articles (in *The Evening Post* and *The New York Times*) on the activities of the young Society, interested and amused us all. He was the adviser of the New York Public Library for the purchase of scientific books, and wrote the mathematical definitions for the *Century Dictionary*. He was always hard up, living partly on what he could borrow from friends, partly on what he got from odd jobs like writing for the newspapers. He seemed equally brilliant whether under the influence of liquor or otherwise. His company was prized by the various organizations to which he belonged; and so he was never dropped from membership even though he failed to pay his dues. He infuriated Charlotte Angus Scott by contributing to the *Evening Post* an unsigned obituary of Arthur Cayley, in which he stated, upon no grounds whatsoever, that Cayley had inherited his genius from a Russian mother.

Now Cayley's mother was English. His father and uncle were both English merchants in St. Petersburg. Arthur was born during a visit of his parents in England and he did not return to England until he was eight years old. Fiske continues with the following statement:

At a meeting of the Society in November 1894 in an eloquent oration on the nature of mathematics, C. S. Peirce proclaimed that the intellectual powers essential to the mathematician are "Concentration, imagination, and generalization." Then, after a dramatic pause, he cried, "Did I hear someone say demonstration? Why, my friends," he added, "demonstration is but the pavement on which the chariot of the mathematician rolls."

Fiske's recollection of Peirce's service to the Astor Library in New York brings to mind the copy of the letter in the files of that institution from J. M. Markoe to Peirce written on 4 June 1890. It reads: "I write to thank you on behalf of the Astor Library for your very full and valuable lists of works on mathematical subjects which you deem worthy of a place in our Collection. It is a great help to us in selecting books to have such a careful and thorough examination made for us by an expert, and we would be glad at any time to receive suggestions from you in the future." That mathematics collection is still, incidentally, of great use to mathematicians.

   We learn from the first volume of the *Bulletin of the New York Mathematical Society* that "Mr. Charles S. Peirce attended a regular meeting of the Society on Saturday afternoon November 7, 1891." But of still greater interest was his active participation in the presentation of not one but two papers during the year 1894. At the meeting on 7 April

Peirce exhibited an arithmetic of 1424 from the valuable collection of Mr. George A. Plimpton of New York. It is an extensive manuscript work written in Latin, and has been entirely unknown to the historians of mathematics. The author was Rollandus, a Portuguese physician, known for a work upon surgery and another upon physiognomy. He was a minor canon of the Sainte-Chapelle and a protégé of John of Lancaster, to whom the arithmetic bears a flowery dedication.

Peirce's correspondence with Thomas Fiske and H. B. Fine and E. H. Moore and other prominent mathematicians associated with the Society that became the American Mathematical Society in 1894 will be treated in a later place. But one communication from Fiske to Peirce on behalf of the Committee on Publication (27 February 1894) deserves mention here. Fiske wrote:

Ever since we began the publication of our Journal, *The Bulletin of the New York*

Mathematical Society, we have been very desirous of securing for publication some contribution from your pen.

We hope that in the near future you may find it convenient to favor us in this manner.

Would it not be possible for us to reap the advantage of your experience and observations in connection with your work on the *Century Dictionary* in an article, to be written by you, and entitled, say, "English Mathematical Nomenclature."

In April, Fiske again invited Peirce to "throw" his remarks on Rollandus "into a form for publication in the *Bulletin*." Peirce had already written a report of the meeting and had included in it his own translation from the Latin of the "flowery dedication" to John of Lancaster. This story was published in *The New York Times* on Sunday, 8 April.

Hence one concludes that Peirce's interest in attendance at meetings was that of the professional mathematician and that he was influenced in his thought in those years by what was presented there. Particularly important to the story of that influence on Peirce's educational philosophy was the advent of Felix Klein on the American scene. Klein had come to deliver the inaugural address on 21 August 1893 at the general session of the International Congress of Mathematicians and Astronomers in Chicago held in connection with the International Exposition there, and these remarks were available to all in the October issue of *The Monist* under the title "The Present State of Mathematics." Klein was the Honorary President of the Mathematical Congress and W. E. Story, the President. The Evanston Colloquium was sponsored by Northwestern University and Klein delivered his famous series of lectures there from 28 August to 9 September. Moreover on 30 September, a meeting of the New York Mathematical Society was called for the special purpose of giving its members an opportunity to meet Klein. Klein addressed them on a non-Euclidean development of spherical trigonometry by Dr. Schilling "in which the fundamental formulae found a real geometrical interpretation when applied to a generalized spherical triangle whose sides and angles have complex values." He then outlined the then recent investigations by himself and Professor Study of the University of Marburg. Klein was present again at another meeting of the Society in October 1896 at Princeton, in connection with the sesquicentennial celebration of that University.

The Society brought Klein's philosophy and influence to bear on the course of mathematics and its teaching in America by publishing in the July *Bulletin* of 1893 an English translation of Klein's Erlanger Programm, his dissertation on entering the Philosophical Faculty and the

Senate of the University of Erlangen in 1872 now entitled "A Comparative Review of Recent Researches in Geometry." It is therefore to be assumed that Peirce was well aware of the philosophy of this great teacher and organizer of the then current developments in mathematics. Klein's mission became that of publicizing such mathematical advances to all persons whose business was mathematics. It was Klein who generalized Cayley's demonstration that Euclidean metrics may be regarded as a special aspect of projective geometry in his own description of three metric geometries, the *elliptic* (Riemann), the *hyperbolic* (Lobachevsky), and the *parabolic* (Euclid). Indeed Peirce owned a copy of the lithographed lectures of Klein on *Nicht-Euklidische Geometrie* I and II, given at Göttingen during the winter-session 1889-1890, and the summer of 1890. It reposes, with his marginal notations, in the Harvard University Library today. A companion piece, *Riemannische Flächen*, Vorlesung von F. Klein, is also there as a gift from Mrs. Charles Peirce. The many uncut pages seem to imply a tepid reception on Peirce's part. He also owned a copy of the translation into English by George G. Morrice of Klein's *Lectures on the Ikosahedron*. Peirce had undoubtedly been acquainted with the subject matter much earlier since "Klein's Ikosaheder" by F. N. Cole appeared in the *American Journal of Mathematics* IX (1886-1887).

Evidence of Klein's influence runs all through Peirce's manuscripts as he attempts to follow Klein's suggestions. A few of Peirce's scattered notations remain in the last-mentioned book, which in the rebinding has had many of the marginal notations cut away. On page 30, Peirce directs one to see the fly-leaf at the end that is, alas, no longer there.

But Peirce was undoubtedly influenced in his mathematical and educational philosophy by the many *Bulletin* items that reflected the new revolution in mathematical thought, especially in geometry. A hasty sampling of some of the papers brings to light, for example, Newcomb's "Modern Mathematical Thought," an address delivered at the annual meeting of the Society, 28 December 1893, and printed in the January 1894 issue. He is quoted as saying:

The mathematics of the twenty-first century may be very different from our own; perhaps the schoolboy will begin algebra with the theory of substitution-groups, as he might now but for inherited habits. But it does not follow that our posterity will solve many problems which we have attacked in vain, or invent an algorithm more powerful than the calculus.

Earlier in the paper Newcomb took the same stand one finds in a letter to Peirce, 24 December 1891, and published by the editor in the "Charles

S. Peirce-Simon Newcomb Correspondence" (*Proceedings of the American Philosophical Society* 101: 5). Newcomb disapproved of the "concept of what is sometimes called curved space," as he did not see "how space itself can be regarded as curved. Geometry is not the science of space, but the science of figures in space, possessing the properties of extension and mobility which we find to be common to all material bodies. The question raised here is a very old one, and in a general way its history is familiar." This was the voice of scientific conservatism with which Peirce was inclined to be in open rebellion.

Other papers of undoubted interest to Peirce in those years were G. W. Hill's "Application of Analysis to Polyhedra" read at a meeting, 2 December 1893; Vasiliev's "Lobachevsky as Algebraist and Analyst," June 1894; E. McClintoch's "On the non-Euclidean geometry," *Bulletin* II, 1892-1893, and his "On the Early History of the Non-Euclidean Geometry," *Bulletin*, March 1893; W. Woolsey Johnson's "A Case of non-Euclidean geometry," April 1893; Maxime Bôcher's address on 4 June 1892 on "Collineation as a Mode of Motion," in which Clebsch and Klein are prominently referred to.

Peirce undoubtedly was influenced also by the work of George Bruce Halsted, the prolific American writer on non-Euclidean geometry who took his post-graduate work under Sylvester at the Johns Hopkins University after his graduation from Princeton in 1875 and who was later to inspire L. Dickson, R. L. Moore, and H. B. Fine to aspire to careers in mathematics. In his biographical statement on Felix Klein in *The American Mathematical Monthly* 1 (December 1894), Halsted called attention to Peirce in speaking of Klein's five theses in his doctoral dissertation. "It may be interesting, as characteristic of this germinating state, to note that of his five theses, the second calls attention to one of Cauchy's slips in logical rigor, slips now known to be so numerous that C. S. Peirce makes of them a paradox, maintaining that the fruitfulness of Cauchy's work is essentially connected with its logical inaccuracy." Halsted's articles on non-Euclidean geometry were run serially during 1894 and 1895, in volumes I and II of *The American Mathematical Monthly* under the title of "Non-Euclidean Geometry, Historical and Expository." He published an account of "Lambert's non-Euclidean Geometry" in the *Bulletin* (1893-1894), and "The non-Euclidean Geometry Inevitable" in volume IV of *The Monist* (1893-1894), a journal to which Peirce was also a contributor. He was to translate later into English, from the Italian, Doria's "Sketch of the Origin and Development of Geometry Prior to 1850" (in *The Monist* 13 [1902-1903]). Halsted published several textbooks in geometry after he became a professor of mathematics at the University of Texas at Austin, and his *Elementary Synthetic Geometry* was praised at home and abroad for its originality. His English translation of *Nicholaus Lobatschewsky's Non-Euclidean Geometry* appeared in 1891 and of *John Bolyai's Science Absolute of Space* in 1893. His translation of *Girolamo Saccheri's Euclides Vindicatus* did not appear until 1920. He published an extensive "Bibliography of Hyper-space and non-Euclidean Geometry" in the very first volume of the *American Journal of Mathematics*. A copy of Halsted's article-review in *Science* (9 June 1899) of *Urkunden zur Geschichte der nichteuklidischen Geometrie, I. Nikolai Ivanovitsch Lobatschefski* by F. Engel and P. Staeckel are among the Peirce items presented to the Widener Library by Peirce's widow.

The foregoing gives some awareness of the persons and the publications that helped to shape Peirce's thought on the "new mathematics" of his time. In depicting him as a mathematician it will help also to examine references that were made to his mathematical talents by his peers. One recalls Sylvester's belief that Charles's mathematical talents might indeed have exceeded those of his father, Benjamin. Max Fisch tells that E. L. Youmans in a letter to his sister from London (29 October 1877) said that "Charles Peirce isn't much read on this side. Clifford, however, says he is the greatest living logician, and the second man since Aristotle who has added to the subject something material, the other being George Boole, author of *The Laws of Thought*."

Yet Peirce felt that his real power lay in logic rather than in mathematics. That was said at a time when the lines between the two fields were tightly drawn in terms of medieval categorization. Peirce's kind of logic, that of Boole, is today an acknowledged part of the mathematical discipline. He himself once wrote, "It does not seem to me that mathematics depends in any way upon logic.... On the contrary, I am persuaded that logic cannot possibly attain the solution of its problems without great use of mathematics. Indeed all formal logic is merely mathematics applied to logic."

It is baffling to today's scholar to find so reliable an authority as Smith and Ginsburg in *A History of Mathematics in America before 1900* overlooking, perhaps as a result of Peirce's underestimation of his own mathematical powers, the very real mathematical contributions that Peirce made, even in the applied field. For example, they list the American mathematicians who gave particular attention to the problem of the pendulum. Bowditch, Adrain, Farrar, Newcomb, Mendenhall are all mentioned. But there is no reference in any form to C. S. Peirce whose geodetic researches in his time won the acclaim of the international community of geodesists and mathematicians. He was the Assistant of the Coast Survey in charge of the measurement of gravity and the determination of the figure of the earth. Not only was he conversant with the mathematical tricks of that trade but in meeting challenging new problems he was most inventive in the use of the calculus of finite differences. In a Coast Survey report dated 23 September 1875 he speaks of having "assisted at the seances of the International Geodetical Association and also of the Permanent Commission, where the subject of pendulums has been minutely discussed," while he was on a Coast Survey mission in Paris. He had been invited to attend these meetings as an individual and subsequently made a lasting contribution in a twenty-three page report entitled "De l'influence de la flexibilité du trépied sur l'oscillation du pendule à reversion," which was read for him at Geneva on 27 October 1877, and in which he confirmed his original criticisms. The recent researches and writings of Victor Lenzen on this subject highlight Peirce as a leader in this field. Then, too, there was his clever use of an elliptic function in his invention of the quincuncial map projection which was originally published by the Coast Survey in Appendix 15 (1877) as well as in the *American Journal of Mathematics* (1879). Further details may be found in "Charles S. Peirce and the. Problem of Map-Projection" by the editor in *Proceedings of the American Philosophical Society* 107:4.

One finds in the D. E. Smith correspondence in Special Collections at Columbia University that Smith was chided by both Cajori and J. Coolidge for not having fully appreciated the talents of this son of Benjamin. Coolidge complained in a letter dated 21 March 1934 that though he liked Smith's treatment of Benjamin Peirce in the book mentioned above, he felt that Smith could have given more credit to the "erratic" son, Charles Sanders. Cajori wrote on 27 October 1926 about a list of mathematicians that Smith had drawn up. The most serious omission, he felt, was that of C. S. Peirce whom Sylvester, he recalled, had considered an abler mathematician than Benjamin himself.

In Cajori's *History of Mathematics* Charles Peirce's work is noted in several places. In the matrix section, Cajori speaks of Peirce's representation of Grassmann's system in the logical notation. In the analytic geometry section, Cajori writes, "Thus Newcomb showed the possibility of turning a closed material shell inside out by simple flexure without either stretching or tearing; Klein pointed out that knots could not be tied; Veronese showed that a body could be removed from a closed room without breaking the walls; C. S. Peirce proved that a body in four-fold space either rotates about two axes at once, or cannot rotate without losing one of its dimensions." Smith's critical yardstick was apparently not used in all of the contemporary critical thought of his time.

George Birkoff in his "Fifty Years of American Mathematics" noted that "Although the logician and philosopher, C. S. Peirce, son of Benjamin Peirce, contributed to Boolean Algebra, definite mathematical work on this subject may be said to have begun in this country with E. V. Huntington's set of postulates of 1904." Now E. V. Huntington had published "Sets of Independent Postulates for the Algebra of Logic" in the *Transactions of the American Mathematical Society* in July 1904. The opening sentence speaks of "the algebra of symbolic logic, as developed by Leibniz, Boole, C. S. Peirce, E. Schröder, and others." It was described by Whitehead as "the only known member of the non-numerical genus of universal Algebra." In a later explanation regarding the similarity of certain of his postulates to fundamental propositions in Schröder, Huntington says: "For the possibility of this simplification I am especially indebted to Mr. C. S. Peirce who has kindly communicated to me a proof of the second part of the distributive law (22a, b) on the basis of postulate 9." Again, in the second edition of his *The Continuum and other Types of Serial Order* he writes that "Cantor has proved that when any class is given, a class can be constructed which shall have a greater cardinal number than the given class," and footnotes the names of Cantor, Borel, and C. S. Peirce, the latter's *Monist* article in vol. 16 (1906) being cited. Peirce's name did not appear, however, in the original article in the *Annals of Mathematics* (1905).

Although Peirce's name is here associated with that of Borel, he was to complain later (24 May 1908), in a note to an *Open Court* article that had been published earlier, that he had been unable to procure a copy of a particular paper by Borel that might justify his position on the matter of there being room on a line for *any* multitude of points. He admitted to not being fully satisfied with his own demonstration because it was based on a logical analysis and not on mathematical demonstration. Manuscript 203 tells of his lack of acquaintance with Borel's work.

George Birkhoff also noted that "Although the idea of lattices goes back partially to C. S. Peirce and Ernst Schröder, it was Richard Dedekind who first saw their true nature and importance." Indeed credit for basic assumptions and notations is given to Peirce in several references by Garrett Birkhoff in his *Lattice Theory*.

Benjamin's opinion of Charles's contribution to his own field may be sensed from what he says in "On the Uses and Transformations of Linear

Algebra" in the *Proceedings of the American Academy of Arts and Sciences*, an address given on 11 May 1875. Benjamin refers to the letters or units of the linear algebra, "or to use the better term proposed by Mr. Charles S. Peirce, the *vids* of these algebras," as being fitted to perform a certain function. He says that "The best definition of quadrates is that proposed by Mr. Charles S. Peirce." And again he claims that "Mr. Peirce has shown by a simple logical argument that the quadrate is the legitimate form of a complete linear algebra, and that all the forms of the algebras given by me must be imperfect quadrates, and has confirmed this conclusion by actual investigation and reduction. His investigations do not however dispense with the analysis, by which the independent forms have been deduced in my treatise, but they seem to throw much light upon their probable use." More will be said of C. S. Peirce's contributions to this field in the Introduction to Volume 3.

The foregoing represents, then, an outline of Peirce's exposure to the mathematical influences of his time. Mention has already been made of that other form of mathematical productivity — that of bringing to the student and general reader an explanation of current mathematical methodology, the writing of mathematical textbooks. In this Peirce was also an expert. But unlike other experts, he suffered from foreseeing needs that would be recognized three quarters of a century after his time when drastic attempts would be made to fill them. His own contemporaries were in no position to judge the value of his textbook output which never reached the publication stage.

Indeed the French influence in school textbooks was so strong in the U.S.A. in Peirce's time that Legendre's *Éléments de géométrie* and his *Traité de trigonométrie* served as models to textbook writers. Legendre was first translated into English by John Farrar of Harvard (1819) and was revised by Thomas Carlyle and again by Charles Davies. Charles's father also wrote elementary textbooks as did Simon Newcomb and George Halsted. The successful Beman and Smith *Geometry* appeared in 1895.

Farrar further translated the *Éléments d'algèbre* of Bourdon (1831). Charles Davies was the third person to translate Lacroix's *Éléments d'algèbre*, which met with great success. Farrar also translated Lacroix's trigonometry, his arithmetic, and the calculus of Bézout, while Davies translated Bourdon's *Application de l'algèbre a la géométrie* in his *Analytical Geometry* (1836) which went through several editions. In the Smith and Ginsburg *History* mentioned above, Benjamin Peirce is quoted as saying: "The excellent treatises on Algebra ... containing as they do the best improvements of Bourdon and the other French writers, would seem to leave nothing to be desired in this department of mathematics…. The investigation of each proposition has been conducted according to the French system of analysis." Smith and Ginsburg also tell of Charles Davies's presentation of one of his books to Lieutenant-Colonel S. Thayer, superintendent of the military academy at West Point, with the inscription: "In the organization of the military Academy under your immediate superintendence, the French methods of instruction, in the exact sciences, were adopted; and near twenty years experience has suggested few alterations in the original plan." Textbooks written and used in elementary mathematics in America up to the time of C. S. Peirce's involvement in the problem reflected little of the revolutionary mathematical thought of the mid-nineteenth century.

However by the end of the century the need of a review of mathematical curriculum and instruction throughout the world became apparent, and steps were taken at the International Congress of Mathematicians in Rome in 1908 to implement just that. A commission with Felix Klein at the head was appointed to make recommendations for the necessary changes.

Peirce anticipated such revision in his own textbook writing, as will be seen in Volume 2. His logical development of subject matter, his fruitful symbolism, his inventiveness as exemplified in existential graphing, his careful nomenclature — reflecting his work as a linguist and a contributor to dictionaries — his deep appreciation of topological structure at a time when nothing was being written to introduce the basic topological ideas on the lower school level, and little on a higher level, his fascination with non-Euclidean notions that is reflected in the appearance of the Moebius strip in his geometry even though Klein himself had advised against the introduction of non-Euclidean concepts on so low a level in his Evanston lectures, all tend to make of C. S. Peirce a mathematical prophet, as well as a superb mid-twentieth century teacher.

Actually topology began to develop only with the work of Brouwer after the first decade of the twentieth century. In the Epilogue of his *History of Geometrical Methods* (1940) Julian Coolidge says that "the subject of topology, which has scarcely been mentioned in the preceding pages, has come in the third and fourth decades to be one of the most eagerly and fruitfully studied of all the mathematical fields. It may one day be looked upon as a separate domain to be classified under no particular heading except that of Mathematics." Yet topology in the 1890s, like non-Euclidean geometry, had not reached textbook recognition; unlike the non-Euclidean materials, little of it was to be found in widely circulated research papers.

David Eugene Smith, who had a long experience in writing popular mathematical textbooks, once wrote of having been both a radical reformer and a conservative one as well, but that only in the latter role can one meet with success in a textbook. He had learned that radical reforms belong in books for teachers and in speeches, but that they are "dead weights" in a book for pupils. Therein lies, perhaps, the explanation of Peirce's inability to get a hearing on his textbooks for the past seventy-five years, diverging as he did from the earlier practices of our times as well as of his own. It will be obvious that Peirce's "radical" ideas have become the "conservative" ones at last.

INTRODUCTION TO VOLUME 1

On Thanksgiving day, 1888, Charles Peirce wrote a letter to his brother James Mills Peirce (Jem) in which he told of having read Dee's preface to *Euclid*, Thiriot's *History of Arithmetic*, and of having examined some Arithmetics from the past as well as other rare books. We learn from a letter to his wife Juliette a year later (December 6) that Peirce had dined at the Pinchot's in New York and that Pinchot, hearing of a new Peirce arithmetic project, had exclaimed that Peirce's "Arithmetic will be better than Butler's iron-mine." In a general estimate of his possible earnings from the writing of textbooks, Peirce felt that this one book alone could bring him $1000 a year in royalties.

Just after Peirce's enforced resignation from the Coast and Geodetic Survey on 1 January 1891, Jem tried to help get the project started by offering arithmetic textbook suggestions. He was in New York City at the time of what he called "the splendid conflagration in the Fifth Avenue Theatre" and in a letter dated 3 January 1891 suggested Wentworth and Hill's Arithmetic, "to which Hill made some good contributions, published by Ginn, Boston.... Also in Sonnenschein and Nesbitt's Arithmetic.... Is there a German Arithmetic by Richard Baltzer?"

Peirce was seeking advice on other fronts as well. Allan Douglas Risteen had been a computing assistant to Peirce in pendulum experimentation in the Coast Survey and had become Peirce's assistant as well in the preliminary research for Peirce's *Century Dictionary* contributions in mathematics, mechanics, astronomy, weights and measures, and logic and metaphysics. By 1891 Risteen was employed by the Hartford Steam Boiler Inspection and Insurance Company in Hartford, Connecticut, and hence his assistance was restricted to hours away from his regular job. His devotion to Peirce and his own talent and diligence enabled him to qualify for a Ph.D. at Yale under Gibbs by the summer of 1903 and he later became a member of the Department of Physics at the University of Pennsylvania. He was devoted to Peirce to the end, the correspondence between them flourishing in the period 4 August 1887 to 21 September 1913. The seriousness of purpose with which Peirce was approaching the composition of his *Arithmetic* is revealed in letters between the two men. Risteen wrote: "Regarding the Arithmetic. I have been busy at it in my spare hours, though I have not written you much about it. I will send shortly, a skeleton of it, for criticism and revision" (3 March 1891); "The Arithmetic is still coming on as well as possible, considering that I can devote only my spare time to it" (24 March 1891); "I send you your manuscript on the Arithmetic by today's express.... Just before I went away I destroyed a considerable part of my own work, foolishly perhaps, but the fact is as I read it over it was really unbearable, and would never do at all. I am not logical enough to arrange the early part of the book in a shape intelligible to a youngster and I ought to have known better than to try it." He suggested that Peirce do the text and that he, Risteen, would supply the examples, with himself supplying text and examples for the commercial part (16 October 1891).

Another friend who was to play a role in this venture was Judge Francis Russell of Chicago. In a letter to his wife (7 February 1893) Peirce tells of his projected visit to his friend in Chicago on the morrow and that matters had been so arranged that he could see his way to writing his arithmetic. The "way" was apparently to be through Edward C. Hegeler, publisher of *The Monist* and of *The Open Court* who had become interested in sponsoring the new project. As a stipend of $2000 during the next year seemed to be necessary to enable Peirce to write his book it must be inferred that no completed manuscript was on hand at the time of Peirce's visit. By 9 March 1893, Peirce was complaining to his wife in a letter from Albany that the LaSalle visit with Hegeler had not met with the success he had hoped for. Nevertheless on 22 May 1893 a report on the state of his work was sent to Hegeler. A year later (5 April) Peirce was still writing to Jem that "Of course the arithmetic is the first thing to be done, *could it be done....* I can't finish my arithmetic till I can get ahead of my expenses by $500 at least."

Further details come to light in an undated letter to Russell in which Peirce explains that the "arithmetic has been finished also, all but the examples and parts of the advanced book. But it had been rewritten and rewritten in the effort to adapt it to children and is now in the hands of a lady for criticism. I am rushing everything to try to get that to press. But my idea is to finish the geometry first and I hope it won't take me much longer." Five months later, 5 September 1894, Peirce complained that Hegeler had changed his mind about publishing Charles's papers and flatly refused to keep his promise to do so. "My arithmetic was unavoidably delayed," he wrote. "I shall soon be in condition to repay all I owe to Hegeler, pack up the books and send them to him, and go about my proper business of making the exposition of my philosophy." Indeed a letter to Russell on 8 September reveals the startling fact that "the arithmetic is out of" his hands and another letter on 23 September told of his inability to understand Hegeler's antagonism. "I am inclined to think that it is because I did not finish my arithmetic within the time specified." With personal misfortunes engulfing him during those months, Peirce could still write to his brother on 3 March 1895 that his arithmetic will be profitable — "very profitable but only after a long time."

Unhappy litigation had apparently ensued. But as late as 7 March Peirce was still hoping "to square accounts with Hegeler" and then to recover "The manuscript of my arithmetic which was seized long ago ... and I am afraid Hegeler has it and is determined not to let me have it." On 28 September 1896 he reminds Judge Russell of the Arithmetic "seizure" two years before; "and if I don't have the money to get that back soon, it will be gone forever."

The report of 22 May 1893 to Hegeler gives the clue as to the contents of the *Arithmetic* and makes it possible to carry out Peirce's intentions by a proper selection from the extant manuscripts in the Houghton Library. For the materials used in this edition conform exactly to the descriptions of them given out by Peirce at that time. It may well be that these were the very materials sent to Hegeler later but listed by Peirce in the following terms:

The following MS. is in my hands for my arithmetics

Copy for Primary Ar.		
About 50 pages, with very numerous rough sketches for illustrations, equivalent to about	5000 words	
Copy for Advanced Ar.		
About 20 pages typewritten 60 lines, or 1000 words to page, say	20000 „	
About 50 [pages] written, about 120 words to page, say	6000 „	
Total copy	about 31000 words	

Preparation for copy			
Detailed notes for Primary Arithmetic	50 pages, about		
Examples mostly statistical for Advanced A.	50 „	„	
Calculations for physical examples	30 „	„	

In addition to the above, there is a quantity of MS, which, though it will not serve for copy for the arithmetic, was prepared to guide me in writing it, and out of which one or two articles can be made. Namely there are

> Notes on previous arithmetics. About 40 textbooks now in the schools are carefully noticed (I much regret not having German, French, and Italian textbooks). About 20 older books are noticed. In all about 150 pages MS.
> Notes on apparatus to be used in teaching arithmetic, on the psychology of the subject, on my method of teaching each operation, various attempts at laying out the work so as to get the whole subject into moderate compass. Memoranda of matters to be introduced, etc. About 100 pages MS. In all there are about 500 pages MS.

The work is in rather a backward condition, but by no means desperately so.

Yours very truly
C. S. Peirce

On an isolated sheet one finds a further breakdown of the 500 pages as Peirce estimated it. It runs as follows:

> 20 Pages typewritten copy for Advanced Arithmetic
> 50 Pages written copy for Advanced Arithmetic
> 50 Pages examples for Advanced Arithmetic
> 30 Pages calculations for examples for Advanced Arithmetic
> 50 Pages for Primary Arithmetic
> 50 Pages detailed notes for same
> 150 Pages notes on Existing arithmetics
> 100 Pages Remarks on methods, apparatus, Plan of the Work
> —————
> 500 pages of MS.

The story has a sequel beginning in 1900. Edward S. Holden, apparently in answer to a letter from Peirce, felt that *two* school arithmetics were needed to cover the whole ground. He advised Peirce to send the arithmetic manuscripts to him for review by publishers for joint publication by himself and Peirce with both sharing profits equally (18 October 1900). And in January 1901, Peirce sent Holden a full review of his arithmetic materials. Holden, in turn, listed the manuscripts he had received from Peirce and that list corresponds roughly to the materials now in the Houghton Library and to that appearing in the early report to Hegeler. Holden's letter (28 January 1901) reads as follows:

My dear Peirce,

I've gone over your Arithmetic papers and sorted them (and let me say it has been an intellectual pleasure to find ideas and a man in all the writing!) into

   I   Primary Arith. ms. 31 pp. pretty well complete to counting by eight.

  II   Misc. pp. of Primary Arith. perhaps 100 — thro Multipl^n and Div^n — but needing, I think now, some changes.

 III   Practical Arith^c — perhaps 15 typewritten pages.

 IV   Misc. pp. of notes etc. — all useful in their place and time.

      (I enclose a page of MS. that I think is in the wrong Box.)

I should say that pretty much all the Practical Arith^c — was still to write; and the Primary A. perhaps more than half done. As soon as you can find the rest of your Ms. you'd better send it to me — and then we can see what to do.

I saw your review of Herschel; but I've not seen Sime's book yet. "Chevalier" made me laugh.

Let me have the Ms. when you can. In the meantime, I'm yours faithfully,

Holden

Over the years Peirce had apparently mislaid what he considered "the principal piece." For he told Holden it had been lost. However, Manuscript 189 in the Peirce Collection fits perfectly the description given by Peirce and thus is reinstated to its rightful position in this collection.

On 5 April 1901 Holden returned the manuscript — collect. He explained to Peirce that he had "spoken to Brett (MacMillan Co.) again about the plan and he is interested." He also volunteered to speak to Ginn and Co. and to others and, as occasion arose, would "try to have them bidding against each other." With these words, Holden seems to have ended his association with the project.

In a letter to Albert Stickney that Max Fisch dates circa 15 October 1906, Peirce speaks of the disposition of his estate, were he to pass on, and mentions his lack of interest in his nephews and nieces. He continues, "Should my arithmetic bring me a considerable sum, — a lack of dollars, — (I have more than that already in my impregnable *lack* thereof), I might do *something* for some of them; but it is highly improbable that I or Juliette shall live to get one dollar's profit from the Arithmetic though it be worth half a million, as I am inclined to think it will be. In any case, I should not wish to give them over one fifth of the net profits, be they large or small." The letter continues,

But now as to Arithmetic, which, properly speaking, has nothing to do with *arithmetic*, the mathematics of number, but solely with the art which Chaucer and others of his time called *augrim*, the art of using the so-called "Arabic" numeral figures, 0, 1, 2, 3, 4, 5, 6, 7, 8, 9. It is a great pity that the word "augrim" has become obsolete, without leaving any synonym whatever. The nearest is "*logistic*", which means the art of computation generally, but more especially with the Greek system of numeral notation. "*Vulgar arithmetic*" is a rather incorrect and decidedly uninviting sign for a book to put out on its title page. *"Practical Arithmetic"* is a phrase inevitably to be universally misunderstood, and supposed to be a sort of self-puff, which no self-respecting writer would indulge in, and which consequently is much the same as if one were to give this title

THE CIPHERING ART:
A Humbug Treatise on this Subject

If I could find a really good title in the Elizabethan taste, I would adopt it, I think. Recorde's book of augrim, which was *the* book in England on the subject for more than a century, its first edition being of date 1540, and its last of 1699, was very charmingly and veritably entitled

The Ground of Artes

Well, to recover my grammar in a new breath, my Augrim is at present in the following condition: *firstly*, a plan of the whole work fills a quarto blankbook of 48 pages and runs into another. But were it now rewritten, it would be longer; and a provisional table of Contents of the Second Book, — for it is to be a "Two-Book" arithmetic, — has been drawn up. It includes processes of which ordinary arithmetics give no account. For one example among many, I will, on a slip which I will insert herewith, do twice over this sum "Give, correctly to the thousandth part of itself, the number whose fifth power exceeds a hundred times its cube by 1." There is nothing particular about this problem. I have just invented it to illustrate what I was saying just now.

But no undue stress will be placed on out of the way methods. On the contrary, the greatest point in the first volume is to make the matter interesting to the little tots, and trial by practical teachers has more than once shown that it is successful in this and in training them in addition and the other operations. In both volumes but more particularly in the *second*, whole numbers and decimals are everywhere treated, as being purely *ordinal*, without reference to the values of the intervals, yet *at the same time* as being *quotal* that is as concerning the question "How many?" For number is treated entirely from the point of view of counting.

Addition is the operation of finding how many in all there are in two or more mutually exclusive collections.

Multiplication is the operation of finding how many *pairs* there are of which one member comes from one and the other from another collection. Continued multiplication finds how many *sets* there are of which one member is drawn from a collection of given *quotal* number. Thus, twice three is

Fig. 1 (6 ways)

Involution is the operation of finding in how many ways every member of one collection can be paired with a member of another collection. Thus 2^3 is as follows

Fig. 2 (8 ways)

while 3^2 is as follows

Fig. 3 (9 ways)

Factorials are treated in the same way. Thus $4 \underline{|3}$ [4·3!] is the number of ways in which 3 objects can be paired each with a *different one* of 4 other objects. Thus [18 of the 24 ways]:

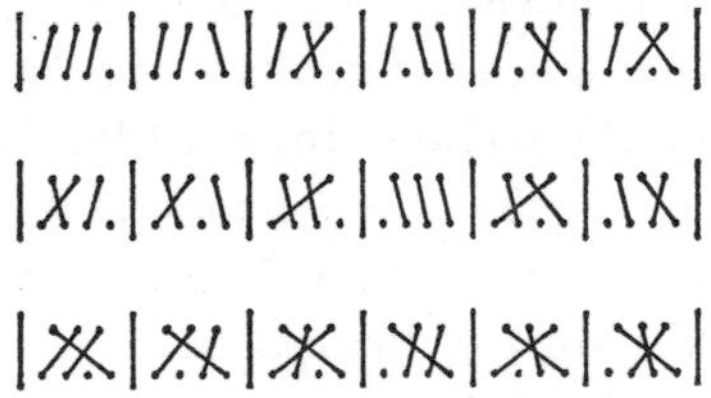

Fig. 4 (24 ways)

The editor believes that Peirce had in mind at that time a Primary Arithmetic consisting of the Elementary Arithmetic as given in MS. 189 (Lydia Peirce's Primary Arithmetic) and MS. 181 (Primary Arithmetic — MS. 182 is a draft of 181 with Suggestions to Teachers); a Vulgar Arithmetic, as developed in MS. 177 (The Practice of Vulgar Arithmetic) for students and in MS. 178 (C. S. Peirce's Vulgar Arithmetic: Its Chief Features) for teachers; a Practical Arithmetic, as given in MSS. 167 and 168. In an Advanced Arithmetic he probably intended to encompass number theory as given, for example, in Familiar Letters about the Art of Reasoning (MS. 186) and in Amazing Mazes; and Secundals, the binary number system so popular today.

Peirce had truly made an exhaustive study of arithmetic textbooks. There is still extant a sheaf of pages entitled *Copy and notes for arithmetic* (MS. 1545) in which he registered his reactions to some of the textbooks he had examined. For example, the Wentworth & Hill book is deemed "No doubt the best advanced arithmetic. Most intelligent and bright. Printing tolerably good." And Ray's *New Higher Arithmetic* brings forth: "This has been immensely popular. It contains many tables and everything a little fuller than most arithmetics. Easy to surpass it in all its strong points. Contains a great deal of information. Little useless stuff. Its logic is beneath contempt." Among mathematical works, ancient as well as current in Peirce's time, listed on another sheet is "Peacock, Geo. Arithmetic, 4to. A most valuable work and difficult to obtain separate. I was about five years hunting for mine. The plate referred to is wanting. $6." (MS. 1542). By a happy circumstance this copy was found in the stacks of Widener Library and today is being preserved at Houghton Library. A list of Arithmetics owned by Peirce on 21 March 1893 contains 44 nineteenth-century titles. He owned a dozen rare arithmetics of the sixteenth, seventeenth, and eighteenth centuries. In addition he listed one contemporary and six old titles he had been using. The old ones were probably in the George A. Plimpton Collection in Plimpton's home or in the Astor Public Library.

Since Peirce apparently intended to include secundal numeration in the arithmetic, the editor has taken the liberty of placing the manuscripts on secundals in this arithmetic section. Indeed MS. 64 is a large notebook entitled Notes for *My Treatise in Arithmetic* and dates from his Coast Survey period. There is a notation "1876 Paris Pend. swings. Diffs. of transits right and left." Most of the notebook remains blank but there is a section in which the importance of the idea of separation is stressed and in which secundal arithmetic and its various applications are developed. The advantages of number scales on bases other than ten were well appreciated in those years. For example, a paper on "Octonary Numeration" by W. Woolsey Johnson appeared as the first article in the very first volume of the *Bulletin of the New York Mathematical Society* and Johnson lists the many advantages of that system, advantages that have made possible the IBM machine age in which we now live. Benjamin Peirce had published in 1876, while Consulting Geometer of the United States Coast and Geodetic Survey, a pamphlet entitled "A New System of Binary Arithmetic" as Appendix 6 in the United States Coast Survey Report for that year. Charles, however, with his interest in the work of Boole and in its probability aspects, of necessity would have developed an interest in the binary system. In MS. 812 he wrote of the Boolean Calculus as follows: "This algebra marks the merit of propositions on a scale of two. Good and bad, or true and false are its only grades. It is a system of quantity having but two values; and each of its equations is, as it were, an arithmetical congruence having 2 for its modulus." His own algebra of relatives admitted only two values which he naturally used, for reasoning was to determine whether ideas are true or false.

Moreover, from the standpoint of number theory he found the Gaussian congruence modulo 2 of great interest. That cyclic arithmetic held a particular fascination for Peirce is evident throughout the mathematics manuscripts. It is the basis of his many card tricks and of much of the "Amazing Mazes." It will be seen in Volume 3 of this edition that the secundal notation was indispensable to his purpose in the development of the idea of a primipostnumeral collection. With secundals he made fractions "express nothing but relative places in a linear series" (4.212, 4.338) and this became an important element in his expository methodology.

With the experience of a thirty-year service in the Coast and Geodetic Survey behind him, Peirce was always alert to the possibility of new or shorter or simpler computing techniques. In a letter to H. B. Fine at Princeton University in 1903, Peirce contrived a scheme to find by secundals the millionth fraction in the decimal notation as a special case of the general problem of setting up a one-to-one correspondence between the positive rationals and all the ordinals (see 3,18,c).

Peirce's ingenuity in creating symbols is striking, and this skill can be seen in his attempt to develop a secundal notation. Feeling that it was a violation of good mathematical method to introduce the decimal point between the place of multiples of 10 to the zero power and the places of multiples of ten to negative powers, he contended that a mark should have been used instead to identify units place. He said that "The remarkable facility of the differential calculus is due to Leibniz's mind having been eminently one to whom such hybrids between different kinds of ideas were offensive." However, Peirce finally succumbed to the pressures of current usage and placed the decimal point as we do in the decimal notation.

Although Peirce was interested in the possible development of logic machines and wrote in 1888 about the Jevons and Marquand machines for the *American Journal of Psychology*, he could in no way foresee then the tremendous value of the use of the binary system in the logic and computing machines of the second half of the twentieth century.

CONTENTS

LYDIA PEIRCE'S PRIMARY ARITHMETIC (189)

LESSON I

(The children are not supposed to be able as yet to read. Nevertheless, they will need copies of this book, as will appear, soon. The first lessons are to be read to them by the teacher, who must be provided with a separate copy of the book.)

Once upon a time, many, many, many long years ago, when the world was young, there was a little girl, — a very pretty little girl, she was, too, with eyes like golden thread in the sunshine and hair like the sky in June, — or perhaps it was her hair that was like the gold thread, and her eyes that were more like the sky — which do you think? — who lived in the midst of a great wood; nothing but trees, trees, trees, in every direction for further than I could tell you until you have learned arithmetic, — in a funny little old house, the only one in all that forest, with her poor, old gyammah.

Now this grand-ma was very fond of numbers, she was; and she was always marking numbers against things; because she said there was one right number for everything, and all the other numbers were wrong. She said the right number of meals for people to eat every day was *three*, — breakfast, *one*; dinner, *two*; supper, *three*. But the right number of shoes for a little girl to wear, was *two*, — the right shoe, *one*, the left shoe, *two*. And the right number of mammas for a little girl to have was *one*. There was even a right number of fibs for a little girl to tell every day. "What number was that," asked the little granddaughter in Blue and Gold, whose name, by the bye, was Barbara. "Why, *none*, my dear," said her grandmamma; "I thought you knew that. Didn't you know, little Barbara, that *none* was the right number of fibs to tell?" "Yes, I knew it," said Barbara. "Then why didn't you tell me? It is not a secret, is it?" "I did not know that *none* was a number," said Barbara. "When you get up in the morning, how many meals do you expect to eat before you go to bed, Barbara?" asked her grandma. "Three." "After you have done breakfast, how many more meals do you expect to eat that day?" "Two," said Barbara. "Very good indeed," said the grandma, "one may hope you will soon be very bright about numbers. Now after you have done dinner, how many more meals do you expect that day?" "One," replied Barbara. "Good again. And after you have done supper how many more meals do you expect to eat?" "I don't expect to eat any more," said Barbara. "Yes, that is true. But another way of saying 'I don't expect to eat one' is to say 'I expect to eat none.' So as three is a how many, and two and one are how manies, *none* is another how many. By a *number* we sometimes mean a good many; but we sometimes call any how many a number, whether it is many, or few, or is not any. Now tell me; how many persons hear what I am saying to you? Give me the right number." "None," says Barbara. "What! Well, you don't mean that *you* are not a person, do you?" "One." "Dear me! Am I deaf?" "Two." "Now, my dear Barbara, you are giving me a very wrong answer. You are forgetting God. You must not forget for one single minute that God hears whatever you say and all that you think without saying. There is a right number to everything. The right number of persons who hear what I am saying to you is *three*. Never forget that!"

I am going to tell you more about Barbara and her grandma, another day. But now I am going to ask you some questions.

How many spots are there here?

Cover one, and how many can you see?   Fig. 1

How many ends has this line?   Fig. 2

How many has this line?   Fig. 3

How many has this line?   Fig. 4

How many has this line?   Fig. 5

How many this?   〇   Fig. 6

How many has this line?   Fig. 7

How many has this?   Fig. 8

How many has this line?   Fig. 9

(The teacher to take cards numbered 0, 1, 2, 3 and require various things to be counted by laying 0 card down first, then one of the others against each object counted. The first card is the answer if there is none of the kind sought. Otherwise the last card laid down is the number.)

LESSON II

Do you remember about the little girl who lived with her grandmother in the little old house in the wood? What was the little girl's name? The grandmamma's name was Lydia. What did Lydia say about right and wrong numbers? She said there was a right number for everything. Another day she said, "Barbara, my child, there is a right way of doing everything, or else the only right way is not to do it at all. There are some things we have to do very often; such as getting up in the morning, eating, speaking, playing, learning, sitting down, talking to friends. These things we must be very, very careful to do in the right way; because any wrong way will be apt to turn out badly, and make everybody sorry, ourselves and other people. If we don't want to make people sorry but want to make them glad, we must begin by finding out what the right way is, and then we must learn to do that right way and last we must do what we have to do in the right way. That makes three things: 1st to find out the right way; 2nd to learn the right way and third to do the right way. One of the things that we have to do very often is to find out how many things of the same kind there are in some box or bag, or basket or barrel or bank or basin or bucket, or bureau, or bottle, or bowl, or bunker, or bird's nest, or buffet, or boiler, or barrow, or barn-bay, or book, or be it what it may, or to find out how many times anything happens, or any other kind of how many. To cut a long story short, we very often want to know how many somethings are. Now what is the right way to answer the question, 'How many things there are anywhere?' Can you not tell me, Barbara?" "To count them, I think," said Barbara. "That is right; and it is arithmetic that teaches us the right way to count. Sometimes we have to count in one way and sometimes in another way. But the first way you must learn is plain counting, or numbering by the words *one*, *two*, *three*, and so forth. So dear Barbara," said Lydia, "the right way for me now is to begin by teaching you the right way to do plain counting and the right thing for you is listen closely and try to learn exactly how to number things so as not to make a mistake. I will count these cards.

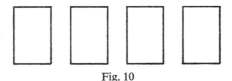

Fig. 10

I first put them where I can reach them, and I put them all face down."

(Just as old Lydia had the cards put down in a row, she and Barbara heard voices in the entry, and immediately the door opened, and in came a gentleman and a little boy, neither of whom Barbara had ever seen. They all uttered exclamations, and the gentlemen came and kissed Lydia and called her "Mother"; so that Barbara knew that they must be her uncle Charles and her cousin Ben. After some talk, the old lady said, "I was just beginning to teach Barbara arithmetic." "I wish you would teach Benjie, too," said Uncle Charles. So it was arranged that Benjie should stay with them, although his father could not stay; and the next day they had another lesson.)[1]

[Lydia continued with the lesson.]

"I then ask myself, 'How many of the cards are turned face up?' I look them over, and answer *None.* If I did not do that, I might make a mistake. I now turn one over, and as I do so I say '*One!*'

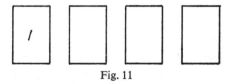

Fig. 11

I now turn another over, saying '*Two*' as I do so.

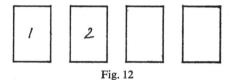

Fig. 12

I next turn another over, saying as I do so, 'Three!'

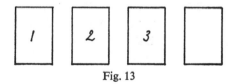

Fig. 13

I next turn another over, saying as I do so, 'Four!'

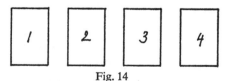

Fig. 14

Now there is no other to be turned over. So the last number that I called, Four, is the number of cards.

"Have you never picked the petals from a daisy and said, 'Big-house, little-house, pigsty, barn; big-house, little-house,' and so forth. Then the last one called is supposed to be your future home. That is like counting.

"To find out who shall be It, one can put all the children in a row, and

---

[1] Lydia, Charles, and Benjamin are all Christian names in the Peirce family. "Barbara" is, of course, a mode in logic.

point at them with the words:

  ☞ Eeny, ☞ Meeny, ☞ Mony, ☞ Méye,
  ☞ Tusca, ☞ Rora, ☞ Bonas, ☞ Try,
  ☞ Cabell, ☞ Broke a well,
  ☞ Wee, ☞ Woe, ☞ Whack!

Or with the words:

  ☞ Peek, ☞ a Doorway, ☞ Tries, ☞ What wore he,
  ☞ Punchy, ☞ Switches, ☞ Caspar Dory,
  ☞ Ash-pan, ☞ Navy,
  ☞ Dash them, ☞ Gravy,
  ☞ Do you knock 'em, ☞ Down!

Or thus:

  ☞ One o' you, ☞ You are a, ☞ Trickier, ☞ Ann,
  ☞ Phil I see, ☞ Fol I see, ☞ Nicholas John,
  ☞ Queevy, ☞ Quavy, ☞ Join the navy,
  ☞ Sting all 'em, ☞ Strangle 'em, ☞ Buck!"

When dear old Lydia was a child, as she was once, she and her playmates used to stand strictly serious while such words were being repeated. There seemed to be in them something solemn and secret and strong. That was the tradition. Do you know what a tradition is? It is anything that older people have commonly taught to younger people from for how long nobody knows. The words are really nothing but numbers or counting words.[2] Thousands of years ago before our grandfather's greatgrandfather's great great great grandfather's people had learned to build houses or do anything but fight and hunt and cook a little, only a few men knew how to count. It was a wonderful thing to know so much; and everybody

---

[2] Or "vocables" as Peirce says throughout the manuscripts.

thought when the last word of the counting came out with snap, that it did something, they didn't know what, but something great.

When they wanted a jury of twelve men to decide any matter, and they had more than twelve men to choose from, they would stand them up and very solemnly count to thirteen and send away the thirteenth man; and they would go on in that way until there was no longer a thirteenth man. Then those that were left were just twelve. They used old traditional numbers for this purpose; and in that way people came to have two curious feelings. One was that there was something strange and strong and secret about those old fashioned number–words. The other feeling they came to have was that the number thirteen was a sign of separation. This feeling was caught by one person from another, like a sickness, and even now when that way of choosing a jury or council has been given up hundreds and hundreds of years ago, many people continue to have these feelings. There is no harm in the feelings if we know there is no truth in them; but in some persons they are much too strong and quite unreasonable. Because after all these words are nothing but old words of numbers, that have got changed since they have been little used so that people forgot exactly how to say them; and all that the number thirteen has to do with separation is because being the number next after twelve, the number generally used for a jury or council, counting to thirteen was a convenient way of separating out the extra persons not wanted.[3]

All the real old jingles of counting out words make thirteen.

[3] A letter to W. W. Newell on May 15, 1904, reads as follows:

"Milford Pa 1904 May 15

My dear Newell:

I have a beautiful theory. All it needs is some facts to support it, of which at present it is almost entirely destitute. Perhaps you could supply them.

It is that in the ancient times and the ages long gone by, men preferred a jury of 12, or any council or committee of 12, and used to count up to 13 to throw out extra candidates or to reduce the panel; and that they used archaic or strange numerals, which would give an air of solemnity to the proceeding.

Now the only facts to support this that I have so far are, 1st, that the number 13 is widely associated with the idea of severance; 2nd, that our childhood's counting-rhymes (as well as I remember) counted up to 13

Eeny, Meeny, Mony, Meye,
1   2   3   4

Tusker, Leaner or Roarer, Boner, Stri,
5   6   7   8

Cabell, Broke a wall,
9   10

Wee, Woe, Whack!
11   12   13

One o'you, You are a, Trickier, Ann,
  1   2   3   4

Phil I see, Fol I see, Nicholas John,
  5   6   7

Queery, Quavy, Royal Navy,
  8   9   10

Sting 'em all, Strangle 'em, Buck!
   11   12   13

Intery, Mintery, Cutery corn,
  1   2   3

Apple seed and apple thorn,
       4

Wire, Briar, Limber lock,
 5   6   7

Five geese in a flock,
     8

Catch 'em Mary
    9

Hold 'em Tom
   10

O u t = out
11 12   13

To be sure, as these cannot be identified with any numerals, there is nothing to show that they preserve the original count; — unless it be that all, or nearly all, the really ancient ones (if such there be) count up to 13. I seem to remember that it was etiquette to be very solemn during such countings.

It seems a natural guess that the panel for a jury would have been reduced to 12 in that way. The only thing wanted is some fact to show it was so, and the 13 superstition *then* will be sufficiently accounted for.

Of course, such count words as children use differ from numerals solely in their limited application. Their want of meaning is not more complete. Numerals differ from all other words in constituting an apparatus for experimentation, and in being nothing else, though the lowest numerals are not *mere* numerals always.

very faithfully
C. S. Peirce

Peter's Daughter Cries Hot water
  1   2   3   4

Punches Witches Hadn't ought to
  5   6   7

Ashpan Never
  8   9

Dash 'em Ever
  10   11

Tweedledee and Dum
  12   13

This is nothing but a counterfeit, to show what I would *like* to find, — or rather something less manifestly artificial is desirable."

LYDIA PEIRCE'S PRIMARY ARITHMETIC[4]

LESSON I

Once upon a time many, many, many years ago, when the world was young, there was a little girl named Barbara, a very pretty little girl she was, too, with hair red gold in the sunshine and eyes like the sky in June, who lived in the midst of a great wood, nothing but trees, trees, trees, in every direction, for a good year's journey, in [a] funny rambling old house, the only house in all that forest, with her poor old gyammah. Now this gyammah was a cheery and active old lady, who enjoyed keeping the house as clean and neat as a pin and arranging the furniture prettily in all its rooms. Of course, there was no butcher nor baker; but water came down in pipes from a spring far up on the side of a neighboring mountain, and came down icy cold with such force that if they let it run through a little turbine wheel, it makes this go round, and makes some machinery move that would do sawing, or hammering, or beating rugs, or ironing, or washing, or ploughing, or almost anything they wished. Then there was a well of natural gas which was led into the house in pipes, furnishing light and heat as much as they wished.[5] There were no roads in the forest; but it was easy to walk under the trees; for there was no great tangle of bushes anywhere. One could not get lost because of telegraph wires that were stretched from tree to tree, at about the height of a low table. Three such wires started from the house, one from the back, two from the front. The two front wires joined a mile from the house; and every wire was joined by other wires at every half-mile, so that by walking along by the side of any wire for three miles from where it joined any other, you would always come back to that same place. And by noticing which way any wire was wound round the trees one could tell which way it ran toward the house. Thus, one could not long be lost.

[4] This is a second draft of the manuscript.
[5] Peirce was very much interested in natural gas at this time.

Barbara and her grandmother, whose name was Lydia, lived alone in the great house. But they had some great dogs and some little dogs; and these dogs were all trained to scrub the floors and wash the windows and do many other things.

But one day when they were wandering in the forest they heard a sound of crying, and going towards it they found a little boy. So they brought him home. He talked a strange language and wore strange clothes. These Lydia took off and found him a suit of clothes; for there was no end to the things that were stored away in closets, and chests, and presses in the great house; and Lydia thought his own clothes ought to be kept in case his parents should ever come. He soon learned to talk as they did, and then told them the strange history of how he came there. They called him Benjy.

LESSON II

Lydia took pleasure in teaching the children whatever they wished to learn and could learn, as well as some other things that they would have great reason to wish they had learned if they should not learn them. Among other things Benjy had been carefully trained to distinguish the mushrooms which could be found growing in places from poisonous toadstools. Therefore, when he said one afternoon, "Gramma Lydia, I know where I could find some mushrooms for supper," she was glad to hear it. "But how will you find the place?" she asked. "I shall go along the left-hand wire in front of the house and say

> Peter's, Daughter, Cries, Hot water,
> Punch's, Witches, Hadn't ought to,
> Ashpan, Never,
> Dash 'em, Ever,
> Tweedledee and, Dum.

I shall call the first tree the wire goes round Peter's, and the next Daughter, and the next Cries, and so on; and the mushrooms are in the grass about the tree where I shall call Dum." So she gave him a small basket, and off he went, and soon returned with the mushrooms. "Now," said Barbara, "I can bring some asparagus, if you like." "How can you find it?" asked Lydia. "Why, I shall follow the wire at the back of the house; and I shall say,

Intery, Mintery, Cutery corn,
Apple seed and apple thorn,
Wire, Briar, Limber lock,
Several geese in a flock,
Catch one Mary,
Hold him Tom,
Blow the bellows,
Old man, Out.

I shall call the trees the wire passes round, first, Intery; then Mintery; then Cutery corn; then Apple seed and apple thorn; then, Wire, then Briar; then, Limber lock; then, Several geese in a flock; then, Catch one Mary; then, Hold him Tom; then, Blow the bellows; then, Old man; then, Out! And round the tree where I shall call Out there grows lots of asparagus." So Barbara was given a basket and a knife, and soon came back with a fine great bunch of asparagus. "Now," said Lydia, "I know where to find some eggs. Come with me, and you shall see what my way is; although it is just like yours." So she went along the right hand wire and the children with her. When she came to a tree that the wire wrapped, she said, "Benjy, what do you call this tree?" "I call it Peter's," said Benjy. "And Barbara, what is your word?" "Intery," said Barbara. "Well, those are very good names. But I call it, One." At the next tree, Benjy without waiting to be asked said, "Daughter;" and Barbara said "Mintery." "Good," said Lydia; "but I will call it, Two." The next tree was called "Cries" by Benjy, and "Cutery corn" by Barbara. Lydia called it, "Three." The next was called "Hot water" by Benjy, and "Appleseed and apple thorn" by Barbara; but Lydia called it "Four." The next was called "Punches" by Benjy, and "Wire" by Barbara; but Lydia called it "Five." The next was called "Witches" by Benjy, and "Briar" by Barbara; but Lydia called it "Six." The next was called "Hadn't ought to" by Benjy, and "Limber lock" by Barbara; but Lydia called it "Seven." The next was called "Ashpan" by Benjy and "Several geese in a Flock" by Barbara; but Lydia called it "Eight." The next was called "Never" by Benjy, and "Catch one Mary" by Barbara; but Lydia called it "Nine." The next tree was called "Dash 'em" by Benjy, and "Hold him Tom" by Barbara; but Lydia called it "Ten." The next was called "Ever" by Benjy, and "Blow the bellows" by Barbara; but Lydia called it "Eleven." The next was called "Tweedledee" by Benjy, and "Old man" by Barbara; but Lydia called it "Twelve." The next was called "Dum" by Benjy, and "Out" by Barbara; but Lydia called it "Thirteen." "This is the same tree," said

Lydia. "I saw several nests of new-laid eggs about here, this morning."
They searched and soon found them, sure enough.

On their way back to the house, Lydia asked, "Benjy, what if the mushrooms had been under the tree before the one they were under? What
would you have done then?" "I should have stopped at Tweedledee,"
said he. "And I," said Barbara, "should have said the asparagus was
at Old man, if it had been near the tree before, and if it had been near
the tree before that I should have said it was at Hold him Tom." "Well,"
said Lydia, "your words in such cases would do just what my words
would do; but you must learn my words. They are the best." Benjy said,
"Why are they the best?" Lydia answered, "Benjy you are going to grow
up to be a man, and you will not always live in this wood, but will live
among men. Your body will be ever so much bigger and stronger than
it is now. You cannot begin to lift now what you will be able to lift
easily. But your mind will grow much, much more than your body; and
you will have thoughts that you cannot now think, at all. You will then
understand reasons that you cannot now understand. For the present,
you must do many things because I tell you it is best to do them, without
being able to understand why. The strongest and greatest reasons why
my words are best you cannot yet understand. But there is one reason
that you can understand. If instead of a few trees, you wished to count
the days that come before your next birthday comes, your words would
be too few. You would get all mixed up, and would not be sure when
your birthday came that it was your birthday. But my words, which are
the words that all grown people use who speak our language, go on without stopping. There is no row that comes to an end that is too long for
them to count. Each of you wants to grow up to be a child of God and
a brother or sister of men and women; and you want to do as other grown
people do, so far as God approves of their ways."

"Benjy, show me your right hand. Barbara, show me your right hand.
Good, you both know which your right hand is. If you had not known,
that would have been the first thing to learn. Now each of you hold out
the right hand with the palm up. That is the *palm*. Now put the tip of
the little finger of the left hand down upon the palm of the right hand and
say, 'One.' Good! Now put the tip of the next finger of the left hand
down upon the right palm along with the little finger, and say, 'Two.'
Good! Now put the tip of the next left hand finger down along with the
others, and say, 'Three.' Now put the tip of the next left hand finger
down along with the others, and way, 'Four.' Now put down the end of
the thumb with the tips of the other fingers, and say, 'Five.' Good. Do

it, now, again! Now again! That is your first lesson. Do it many times today and tomorrow; and when you have learned this well, we will go on to the other numbers.

[MULTIPLICATION][6]

0 time 1 is 0
1 time 2 is 2
2 times 3 are 6
3 times 4 are 12
4 times 5 are 20
5 times 6 are 30
6 times 7 are 42
7 times 8 are 56
8 times 9 are 72

Next remember the "quarter-squares," as they are called.

The quarter square of 0 is 0 time 0, or 0
The quarter square of 1 is 0 time 1, or 0
The quarter square of 2 is 1 time 1, or 1
The quarter square of 3 is 1 time 2, or 2
The quarter square of 4 is 2 times 2, or 4
The quarter square of 5 is 2 times 3, or 6
The quarter square of 6 is 3 times 3, or 9
The quarter square of 7 is 3 times 4, or 12
The quarter square of 8 is 4 times 4, or 16
The quarter square of 9 is 4 times 5, or 20
The quarter square of 10 is 5 times 5, or 25
The quarter square of 11 is 5 times 6, or 30
The quarter square of 12 is 6 times 6, or 36
The quarter square of 13 is 6 times 7, or 42
The quarter square of 14 is 7 times 7, or 49
The quarter square of 15 is 7 times 8, or 56
The quarter square of 16 is 8 times 8, or 64
The quarter square of 17 is 8 times 9, or 72
The quarter square of 18 is 9 times 9, or 81

[6]   This material is on sheets separated from the notebook but belonging to it.

Now, if you want the product of 6 and 7, you must add the factors, giving 13 and subtract the smaller from the larger, giving 1. Then subtract the quarter square of 1, or 0, from the quarter square of 13, or 42, and you have the product.

So if you want 7 times 9, the sum is 16, the difference 2. The quarter square of [16 is] 64 and the quarter square of 2 is 1, which subtracted from 64 leaves 63, the answer.

So if you want 3 times 8, the sum is 11, the difference 5. The quarter square of 11 is 30, and that of 5 is 6, which taken from 30 leaves 24 as the answer.

But you must remember that such devices are merely [to] aid you in learning the multiplication table and to enliven the task, a little, not to serve instead of a knowledge of the multiplication-table. That must be learned so that you do not recognize a letter of the alphabet quicker than you remember the product of two numbers less than 10.

The multiplication-table is learned, and we ought to have a festival. But today I want to teach you *long multiplication*.

From the beheading of Charles I to the Declaration of Independence was 127 years and a fraction. Supposing each year had 365 days, that would be how many days? We have to multiply 365 by 127. Call 365 multiplicand, 127 multiplier. Write the multiplier directly under the multiplicand, units exactly under units, tens exactly under tens, hundreds exactly under hundreds, and draw a line under the multiplier, thus:

$$
\begin{array}{r}
365 \\
127 \\
\hline
\end{array}
$$

Multiply each figure of the multiplicand by every figure of the multiplier and set down the product so that its units place shall be that number of places to the left of the units place of the factors which is the sum of the numbers of places by which the two figures multiplied are to the left of the units' place. Thus, 1 time 3 is 3; the 1 is 2 places to the left of the units, the 3 is 2 places to the left of the units. 2 and 2 make 4. So we set down the 3, the product, 4 places to the left of the units, thus:

$$
\begin{array}{r}
365 \\
127 \\
\hline
3 \quad\quad\quad\quad
\end{array}
$$

Next, 1 time 6 is 6. The 1 is 2 places to the left of the units, the 6 is 1 place

to the left of the units. 2 and 1 make 3. So, the 6 is set down 3 places to
the left of the units, thus:

```
 365
 127
─────
 36
```

Next, 1 time 5 is 5. The 1 is 2 places to the left of the units, the 5 is 0 place
to the left of the units. 2 and 0 make 2. So the 5 is set down 2 places to
the left of the units, thus:

```
 365
 127
─────
 365
```

Next, 2 times 3 make 6. The two is 1 place to the left of the units, the 3
is 2 places to the left of the units. 1 and 2 are 3. So the 6 is set down
3 places to the left of the units, thus:

```
 365
 127
─────
 365
 6
```

Next, 2 times 6 make 12. The 2 is 1 place to the left of the units, the 6
is 1 place to the left of the units. 1 and 1 make 2. So the 12 is set down
with its units 2 places to the left of the units of the factors, thus:

```
 365
 127
─────
 365
 6
 12
```

Next, 2 times 5 make 10. The 2 is 1 place to the left of the units, the 5
is 0 places to the left of the units. 1 and 0 make 1. So the 10 is set down
with its units 1 place to the left of the units of the factors, thus:

```
 365
 127
─────
 365
 6
 12
 10
```

Next, 7 times 3 make 21 the 7 is 0 place to the left of the units, the 3 is 2 places to the left of the units. 0 and 2 make 2. So, the 21 is set down with its units 2 places to the left of the units of the factors, thus:

$$
\begin{array}{r}
365 \\
127 \\
\hline
365 \\
6 \\
12 \\
10 \\
21 \\
\end{array}
$$

Next, 7 times 6 make 42. The 7 is 0 place to the left of the units, the 6 is 1 place to the left of the units. 0 and 1 make 1. So the 42 is to be set down with its units 1 place to the left of the units of the factors, thus:

$$
\begin{array}{r}
365 \\
127 \\
\hline
365 \\
6 \\
12 \\
10 \\
21 \\
42 \\
\end{array}
$$

Next, 7 times 5 make 35. The 7 is 0 place to the left of the units, the 5 is 0 place to the left of the units. 0 and 0 make 0. So, the 35 is to be set down with its units 0 place to the left of the units of the factors, thus:

$$
\begin{array}{r}
365 \\
127 \\
\hline
365 \\
6 \\
12 \\
10 \\
21 \\
42 \\
35 \\
\end{array}
$$

Now draw a line under these numbers and add them up.

```
  365
  127
 ────
  365
    6
   12
   10
   21
   42
   35
 ─────
46355
```

Then 46355 are the number of days in 127 years of 365 days each, and somewhat less than the number of days between the execution of Charles I and the Declaration of Independence."

"But Lydia," said Benjie, "why do you set down the products in those places?"

"Why, can't you see for yourself?"

"I don't know."

"How much is 6 times 7?"

"42."

"And how much is 6 times 70?"

"Ten times as much, that is, 420."

"And how much is 60 times 70?"

"Ten times as much, 4200."

"Well, that makes the whole thing clear does it not."

"I must think over that," said Benjie.

———

"But Lydia," said Benjie, "why are those products added up to get the answer?"

"Why, you see 2 times 7 and 3 more times 7 make, in all, 5 times 7, don't they?"

"Yes."

"So 7 times 2 and 7 times 3 make 7 times 5, don't they?"

"Yes."

"Then, 100 times 365 and 27 times 365 make 127 times 365, don't they?"

"Yes."

"And 100 times 300 and 100 times 65 make 100 times 365. And 27 times

300 and 27 times 65 make 27 times 365. So:

        100 times 300
    and 100 times 65
    and 27 times 300
    and 27 times 65

make 127 times 365. Now 100 times 60 and 100 times 5 make 100 times 65. And 20 times 300 and 7 times 300 makes 27 times 300. So:

        100 times 300
    and 100 times 60
    and 100 times 5
    and 20 times 300
    and 20 times 60
    and 20 times 5
    and   7 times 300
    and   7 times 60
    and   7 times 5

make 127 times 365."

"Oh, yes, I see it," said Benjie.

"Now," said Lydia, "I will show you a quicker way of doing long multiplication. Set down the factors, as before, one exactly under the other, units under units, tens under tens, and hundreds under hundreds, and draw a line below, thus:

        365
        127
        ———

Now, begin at the right, and say 7 times 5 make 35. Set down the 5 in the units place and carry the 3 for the tens place, thus:

        365
        127
        ———
          5
        3

Then say 7 times 6 make 42; and 3 added makes 45. Set down the 5 in the tens place and carry the 4 for the hundreds place, thus:

        365
        127
        ———
         55
        43

Now say 7 times 3 make 21; and 4 added makes 25. Set it down, thus:

```
 365
 127
────
2555
 4 3
```

Now, say 2 times 5 make 10. Set down the 0 under the 2 in the tens place and carry the 1 for the hundreds' place, thus:

```
 365
 127
────
2555
 4 3

   0
 1
```

Then, you say 2 times 6 make 12; and 1 added makes 13. Set down the 3 in the hundreds' place and carry the 1 for the thousands' place, thus:

```
 365
 127
────
2555
 4 3

  30
 1 1
```

Then, you say 2 times 3 make 6; and 1 added makes 7. Set it down, thus:

```
 365
 127
────
2555
 4 3

 730
 1 1
```

Now you say 1 time 365 makes 365. Set it down, with the units under the 1, thus:

```
 365
 127
────
2555
 730
 365
```

Now, draw a line and add, thus:

```
  365
  127
  ____
 2555
  730
  365
 _____
46355
```

Now, I will show you a way which is still shorter, sometimes. Say, 5 times 7 make 35. Set down the 5 and carry the 3.

```
365
127
___
  5
```

Say 7 times 6 make 42, and 2 times 5 make 10; 42 and 10 and 3 make 55. Set down the 5 and carry the 5.

```
365
127
___
 55
```

Say 7 times 3 make 21, 2 times 6 make 12, 1 time 5 makes 5. 21 and 12 and 5 and 5 make 43. Set down the 3 and carry the 4.

```
365
127
___
355
```

Say 2 times 3 make 6, and 1 time 6 makes 6. 6 and 6 and 4 make 16. Set down the 6 and carry the 1.

```
 365
 127
 ____
6355
```

Say 1 time 3 makes 3. 3 and 1 make 4. Set down the 4.

```
  365
  127
  ____
46355
```

But the second way is the best way; because this third way is too hard. You are apt to make mistakes. But if there are only two figures, it is a good way. Thus, how much is 27 times 13. Set down the factors

27
13

Now say 3 times 7 are 21. Set down the 1 and carry the 2. 3 times 2 make 6, and 7 makes 13, and 2 makes 15. Set down the 5 and carry the 1. 2 and 1 are 3. So 351 is the answer.

If there are decimals, you follow the rule of putting the units of the product that number of places to the right of the units place which is the sum of the places by which the factors are to the right.

If gold is worth 62 cents a gram, how much is 16.042 grams worth?

$$
\begin{array}{r}
16.042 \\
.62 \\
\hline
.32084 \\
9.6252 \\
\hline
9.94604
\end{array}
$$

Answer: nearly $9.95.

But, in fact, gold is worth over 62.3 cents a gram. Then we correct the calculation, thus:

$$
\begin{array}{r}
16.042 \\
.623 \\
\hline
.32084 \\
9.6252 \\
48126 \\
\hline
9.994166
\end{array}
$$

Answer: $9.99."

DIVISION

"Tell me, Lydia dear, if I deal 38 cards into 7 packets, how many cards will there be in each packet?"

"Your multiplication table tells you how many cards it will take to make 7 packets of 5 cards each. How many is it?"

"35."

"And how many cards will it take to make 7 packets of 6 cards each?"

"42."

"Then if you deal out 38 cards, when you have dealt 35 of them you will have put 5 cards into each of the 7 packets. Now after you have dealt 35 cards from 38, how many will you have left?"

"3."

"So if you deal out 38 cards into 7 packets 3 of the packets will have 6 cards and the rest 5. This is called *division*. The 38 is called the *dividend*; the 7 the *divisor*, the 5 the *quotient*, and the 3 the *remainder*, which is *left over*."

"Benjie," said Lydia, "there are 24 hours in a day. If I give just as much time to sleep that I do to eating and play and just as much time to work, also, how many hours shall I give to each?"

"Eight," said Benjie.

"Good. Now if I have in those 8 hours, 3 kinds of work to do, housekeeping, teaching, and writing, and I give just as much time to one as to another, how many hours shall I give to each?"

"2, with a remainder of 2 hours left over."

"Yes, but I want to work the whole 8 hours, without having any left over."

"Then you must write part of the two hours and teach part of them and keep house part of them."

"Yes, but how much?"

"I shall have to think over that," said Benjie.

"Well, tell me tomorrow," said Lydia. "Only, you must suppose that I know how to divide an hour into any number of equal parts."

The next day, Benjie said: "Lydia dear, you said you could divide an hour into any number of equal parts."

"Yes, Benjie."

"Well, if you divide those 2 hours each into 3 equal parts, and then give 2 hours and 2 parts to housekeeping, and the same to teaching, and the same to writing, that will just make 8 hours in all."

"That is right, Benjie. I thought you would find it out, though if you had not I should not have been surprised. When an hour or anything else is divided into 3 equal parts, those parts are called *thirds*. So you should say 2 hours and 2 thirds. And it is written

$$2\tfrac{2}{3}$$

If a thing is divided into 4 equal parts, each part is called 1 *fourth*, written $\tfrac{1}{4}$; if into 5 equal parts, each part is called 1 *fifth*, written $\tfrac{1}{5}$; if into 101 equal parts, each part is called 1 one hundred and oneth, or 1 one hundred and first, written $\tfrac{1}{101}$, and so on. If a thing is divided into two equal parts, each part ought to be called 1 twoth; if people liked that word; but people prefer to say 1 *half*, written $\frac{1}{2}$.

2 halves, or $\frac{2}{2}$, is a whole one, or unit; so is 3 thirds, $\frac{3}{3}$; so is 4 fourths, or quarters, $\frac{4}{4}$; and so on.

3 halves, $\frac{3}{2}$, is 2 halves, $\frac{2}{2}$, and 1 half, $\frac{1}{2}$, or one and a half, $1\frac{1}{2}$.

4 thirds, $\frac{4}{3}$, is 3 thirds, $\frac{3}{3}$, and 1 third $\frac{1}{3}$, or one and a third, $1\frac{1}{3}$.

5 quarters, $\frac{5}{4}$, is 4 quarters, $\frac{4}{4}$, and 1 quarter $\frac{1}{4}$, or one and a quarter $1\frac{1}{4}$.

And so on.

$\frac{7}{5}$ is $\frac{5}{5}$ and $\frac{2}{5}$, or $1\frac{2}{5}$.

$\frac{11}{8}$ is $\frac{8}{8}$ and $\frac{3}{8}$, or $1\frac{3}{8}$.

$\frac{19}{13}$ is $\frac{13}{13}$ and $\frac{6}{13}$, or $1\frac{6}{13}$.

And so on.

$\frac{10}{5}$ is 2. $\frac{15}{5}$ is 3. $\frac{20}{5}$ is 4, $\frac{25}{5}$ is 5, and so on.

$\frac{14}{7}$ is 2. $\frac{21}{7}$ is 3. $\frac{28}{7}$ is 4, $\frac{35}{7}$ is 5, and so on."

"Benjie," said Lydia, "a week has 7 days; a common year has 365 days. How many weeks, then, are there in a year?"

"That is a pretty hard question," said Benjie.

"Yes," said Lydia. "We find that out by *short division*. So I must show you how to do short division. You want to divide 365 by 7. The dividend is 365, the divisor is 7; we want to find the quotient and the remainder. You write down the dividend and draw a line under it. You make a curve to the left of it and to the left of that you write the divisor, thus:

7)365

Now you say, what whole number of times does 7 go into 3. It does not go in once. Then take the first two figures of the dividend, 36. What whole number of times does 7 go into 36, or thirty-six? We know that 5 times 7 is 35. So it goes in 5 times and 1 over; because 35 subtracted from 36 leaves 1. Then we set down the 5 under the 6 and write the 1 small over the 6, thus:

7)365
5

Now, you ask how many times does 7 go into 15? We know that 2 times 7 make 14. And 14 from 15 leaves 1. So it goes in 2 times, with 1 over. Then we set down the 2 under the 5 and write a little 1 over the 5, thus:

7)365
52

Now the answer is 52 weeks and 1 day, or $52\frac{1}{7}$ weeks.

Or, we can add some decimal places, thus:

1 1
7) 365.000000000000000000
————————————
   52

Now, you can ask how many times 7 goes into 10. Answer."

"1 time and 3 over."

"Right. Make the decimal point and set down 1 under the first 0 and a little 3 above it, thus:

1 1 3
7) 365.000000000000000000
————————————
   52.1

Now, you go on in the same way. 7 into 30 goes 4 times and 2 over and so on and you get

1 1 3 2 6 4 5 1 3 2 6 4 5 1 3 2 6 4 5 1
7) 365.000000000000000000
————————————
   52.142857142857142857

You see these 6 figures 142857 keep coming round and round. So 365 divided by 7 gives

$$52\frac{1}{7}$$

or $52.1\frac{3}{7}$, that is, 52.1 and $\frac{3}{70}$,

or $52.14\frac{2}{7}$, that is, $52.14\frac{2}{700}$,

or $52.142\frac{6}{7}$, that is, $52.142\frac{6}{7000}$,

or $52.1428\frac{4}{7}$, that is, $52.1428\frac{4}{70000}$,

and so forth.

We also write this

$$52.1\overset{\cdot}{4}285\overset{\cdot}{7}$$

where we put dots over the 1 and 7, to show that those figures and all between them come round over and over again. That is called a circulating decimal.

Express $\frac{1}{2}$ in decimals; that is, divide 1.0000 by 2

0 0 0 0 0 0
2) 1.000000
————————
  .500000

Then, $\frac{1}{2}$ is the same as .5 or 0.5

Express $\frac{1}{3}$ in decimals; that is divide 1.000 by 3

$$\begin{array}{r} {\scriptstyle 111111} \\ 3)\overline{1.000000} \\ \hline .333333 \end{array}$$

Then, $\frac{1}{3}$ is 0.3, that is 0.33333$\frac{1}{3}$

Express $\frac{1}{4}$ in decimals; [also] $\frac{1}{5}$, $\frac{1}{6}$, $\frac{1}{7}$, $\frac{1}{8}$, $\frac{1}{9}$."

AVERAGE

"Benjie, my boy," said Lydia, "I am going to explain to you what is meant by an *average*, or *arithmetical mean*. A common year has 365 days. But besides common years, there are leap years which have 366 days. Commonly, there come three common years and then a leap year then three more common years and then a leap year. Now, I must tell you that there are two ways of counting time, called *Old Style* and *New Style*. *Old style*, called also the *Julian calendar*, is used in Russia and in Greece, and used, 200 years ago, to be used here. *New style*, called also the *Gregorian calendar*, is used here and in England, France, Germany, Spain, Italy, and many other places. This has nothing to do with the average; but I am going to talk about Old Style and New Style in order to explain what an average is.

In the Julian calendar every fourth year is always a leap year. Then if we take 365 and multiply it by 4, it will be one day less than any four successive years of the Julian calendar.

Let us multiply 365 by 4

$$\begin{array}{r} 365 \\ 4 \\ \hline {\scriptstyle 22} \\ 1460 \end{array}$$

Now let us add one day for the leap year, and we get 1461, which is the number of days in 4 successive years of the Julian calendar. Let us divide 1461 by 4

$$\begin{array}{r} {\scriptstyle 221\ 20} \\ 4)\overline{1461.000} \\ \hline 365.25 \end{array}$$

Then, 365.25 is the length which a year would have, if all years were alike, and if four of them were equal to four successive years of the Julian calendar. Such a year of 365.25 days is called an average Julian year. An average is a number which is what several numbers would become if they were all made equal and if their sum were to remain unchanged.

A hundred years are called a century. In a Julian century there are 36525 days. In any four successive Gregorian centuries, there are 3 days less, than in 4 Julian centuries. In four Julian centuries, there are how many days? Let us see.

$$\begin{array}{r} 36525 \\ 4 \\ \hline \scriptstyle 2\,2\,1\,2 \\ 146100 \end{array}$$

Now subtracting 3, we get 146097 for the number of days in 4 successive Gregorian centuries. What is the average number of days in a Gregorian century?

$$\begin{array}{r} \scriptstyle 2\,2\,0\,1\,1\ 2\,0 \\ 4\,)\,146097.00 \\ \hline 36524.25 \end{array}$$

Then, what is the average number of days in a Gregorian year? Answer." "365.2425."

LONG DIVISION

"Lydia," said Benjie, "there are 365.2425 days in an average year, aren't there?"

"Yes."

"And there are 12 months in each year, aren't there?"

"Twelve calendar months, yes."

"Then, how long is an average calendar month?"

"Ah, that is a question in *long division*. I must show you how to do it. You set down the dividend and divisor as before, only you draw a line above the dividend, and set down the figures of the quotient, as fast as you find them, above that line, thus:

$$12\ \overline{)\,365.2425}$$

Now you take the successive multiples of the last figure of the divisor, and write the last figures of nine of them successively under the last figure of the divisor and every time the first figure changes, you make a dot in the tens' place, thus:

```
12 |365.2425
 4
 6
 8
.0
 2
 4
 6
 8
.0
```

Now you successively add the next figure to the right, adding one more whenever you come to a dot, thus:

```
 12 |365.2425
 24
 36
 48
 60
 72
 84
 96
108
120
```

Here you have the successive multiples of the divisor, and you know they are right, if the tenth is ten times the first. You number them on the right from 1 to 9, omitting the tenth, thus:

```
1      12 |365.2425
2      24
3      36
4      48
5      60
6      72
7      84
8      96
9     108
      120
```

The divisor, 12, is larger than 3, but less than 36. You look for the largest multiple of 12, which is as small as 36. It is the 3rd. You set it down under the 36 writing the 3 above, and then you subtract it from the 36, thus:

```
                    3
1      12 |365.2425
2      24  36
3      36   0
4      48
5      60
6      72
7      84
8      96
9     108
      120
```

You now say 12 into 5 goes 0 time. You write 0 above the 5, and say 12 into 50 how many times? Your table of multiples shows that 4 times 12 is 48. You set down the 4 above the units of 52 and the 48 below and subtract it, thus:

```
                  30.4
1      12 |365.2425
2      24  36
3      36   048
4      48     4
5      60
6      72
7      84
8      96
9     108
      120
```

You now ask, 12 into 44 how many times? Your table of multiples shows 3 times 12 is 36. You set down the 3 above the units of 44, set down the 36 below, and subtract, thus:

```
                    30.43
1         12  |365.2425
2         24   36
3         36   048
4         48    4
5         60    36
6         72     8
7         84
8         96
9        108
         120
```

You now ask, 12 into 82 how many times? Your table of multiples shows that 6 times 12 are 72. You set down the 6 above the units of the 82 and set down the 72 below and subtract, thus:

```
                    30.436
1         12  |365.2425
2         24   36
3         36   048
4         48    4
5         60    36
6         72     8
7         84    72
8         96    10
9        108
         120
```

Proceeding in the same way we get

```
                    30.436875
1         12  |365.2425
2         24   36
3         36   048
4         48    4
5         60    36
6         72     8
7         84    72
8         96    10
9        108    96
         120     9
                84
                 6
```

Here is a better example. How many average Gregorian years are there
in an average Julian Year. The first step gives

$$365.2425\ \overline{|365.25}$$

.0
5
.0
5
.0
5
.0
5
.0

The next step gives

$$365.2425\ \overline{|365.25}$$

50
75
.00
25
50
75
.00
25
50

The next step gives

$$365.2425\ \overline{|365.25}$$

850
.275
700
.125
550
975
.400
825
.250

The next step gives

```
365.2425 |365.25
    .4850  ——————
    .7275
    .9700
   ..2125
    .4550
    .6975
    .9400
   ..1825
    .4250
```

The next step gives

```
365.2425 |365.25
  .0.4850  ——————
  5.7275
  .0.9700
  6.2125
  .1.4550
  6.6975
  .1.9400
  7.1825
  .2.4250
```

The next step gives

```
365.2425 |365.25
  .30.4850  ——————
  95.7275
  .60.9700
  .26.2125
  91.4550
  .56.6975
  .21.9400
  87.1825
  .52.4250
```

The next step gives

1	365.2425	365.25
2	730.4850	
3	1095.7275	
4	1460.9700	
5	1826.2125	
6	2191.4550	
7	2556.6975	
8	2921.9400	
9	3287.1825	
	3652.4250	

We now go on [as in the previous example]."

THE RULE OF THREE

"Lydia," said Benjie, "addition and multiplication both make numbers greater, don't they?"

"Yes, that is so, if you are speaking of positive whole numbers."

"But," said Benjie, "addition increases a number by putting something to it, multiplication increases a number by increasing every part of it and all parts alike. For instance, here are three dots

. . .

Now make every single dot a two

:::

There is three multiplied by two."

"That is true," said Lydia. "Now here is an india rubber band. I cut it open and lay it down on this ruled paper and make 5 pen-lines so as to mark off 4 spaces equal to the spaces between the lines on the paper."

"Does equal mean just as large?" asked Benjie.

"Yes. Now I stretch the rubber, so that each space is equal to 2 spaces on the paper, and now, of course, the whole 4 spaces on the rubber are equal to 8 spaces on the paper. The 4 has been multiplied by 2. So, stretching is multiplication, that is, supposing all the parts are stretched alike."

"But," said Benjie, "suppose you don't stretch the rubber so much. Suppose you only stretch it to make 2 stretched spaces cover 3 unstretched ones. Then, 4 stretched spaces will cover 6 unstretched ones. That stretching isn't multiplication, exactly, is it?"

"Why, certainly," said Lydia. "That is multiplying by 1.5; for 2 multiplied by 1.5 gives 3, and 4 multiplied by 1.5 gives 6."

"So it does," said Benjie.

"Now, Benjie," said Lydia, "suppose a dozen bananas cost 10 cents, how many will 18 cost?"

"A dozen is 12, is it not?" asked Benjie.

"Yes."

"Then if 12 are stretched so as to become 18, you want to know how much 10 will be stretched to?"

"Yes."

"Let me think," said Benjie. "If 12 are stretched so as to become 18, every one of the 12 will become $\frac{1}{12}$ of 18. Now 12 goes into 18 1.5 times. So every 1 will be stretched to 1.5 and 10 will be stretched to 15."

"That is right," said Lydia. "Now let me ask you another question. If 42 is stretched to 66, how much will 105 be stretched to?"

"Let me see," said Benjie. "I divide 66 by 42.

```
                  1.5714
  1      42 |66
  2      84  42
            ___
  3     126  24
  4     168  210
            ___
  5     210  300
  6     252  294
            ___
  7     294   60
  8     336   42
            ___
  9     378  180
         420  168
            ___
              12
```

Call it 1.5714. Now I multiply this by 105.

```
    1.5714
      105
    _____
    7.8570
 157.14
 _____
 164.9970
```

It is 164.9970."

"Not exactly," said Lydia, "because you neglected some figures in the division. You had to divide 66 by 42 and multiply by 105. It will come to the same thing to multiply by 105 first and then divide by 42 ...

$$
\begin{array}{r}
66 \\
105 \\
\hline
330 \\
66 \\
\end{array}
$$

42|6930|165

$$
\begin{array}{r}
42 \\
\hline
273 \\
252 \\
\hline
210 \\
210 \\
\end{array}
$$

"_____

[CARD PROBLEMS][7]

Another day Lydia had the cards dealt in 3 piles and had the children read them off in turn.

Benjie. Third pile:

3	6	9	12	15	18	21	24	27	30
33	36	39	42	45	48	51	54	57	60
63	66	69	72	75	78	81	84	87	90
93	96	99							

Eulalia. First pile:

						1	4	7	10
13	16	19	22	25	28	31	34	37	40
43	46	49	52	55	58	61	64	67	70
73	76	79	82	85	88	91	94	97	100

George. Second pile:

		2	5	8	11	14	17	20
23	26	29	32	35	38	41	44	47	50
53	56	59	62	65	68	71	74	77	80
83	86	89	92	95	98	101.			

Another day Lydia made them deal the cards into 4 piles and to read off the cards in each pile, in turn.

[7] We find here the beginning of Peirce's preoccupation with cards numbered 1-101. This will be the basis for the cyclic tricks in "Amazing Mazes."

Benjie. 4th pile:

4	8	12	16	20
24	28	32	36	40
44	48	52	56	60
64	68	72	76	80
84	88	92	96	100

	3	7	11	15
19	23	27	31	35
39	43	47	51	55
59	63	67	71	75
79	83	87	91	95
99				

		2	6	10
14	18	22	26	30
34	38	42	46	50
54	58	62	66	70
74	78	82	86	90
94	98			

			1	5
9	13	17	21	25
29	33	37	41	45
49	53	57	61	65
69	73	77	81	85
89	93	97	101	

[When the cards are dealt into 5 piles]

5th pile:	4th pile:	3rd pile:	2nd pile:	1st pile:
5	4	3	2	1
10	9	8	7	6
15	14	13	12	11
20	19	18	17	16
25	24	23	22	21
30	29	28	27	26
35	34	33	32	31
40	39	38	37	36
45	44	43	42	41
50	49	48	47	46
55	54	53	52	51
60	59	58	57	56
65	64	63	62	61
70	69	68	67	66
75	74	73	72	71
80	79	78	77	76
85	84	83	82	81
90	89	88	87	86
95	94	93	92	91
100	99	98	97	96
				101

Lydia. George, how do those in the three-pile end?

George. In 3 and 8.

Lydia. Eulalia, how do those in the two-pile end?

Eulalia. In 2 and 7.

Lydia. Benjie, how do those in the one-pile end?

Benjie. In 1 and 6.

Lydia. Now, Eulalia, when they are dealt in 2 piles, take the one-pile and tell me the cards that are in places whose numbers end in one and six. I mean what are the 1st, 6th, 11th, 16th, 21st, 26st, 31st, 36th, and so forth cards?

Eulalia. The cards are 1, 11, 21, 31, 41, 51, 61, 71, 81, 91, 101.

Lydia. Benjie what are the 1, 6, 11, 16, and so forth cards in the second pile?

Benjie. They are 2, 12, 22, 32, 42, 52, 62, 72, 82, 92.

Lydia. George what are the 2nd, 7th, 12th, 22nd, 27th, and so forth cards of the one-pile?

George. They are 3, 13, 23, 33, 43, 53, 63, 73, 83, 93.

Lydia. Eulalia what are the 2nd, 7th, 12th, 17th and so forth cards in the second pile?

Eulalia. They are 4, 14, 24, 34, 44, 54, 64, 74, 84, 94.

Lydia. Benjie, what are the 3rd, 8th, 13th, 18th, and so forth cards in the first pile?

Another day the cards were dealt in 6 piles, and read off.

Benjie. 6th pile:

6	12	18	24	30
36	42	48	54	60
66	72	78	84	90
96				

1	7	13	19	25
31	37	43	49	55
61	67	73	79	85
91	97			

2	8	14	20
26	32	38	44	50
56	62	68	74	80
86	92	98		

3	9	15
21	27	33	39	45
51	57	63	69	75
81	87	93	99	

4	10
16	22	28	34	40
46	52	58	64	70
76	82	88	94	100

5
11	17	23	29	35
41	47	53	59	65
71	77	83	89	95
101				

Another day Lydia had the cards dealt into 7 piles and had the children read off the cards in each pile.

Benjie. Seventh pile: 7 14 21 28 35 42 49 56 63 70
         77 84 91 98

Eulalia. Fourth pile: 4 11 18 25 32 39 46 53 60
        67 74 81 88 95

George. First pile: 1 8 15 22 29 36 43 50
       57 64 71 78 85 92 99

Benjie. Fifth pile: 5 12 19 26 33 40
       47 54 61 68 75 82 89 96

Eulalia. Second pile: 2 9 16 23 30
       37 44 51 58 64 72 79 86 93 100

George. Sixth pile: 6 13 20
       27 34 41 48 54 62 69 76 83 90
       97

Benjie. Third pile: 3 10
       17 24 31 38 44 52 59 66 73 80
       87 94 101

Another day Lydia dealt the cards into 9 piles, and bade the children read off the cards in each pile in turn.

Benjie. 9th pile: 9 18 27 36 45 54 63 72 81 90
       99

Eulalia. 7th pile: 7 16 25 34 43 52 61 70
       79 88 97

George. 5th pile: 5 14 23 32 41 50
       59 68 77 86 95

Benjie. 3rd pile: 3 12 21 30
       39 48 57 66 75 84 93

Eulalia. 1st pile: 1 10
       19 28 37 46 55 64 73 82 91 100

George. 8th pile: 8 17 26 35 44 53 62 71 80
       89 98

Benjie. 6th pile: 6 15 24 33 42 51 60
       69 78 87 96

Eulalia. 4th pile: 4 13 22 31 40
       49 58 67 76 85 94

George. 2nd pile: 2 11 20
       29 38 47 56 65 74 83 92 101

Lydia. The first card in the pile containing 30 is 3. What comes between?

George. 12 and 21.

Lydia. The first card in the pile containing 40 is 4. What comes between?

George. 13, 22, 31.

Benjie. Please; I want to tell you. The figures on the first two cards in the first pile count up to 1 and the rest to 10.

The first 3 cards in the 2nd pile count up to 2; the rest to 11.

The first 4 cards in the 3rd pile count up to 3; the rest to 12.

The first 5 cards in the 4th pile count up to 4; the rest to 13.

The first 6 cards in the 5th pile count up to 5; the rest to 14.

The first 7 cards in the 6th pile count up to 6; the rest to 15.

The first 8 cards in the 7th pile count up to 7; the rest to 16.

The first 9 cards in the 8th pile count up to 8; the rest to 17.

The first 10 cards in the 9th pile count up to 9; the rest to 18.

Eulalia. The figure in the tens place [in each pile]

　of the 1st card is 0,

　of the 2nd card is 1,

　of the 3rd card is 2, except the 1st pile, where it is one less,

　of the 4th card is 3, except the first 2 piles, where it is one less,

　of the 5th card is 4, except the first 3 piles, where it is one less,

　of the 6th card is 5, except the first 4 piles, where it is one less,

　and so forth.

George. And where the ten's figure is two less than the number of the card is just where the two count up to more than the number of the pile.

Benjie. So the figures on every card in the 9th pile count up to 9, don't they?

George. The figures of 99 don't count up to nine.

Benjie. How much do they count up to?

George. Why, 18, of course; because 18 is the next card after 9.

Eulalia. Well the figures of 18 count up to 9. So, if the figures on cards in the 9th pile count up to a number written with one figure it is 9, and if not it is some other number in the 9th pile. Keep counting up the figures and you will get to 9 at last.

Benjie. What do the figures on the cards of the 8th pile count up to?

Eulalia. Why to one less than those in the 9th, of course.

George. The figures of cards of the 8th pile count up to 8.

Eulalia. Yes; and those of the 7th pile to 7 and so on.

Benjie. How about 97?

George. Why 9 and 7 count to 16; because 16 is the card after 7 in dealing by 9s; and 1 and 6 count up to 7.

Lydia. Yes that is quite true. But now answer me this, George, without looking at the cards. What number ending with 0 comes into the first pile?

George. 10 and 100.

Lydia. How do you know?

George. Because the figures add up to 1.

Lydia. Where do 20, 30, 40, 50 come?

George. In the 2nd, 3rd, 4th, 5th piles.

Lydia. So the first card in the pile containing 20 is 2. What comes between?

George. 11.

Lydia. We dealt the cards out into nine piles, and here are the cards in the ninth pile:

9   18   27   36   45   54   63   72   81   90   99

Let us lay them down five one under another and then one over another, thus:[8]

```
      99
   9  90
  18  81
  27  72
  36  63
  45  54
```

Let us put down 9 beans to represent the 1st card

Take away one bean and put it in the tens' place

This represents the second card

Move over another, and you get the third card:

Move over another, and you get the fourth card:

Move over another, and you get the fifth card:

Move over another, and you get the sixth card:

Move over another, and you get the seventh card:

Move over another, and you get the eighth card:

Move over another, and you get the ninth card:

Move over another, and you get the tenth card:

Now there is not another to be moved over; so instead, put down nine in the units' place and you get the eleventh card

---

[8] Peirce shows in the primitive "set" arrangements the basic symmetry in the pairing of numbers on the cards as indicated.

Lydia. Well, Benjie, what is the 5th card of the 4th pile?[9] *Benjie.* 40.
Lydia. What is the 3rd card of the 6th pile. *Benjie.* 24.
Lydia. What is the 6th card of the 3rd pile. *Benjie.* 48.
Lydia. Very good. Eulalia, where is 41? *Eulalia.* The 5th card of the 5th pile.
Lydia. George, where is 67?
George. The 4th pile, 8th card.

[When the cards are dealt into ten piles]

10th pile:	9th pile:	8th pile:	7th pile:	6th pile:	5th pile:	4th pile:	3rd pile:	2nd pile:	1st pile:
10	9	8	7	6	5	4	3	2	1
20	19	18	17	16	15	14	13	12	11
30	29	28	27	16	25	24	23	22	21
40	39	38	37	36	35	34	33	32	31
50	49	48	47	46	45	44	43	42	41
60	59	58	57	56	55	54	53	52	51
70	69	68	67	66	65	64	63	62	61
80	79	78	77	76	75	74	73	72	71
90	89	88	87	86	85	84	83	82	81
100	99	98	97	96	95	94	93	92	91
									101

Another day Lydia had the cards dealt into 8 piles and bade the children read them off in turn:

Benjie. 8th pile: 8 16 24 32 40
                        48 56 64 72 80
                        88 96

Eulalia. 3rd pile: 3 11 19 27 35
                        43 51 59 67 75
                        83 91 99

[9] No. of pile + {one less than no. of card in pile} × 9 = no. on card.
       4 + 4.9 = 40
       6 + 2.9 = 24
       3 + 5.9 = 48
       5 + 4.9 = 41
       4 + 7.9 = 67

George. 6th pile:

			6	14	22	30
	38	46	54	62	70	
	78	86	94			

Benjie. 1st pile:

			1	9	17	25
	33	41	49	57	65	
	73	81	89	97		

Eulalia. 4th pile:

				4	12	20
	28	36	44	52	60	
	68	76	84	92	100	

George. 7th pile:

				7	15
	23	31	39	47	55
	63	71	79	87	95

Benjie. 2nd pile:

				2	10
	18	26	34	42	50
	58	66	74	82	90
	98				

Eulalia. 5th pile:

					5
	13	21	29	37	45
	53	61	69	77	85
	93	101			

Benjie. Some of the piles are all odd numbers and some all even.

Eulalia. Yes, all the odd numbers are in odd piles and all the even numbers in even piles.

Lydia. It was the same when you dealt them into 10 piles, and when you dealt them into 2 piles.

Eulalia. It is because 2, 8, and 10 are even numbers. For the first card will be in an odd pile if it is odd and in an even pile if it is even; and if there are an even number of piles, the cards won't change from odd to even nor from even to odd, but if there is an odd number they will.

Benjie. When we dealt them into 5 and 9 piles, then the odd places in the odd piles had odd numbers, and so did the even places in the even piles; but the even places in the odd piles and the odd places in the even piles had even numbers.

PRIMARY ARITHMETIC

[With Suggestions to Teachers]   (181 and 182)

It must not be supposed that so long as children learn arithmetic, it makes no difference how they learn it. Many persons know numbers; yet cannot imagine them without such fantastic accompaniments of shapes and colors, that they are greatly hampered in endeavoring to operate upon them with rapidity.

Many persons, — even professors of mathematics, — have no clear idea of what numbers are; though they have been using them all their lives.

The first thing to be done is to convey to the pupil as clear an idea of number as a child can have and to teach him to think of the digits, in simple, useful, and flexible diagrammatic images; and to associate with these the Arabic figures.

LESSON I

All *together*:

> One, two, three!
> *One, two, three!*
> ONE, TWO, THREE!

The teacher drops successive cents, nuts, or other objects familiar to children and to which he already attaches some idea of number, on account of his wishing to possess them; and as he drops he counts:

One cent:	One nut:	One block:	One card:
Two cents:	Two nuts:	Two blocks:	Two cards:
Three cents.	Three nuts.	Three blocks.	Three cards.

The teacher marks spots on the blackboard, writing the Arabic figures beneath.* (*It is not intended to draw the child's attention particularly to the Arabic [numerals]. But if the teacher always [writes them], the child will half-learn them impercept[ibly and will] find it easier to [use them], when the time comes. The "Egyptian" ...)

The first three cards of the pack are now to be produced; and the pupil is required to count various sets of two and three things in the room by laying the first card upon the first thing, the second on the second, and the third on the third, if there is a third, pronouncing at the same time the words one, two three. Then, the cards being laid aside, the following is read from the book:

John Brown   had   a little Indian Boy

1 little Indian   2 little Indians   3 little Indian Boys

Fig. 1

LESSON II

All together:

    One, two, three, four!
    One, two, three, four!
    One, two, three, four!
    One, two, three, four!
    One!
    One-two!
    One-two-three!
    One-two-three-four!
    Three-four! Three-four! Three-four! Three-four!
    One-two-three-four!

The teacher takes four biscuits and puts them up so as to display them, one by one, all counting

One! Two! Three! Four!

The teacher places a card before each, and all say, as he does so:

One! Two! Three! Four!

Teacher: How many biscuits are there?   *Answer*: Four.
The teacher makes a spot on the blackboard.

●

Teacher: How many spots are there?   *Answer*: One!
Teacher: Yes. We will mark it.

●
1

The teacher adds another spot.

● ●
1

Teacher: How many spots are there now?   *Answer*: Two!
Teacher: Let us count them. (Pointing) One, two. Yes, two. We will mark them.

● ●
1   2

The teacher adds a third spot.

● ● ●
1   2

Teacher: How many spots are there now?   *Answer*: *Three*!
Teacher: Let us count them. As I point you count. (The teacher points at them successively.)   *All*: One: two: three.
Teacher: Let us count them backward. (Operation repeated in reverse order.) So, there are three. The *third* must be marked.

● ● ●
1   2   3

The teacher adds a fourth spot.

● ● ● ●
1   2   3

Teacher: How many spots are there now?   *Answer*: Four!
They are counted forward and backward.
Teacher: We must mark the *fourth* spot.

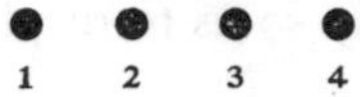

● ● ● ●
1   2   3   4

Here the pupil is exercised in counting sets of things up to 4 in number, using the cards, which he lays in order upon or against the single things as they are counted, at the same time pronouncing [the] numbers.

[In the following figure 2]

How many heads are there [in (a)]?
How many arms have they between them?

How many people are [in (b)]?

How many lines [in (c)]?
How many points [in (c)]?

How many arms to a cross [in (d)]?

How many dots [in (e)]?

How many [in (f)]?

How many [in (g)]?

How many [in (h)]?

How many [in (i)]?

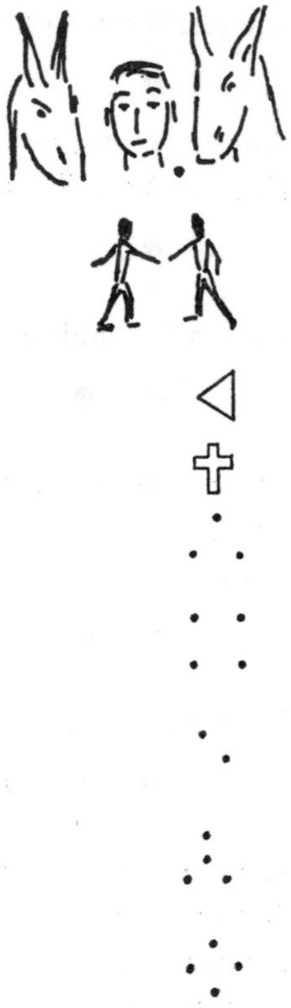

Fig. 2 (a-i)

[How many elements in each picture in figure 3?]

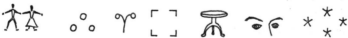

Fig. 3

LESSON III

Teacher: The next number is *five*. Say *five*.   *All*: *Five*.

Four-five! Four-five! Four-five! Four-five! Five!
One-two-three-four-five!
Two-three-four-five!
Three-four-five!
Four-five!
Five!

The teacher makes 5 spots on the board.

● ● ● ● ●

Teacher: How many spots are there?   *Answer*: Five.
Teacher: Let us count them. (He points.)   *All*: One: two: three: four: five.
Teacher: They must be marked.

● ● ● ● ●
1   2   3   4   5

The teacher counts the fingers of one hand with the forefinger of the other; and calls on each one of the class to do the same thing, several times both forward and backward. Then follow exercises in counting with the first 5 cards and with the fingers.

[In the following figure 4]

How many dots are [in (a)]?

How many stars are [in (b)]?

How many lines are [in (c)]?

How many points has this star [in (d)]?
How many lines [in (d)]?

How many crosses are [in (e)]?
How many lines make a cross?
How many arms to a cross?

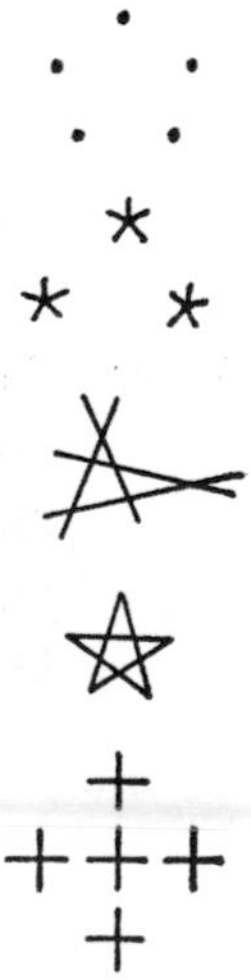

Fig. 4 (a-e)

How many apples are [in (f)]?

How many pears are [in (g)]?

How many eggs are [in (h)]?

Fig. 4 (f-h)

How many toes does your right foot walk on?
How many toes does a dog's foot walk on?
How many toes does a goose's foot walk on?
How many toes does a pig's foot walk on?
How many toes does a horse's foot walk on?

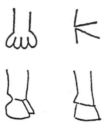

How many petals has a lily?
How many has a laurel-blossom?
How many has an apple-blcssom?

LESSON IV

Teacher: Say *six*!   *All*: *Six*.

One-two-three-four-five!
One-two-three-four-five!
One-two-three-four-five!
One-two-three-four-five-six!
Two-three-four-five-six!
Three-four-five-six!
Four-five-six!
Five-six!
Six!

The teacher makes 6 spots on the board.

● ● ● ● ● ●

Teacher: How many spots are there?   *Answer*: Six.
Teacher: Let us count them. (Points.)   *All*: One: two: three: four: five :six.
Teacher: They must be marked.

● ● ● ● ● ●
1   2   3   4   5   6

Many sets of six and fewer things are now to be counted forward and backward with the cards.

LESSON V

Seven!
Six-seven!
Five-six-seven!
Four-five-six-seven!
Three-four-five-six-seven!
Two-three-four-five-six-seven!
One-two-three-four-five-six-seven!
How many squares are [in Fig. 5(a)]?

◇ ◇ ◇ ◇ ◇ ◇ ◇

Count them. They must be marked [as in Fig. 5(b)].

◇ ◇ ◇ ◇ ◇ ◇ ◇
1   2   3   4   5   6   7

Counting forward and backward and with the cards to be practised here upon articles in the room.

How many spots are [in Fig. 5(c)]?

How many are [in Fig. 5(d)]?

How many are [in Fig. 5(e)]?

How many are [in Fig. 5(f)]?

How many moons are [in Fig. 5(g)]?

How many are [in Fig. 5(h)]?

How many rounds are [in Fig. 5(i)]?
How many crossings?
How many enclosures?

How many rounds are [in Fig. 5(j)]?
How many crossings?
How many enclosures?   Seven!

Fig. 5(a-j)

The days of the week are Sunday   1
                         Monday   2
                         Tuesday   3
                         Wednesday 4
                         Thursday   5
                         Friday   6
                         Saturday   7
How many days are there in all?
   Explanations of this will conclude the lesson.

LESSON VI

Eight!
One!
One-two!
One-two-three!
One-two-three-four!
One-two-three-four-five!
One-two-three-four-five-six!
One-two-three-four-five-six-seven!
One-two-three-four-five-six-seven-eight!
　Two-three-four-five-six-seven-eight!
　　Three-four-five-six-seven-eight!
　　　Four-five-six-seven-eight!
　　　　Five-six-seven-eight!
　　　　　Six-seven-eight!
　　　　　　Seven-eight!
　　　　　　　Eight!

How many hay cocks are there [in Fig. 6(a)]?

Count them. They must be marked [as in Fig. 6(b)].

Fig. 6

Counting objects in the room forward and backward and with the cards is now to be practised. Afterwards, give the child four dress-hooks and ask him how many he has? Then, four eyes for the hooks and [ask] how many he has of them. Then, ask how many hooks and eyes he has in all. Then, taking away the hooks and eyes, give him back a hook and eye attached and ask how many things are there? Then give another hook and eye and ask how many he has in all; and so on up to eight.

How many lines in this figure [7(a)]?
How many points?
How many crossings?

How many black squares [in Fig. 7(b)]?
How many white squares?

How many circles in this wheel [in Fig. 7(c)]?
How many spokes?

How many eggs are [in Fig. 7(d)]?
How many chicks?
How many eggs and chicks together?

How many different figures are [in Fig. 7(e)]?

How many are [in Fig. 7(f)]?

How many are [in Fig. 7(g)]?

How many are [in Fig. 7(h)]?

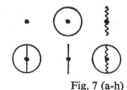

Fig. 7 (a-h)

The teacher now brings out about 247 reddish marbles, with 24 white bags (with strings) to hold 10 marbles each, just comfortably, and 2 or more green bags (with strings) to hold 100 marbles and ten white bags each. He also brings out an abacus, consisting of a frame with seven parallel wires, and *nine* beads on each wire. All the beads on one wire are the same color. Those of the first wire are copper-colored, those on the second wire white or silver, those on the third green (from the green back dollar bill), those on the fourth gold or yellow, those on the fifth light blue, those on the sixth grey, those on the seventh bright red.

The teacher and class together proceed to count the marbles, dropping them one by one into the bag, and pushing forward a copper colored bead for each. At the tenth, the nine copper-colored beads are shoved back, a white bead is pushed forward, and the bag is closed; etc. The numbers are pronounced as follows:

1 One.
2 Two.
3 Three.
4 Four.
5 Five.
6 Six.
7 Seven.
8 Eight.
9 Nine.

On the dropping of the next ball, the white bag is tied up and dropped into the green bag; and the copper-colored beads are all shoved back, and a white one pushed forward. And so at each ten.

10 Ten	20 Two tens	30 Three tens
11 Ten-one	21 Two tens one	31 Three tens one
12 Ten-two	22 Two tens two	32 Three tens two
13 Ten-three	23 Two tens three	33 Three tens three
14 Ten-four	24 Two tens four	34 Three tens four
15 Ten-five	25 Two tens five	35 Three tens five
16 Ten-six	26 Two tens six	36 Three tens six
17 Ten-seven	27 Two tens seven	37 Three tens seven
18 Ten-eight	28 Two tens eight	38 Three tens eight
19 Ten-nine	29 Two tens nine	39 Three tens nine etc.

When 99 has been counted, as nine tens nine, on the next ball being dropped, ten tens is called, the white bag after being tied up is put into the green bag, which is in turn tied up and put into the yellow bag. Meantime, the copper-colored and white beads of the abacus are shoved back and a green one is pushed forward. The counting proceeds.

100 Ten tens	110 Ten tens ten	120 Ten tens two tens
101 Ten tens one	111 Ten tens ten one	121 Ten tens two tens one
102 Ten tens two	112 Ten tens ten two	122 Ten tens two tens two
103 Ten tens three	113 Ten tens ten three	123 Ten tens two tens three
104 Ten tens four	114 Ten tens ten four	124 Ten tens two tens four
105 Ten tens five	115 Ten tens ten five	etc.
106. Ten tens six	116 Ten tens ten six	
107 Ten tens seven	117 Ten tens ten seven	
108 Ten tens eight	118 Ten tens ten eight	
109 Ten tens nine	119 Ten tens ten nine	

200 Two ten tens	210 Two ten tens ten	230 Two ten tens two ten
201 Two ten tens one	211 Two ten tens ten one	221 Two ten tens two ten one

The counting of the marbles is to be practised until the pupils thoroughly understand it, and are perfectly familiar with the numbers.

Teacher (holding up a glove): Is this a shoe? *All*: No.

Teacher: No: it is not, because it is not meant to walk in. What is it? *All*: A glove.

Teacher: Yes. It is meant to wear on the hands. It is called a glove. It *is* a thing meant to wear on the hands, with a place for each finger. *Glove* is its *name*. It is much more convenient to say give me a pair of *gloves*, than to say give me a pair of things to wear on my hands with a place for each finger. (Points to a table.) Is this a chair? *All*: No. *Teacher*: No, because it is not a thing to sit on with a back to it. (Pointing to a stool.) Is this a chair? *All*: No. *Teacher*: No, because it has no back. I would like to sit down. Harry, will you be so kind as to bring me a thing to sit down on with a back? Thank you. It would have been easier for me and for you if I had said, please bring me a *chair*, would it not? *Harry*: Yes, ma'am. *Teacher*: It is a thing to sit on with a back; but its name is *chair*. Some of the numbers have easy names.

Two tens is twenty.   Ten one is eleven.
Three tens is thirty.   Ten two is twelve.
Four tens is forty.   Ten three is thirteen.
Five tens is fifty.   Ten four is fourteen.
Six tens is sixty.   Ten five is fifteen.
Seven tens is seventy.   Ten six is sixteen.
Eight tens is eighty.   Ten seven is seventeen.
Nine tens is ninety.   Ten eight is eighteen.
                                   Ten nine is nineteen.

Ten tens is a hundred.
Ten ten tens is a thousand.

Let us count by bags of ten.

Ten.
Twenty.
Thirty.
Forty.
Fifty.
Sixty.
Seventy.
Eighty.
Ninety.
A Hundred.

Put the white bags in a green bag.

Let us count by bags of ten tens.

A hundred.
Two hundred.
Three hundred.
Four hundred.
Five hundred.
Six hundred.
Seven hundred.
Eight hundred.
Nine hundred.
Ten hundred.

Put the ten green bags in a yellow bag. There are in all a thousand.

Exercises in naming numbers are now to be practised. The bags being shown, and at the same time the beads of the abacus, and the Arabic figures.

The counting of coffee-beans is now to be practised.

Keep your mouth shut in counting; it is the only way to count fast.

To count right is the first merit.

To count fast is the second.

Of those who make no mistakes, the one who counts fastest will be decorated till tomorrow.

Keep up this for several days. A pound of green Java coffee beans will contain 2500, and can easily be counted in a little over half an hour. The countings should gradually be extended to half a pound. Let an ounce first be weighed out to each child (having been counted overnight by the teacher), and thus he will be led to take an interest in the question of how many. An ounce will count from 155 to 160, or thereabouts. From an ounce, proceed to two ounces, and then to four ounces, and finally to eight ounces.

Competitive exercises in counting coffee-beans are now to be practised. The children should be required to keep their mouths shut while doing this; and it should be explained that in that way only can they count very fast. The counting should go up to 2500, which will make a pound of green Java coffee beans. Of course, strict accuracy is the first requirement.

Mixed with these exercises should be others in counting aloud on the large abacus. In the latter, where the pupil will stand behind the abacus, grace and deportment are not to be neglected.

The pupil should now be taught to take the full pack of cards and after arranging them in regular order, beginning at the back, to hold the pack back up and deal out the cards into two piles face up, so that all the odd numbers come successively in the first pile and the even numbers in the other. When all are dealt out, the first pile is to be taken up first and the second at the back of it. The order of the cards is now to be learned *fluently*. Do not go on to the next until this is thoroughly mastered.

Upon this, will follow exercises in counting coffee beans by twos; also in counting up to an odd number singly and then proceeding by twos. Counting by twos aloud at the large abacus should also be practised.

2 4 6 8 10 12 14 16 18 20 22 24 26 28 30 32 34 36 38 40 42 44 46 48 50 52 54 56 58 60 62 64 66 68 70 72 74 76 78 80 82 84 86 88 90 92 94 96 98 100; 1 3 5 7 9 11 13 15 17 19 21 23 25 27 29 31 33 35 37 39 41 43 45 47 49 51 53 55 57 59 61 63 65 67 69 [... 101]

Counting by twos. The counting by two, threes, etc. is the proper method of learning rapid addition. It is, in itself, an irksome task; and at the same time calls for a severe mental exertion. Yet is it indispensable to real facility in arithmetic. Indeed, almost the whole art of computation consists in this. Accordingly, no pains should be spared to make it interesting, and to infuse a spirit of emulation into the exercise. The only limit to the time that should be spent on these exercises is that the children must not be disgusted.

The pupil should be taught to take the full pack of cards, and after arranging them in regular order, beginning from the back of the pack, to hold them back up and deal them out one by one into two piles, so that one shall contain all the odd cards and the other all the even cards in numerical order. The order of the numbers in each pack is now to be learned until they can be said off with the utmost fluency.

2 4 6 8 10 12 14 16 18 20 22 24 26 28 30 32 34 36 38 40 42 44 46 48 50 52 54 56 58 60 62 64 66 68 70 72 74 76 78 80 82 84 86 88 90 92 94 96 98 100;

1 3 5 7 9 11 13 15 17 19 21 23 25 27 29 31 33 35 37 39 41 43 45 47 49 51 53 55 57 59 61 63 65 67 69 71 73 75 77 79 81 83 85 87 89 91 93 95 97 99 101.

Next let counting by twos be practised on the large abacus, both with odd and even numbers. Next must follow competitive exercises in counting coffee-beans by twos; also in counting up to an odd number by ones and going on from that point by twos.

Next counting downward by twos should be practised beginning at 101 and at 100.

How many cards are there in the first pile? How many in the second? Which pile does 3 come in?
Which pile does 4 come in? 11? 22? 30? 35? 47? 56? 68? 79?

A boy had a marble and his mother gave him two more. How many had he then? The next day she gave him two more before breakfast; how many had he then? After breakfast she gave two more: how many had he then? After school, two more: how many then? Before supper two more: how many then? At bedtime, two more: how many then? In the night she came and woke him up and gave him two more; how many then?

A little girl found two pins on Sunday, and two more on Monday; how many was that? She found two more on Tuesday; how many was that? Two more Wednesday; how many? Two more Thursday; how many? Two more Friday; how many? Two more Saturday; how many? Fourteen in one week. She went on the same way for another week.

How many Sunday? Monday? Tuesday? Wednesday? Thursday? Friday? Saturday?

A boy had 34 apples and gave away 2. How many had he left? He gave away two more. How many then? Another two; how many left? Etc.

I hold in my hand 99 coffee-beans. I take out 2. How many have I now? I take out two more. How many now? Etc.

Counting by threes should be taught in the same manner. After the pack is dealt out let the second pile upon which card 101 comes [be] taken first, the first pile at the back of that, and the third [one] at the back of that. (The reason for taking up the piles in a particular order is that thus, for instance, if the pack is successively dealt into 3 piles, 4 piles, 7 piles, into 9 piles; or into 5 piles, 6 piles, [7] piles, and 8 piles; the original order is restored. The rule is to take the pile with 101 first, and then to pass each time as many places to the left as there are piles to the right of 101.) The numbers must be said as fluently as in counting by ones. And so in all the following cases.

Deal the pack into three piles

```
  3   6   9  12  15  18  21  24  27  30 ⎤
 33  36  39  42  45  48  51  54  57  60 ⎥
 63  66  69  72  75  78  81  84  87  90 ⎬ 3rd Pile
 93  96  99                             ⎦

              1   4   7  10  13  16  19 ⎤
 22  25  28  31  34  37  40  43  46  49 ⎥
 52  55  58  61  64  67  70  73  76  79 ⎬ 1st Pile
 82  85  88  91  94  97 100              ⎦

                          2   5   8 ⎤
 11  14  17  20  23  26  29  32  35  38 ⎥
 41  44  47  50  53  56  59  62  65  68 ⎬ 2nd Pile
 71  74  77  80  83  86  89  92  95  98 ⎥
101                                     ⎦
```

Learn these, so as to say them fluently. (But do not let the child become disgusted. Rather give him five or six lessons a day, than fatigue him too much at one.)

Counting by threes on the abacus, beginning with 1, with 2, with [3].

Counting coffee-beans by threes, with decoration for the fastest of those who make no mistakes.

Counting downwards by threes 99, 96, 93, etc. 101, 98, 95, etc. 100, 97, 94, 91, etc.

When the cards are dealt into three piles, how many are there in the first pile? How many in the second? How many in the third? The following questions may be asked, without insisting much upon them. [Ask] the child [to] look and see

In which pile is 1? In which pile is 11? In which pile is 21? In which pile is 31? In which pile is 41? In which pile is 51? 61? 71? 81? 91? 101?
In which pile is 1? In which is 31? In which is 61? In which 91?
In which pile is 11? In which 41? In which 71?
In which pile is 21? In which 51? In which 81?
In which is 2? 12? 22?
            32? 42? 52?
            62? 72? 82?
            92?
In which is 2? 32? 62? 92?
In which is 1? 31? 61? 91?
In which is 12? 42? 72?
In which is 11? 41? 71?
In which is 22? 52? 82?
In which is 21? 51? 81?
In which is 3? 13? 23?
            33? 43? 53?
            63? 73? 83?
            93?
In which is 3? 33? 63? 93?
             2? 32? 62? 92?
             1? 31? 61? 91?
In which is 13? 43? 73?
            12? 42? 72?
            11? 41? 71?
In which is 23? 53? 83?
            22? 52? 82?
            21? 51? 81?
In which pile is 3? 6? 9? 13? 16? 19? 23? 26? 29?
            33? 36? 39? 43? 46? 49? 53? 56? 59?
            63? 66? 69? 73? 76? 79? 83? 86? 89?
            93? 96? 99?

In which pile is 2? 5? 8? 12? 15? 18? 22? 25? 28?
                  32? 35? 38? 42? 45? 48? 52? 55? 58?
                  62? 65? 68? 72? 75? 78? 82? 85? 88?
                  92? 95? 98?
                    1? 4? 7? 11? 14? 17? 21? 24? 27?
                  31? 34? 37? 41? 44? 47? 51? 54? 57?
                  61? 64? 67? 71? 74? 77? 81? 84? 87?
                  91? 94? 97? 101?

I take up 3 coffee-beans, and lay down 2; how many have I? I take up 3 more; how many have I now? I lay down 2; how many? I take up 3; how many now? I lay down 2; how many now?

    I take up 2 coffee-beans, and then two more; how many have I? I lay down 3; how many have I now? I take up 2; how many? I take up 2 more; how many? I lay down 3; how many?

A boy had 3 red marbles, and 3 yellow ones. How many was that? He had besides 3 green ones; how many was that? He had besides 3 blue ones; how many was that? He had besides 3 violet ones; how many was that? He had besides 3 magenta ones; how many was that? He had besides three brown ones; how many was that? He had besides three buff ones; how many was that? He had besides three olive ones; how many was that? He had besides three slate-colored ones; how many was that? He had besides three grey ones; how many was that? He had besides three black ones; how many was that? He had besides three [white] ones ...

Counting by fours. Deal the cards into 4 piles. [The piles should be taken up in this order: 1st, 2nd, 3rd, 4th.]

```
 4   8  12  16  20  24  28  32  36  40 ⎫
44  48  52  56  60  64  68  72  76  80 ⎬ 4th Pile
84  88  92  96 100                     ⎭

                 3   7  11  15  19 ⎫
23  27  31  35  39  43  47  51  55  59 ⎬ 3rd Pile
63  67  71  75  79  83  87  91  95  99 ⎭

 2   6  10  14  18  22  26  30  34  38 ⎫
42  46  50  54  58  62  66  70  74  78 ⎬ 2nd Pile
82  86  90  94  98                     ⎭
```

			1	5	9	13	17	
21	25	29	33	37	41	45	49	53	57
61	65	69	73	77	81	85	89	93	97
101								

1st Pile

Counting by fours on the abacus, beginning with 1, 2, 3, 4. Competitive counting of coffee-beans by fours. Counting downward by fours.

In which pile is   10? 20? 30? 40? 50? 60? 70? 80? 90? 100?

4? 14? 24? 34? 44? 54? 64? 74? 84? 94?

8? 18? 28? 38? 48? 58? 68? 78? 88? 98?

In which pile is 2? 12? 22? 32? 42? 52? 62? 72? 82? 92?

6? 16? 26? 36? 46? 56? 66? 76? 86? 96?

In which pile is 1? 11? 21? 31? 41? 51? 61? 71? 81? 91? 101?

5? 15? 25? 35? 45? 55? 65? 75? 85? 95?

9? 19? 29? 39? 49? 59? 69? 79? 89? 99?

In which pile is 3? 13? 23? 33? 43? 53? 63? 73? 83? 93?

7? 17? 27? 37? 47? 57? 67? 77? 87? 97?

I hold 50 coffee-beans in my hand. I lay down four. How many have I now? I lay down four others; how many have I now? Etc.

There are 52 weeks in a year. After 4 weeks have passed, how many are there to come? After 4 weeks later, how many to come? Etc.

Mrs. Notable had 75 cents. She spent 4. How many had she left? She spent four more; how many had she then? She spent four more; how many had she then? Etc.

Edgar had 25 pigeons; but 4 were lost. How many remained? Four more were lost; how many remained? Etc.

Every President of the United States is President for 4 years, but the same man may be president for two terms of 4 years. The first President was Inaugurated in 1789. What were the years of the others? The presidents were:

George Washington
George Washington
John Adams
Thomas Jefferson

Counting by fives. Deal the cards into 5 piles.

5	10	15	20	25	30	35	40	45	50	5th Pile
55	60	65	70	75	80	85	90	95	100	
4	9	14	19	24	29	34	39	44	49	4th Pile
54	59	64	69	74	79	84	89	94	99	
3	8	13	18	23	28	33	38	43	48	3rd Pile
53	58	63	68	73	78	83	88	93	98	
2	7	12	17	22	27	32	37	42	47	2nd Pile
52	57	62	67	72	77	82	87	92	97	
1	6	11	16	21	26	31	36	41	46	1st Pile
51	56	61	66	71	76	81	86	91	96	
101										

(The piles are to be taken up in this order: 1st, 2nd, 3rd, 4th, 5th.) Counting by fives on the abacus, beginning with 1, 2, 3, 4, 5. Competitive countings of coffee-beans by fives. Counting downward by fives.

In which pile is 1? 11? 21? 31? 41? 51? 61? 71? 81? 91? 101?
In which pile is 2? 12? 22? 32? 42? 52? 62? 72? 82? 92?
In which pile is 3? 13? 23? 33? 43? 53? 63? 73? 83? 93?
In which pile is 4? 14? 24? 34? 44? 54? 64? 74? 84? 94?
In which pile is 5? 15? 25? 35? 45? 55? 65? 75? 85? 95?
In which pile is 6? 16? 26? 36? 46? 56? 66? 76? 86? 96?
In which pile is 7? 17? 27? 37? 47? 57? 67? 77? 87? 97?
In which pile is 8? 18? 28? 38? 48? 58? 68? 78? 88? 98?
In which pile is 9? 19? 29? 39? 49? 59? 69? 79? 89? 99?
In which pile is   10? 20? 30? 40? 50? 60? 70? 80? 90? 100?

Counting by sixes. Deal the cards into 6 piles.

6	12	18	24	30	36	42	48	54	60	6th Pile
66	72	78	84	90	96					
						1	7	13	19	1st Pile
25	31	37	43	49	55	61	67	73	79	
85	91	97								
					2	8	14	20	26	32	38	2nd Pile
44	50	56	62	68	74	80	86	92	98	

```
 3   9  15  21  27  33  39  45  51  57⎤
63  69  75  81  87  93  99             ⎬ 3rd Pile
                                       ⎦

                     4  10  16⎤
22  28  34  40  46  52  58  64  70  76⎬ 4th Pile
82  88  94 100                ⎦

             5  11  17  23  29  35⎤
41  47  53  59  65  71  77  83  89  95⎬ 5th Pile
101                               ⎦
```

(The piles are to be taken up in this order: 5th, 4th, 3rd, 2nd, 1st, 6th.)

Counting by sevens. The piles are to be taken up in this order: 3rd, 6th, 2nd, 5th, 1st, 4th, 7th.

```
7  14  21  28  35  42  49  56  63  70  77  84  91  98
4  11  18  25  32  39  46  53  60  67  74  81  88  95
1   8  15  22  29  36  43  50  57  64  71  78  85  92  99
5  12  19  26  33  40  47  54  61  68  75  82  89  96
2   9  16  23  30  37  44  51  58  65  72  79  86  93 100
6  13  20  27  34  41  48  55  62  69  76  83  90  97
3  10  17  24  31  38  45  52  59  66  73  80  87  94 101
```

3

PEIRCE'S PRIMARY ARITHMETIC
UPON THE PSYCHOLOGICAL METHOD   (part of 179)

My father, Professor Benjamin Peirce, a celebrated mathematician, was very particular to have me taught arithmetic, by the same method by which he had very successfully learnt the art, only with improvements which his experience had suggested. Studies of modern psychology have enabled me still further to perfect this system; and after assuring myself by actual trial of its advantages, I here offer it in a practical form to the teachers of our people.

Miss Sessions was a sweet, dear, jolly old lady, who kept a school for boys and girls. She used to say the children were her gardens, — each child a good spacious garden, not little at all, although the things growing in the garden were little, because it was only spring-time. In every garden, Miss Sessions was trying to make things grow, — beautiful, gay flowers, and sweet-smelling things, and vegetables good to eat, and other little things which seemed very useless, but which would in future years grow up to great shady trees under which many people could find shelter. Then, she had to pull up the weeks, nasty bad-smelling, ugly, and poisonous things, wild grasses, things not so very bad in themselves but which would leave no room for the good things which were to make the garden fine hereafter. Pulling up the weeds always gave the ground pain; but Miss Sessions used to say, "You must bear this little pain, now, my dear garden, for were such weeds allowed to grow, they would have to be pulled up at last with much greater pain, and too late for flowers to take their place."

Miss Sessions wanted to get a dress made for herself. So she went off to the shop, taking with her some of her scholars, Alfred and Beatrice and Eulalia and George and Ned and Ralph and Louisa and Robert and Richard and Daisy and Barbara and Cicely and Deborah and Priscilla and Hugh and Guy and Roger.

They looked at many things and at last Deborah said, "Please, Miss

Sessions, get this blue silk with a white vine upon it." "Would you like to see me wear that?" asked Miss Sessions. "Indeed I should," said Deborah. So it was settled that that should be taken. "How much do you want?" asked the salesman. "Now, what a silly old thing I am. I don't know how much I want," said Miss Sessions. "I must go home and think it over." The salesman promised to keep the piece till the next day. "I'll tell you, how I can find out," said Miss Sessions, on the way back. "When I had my black bombazine made, I had a piece of wine colored muslin, of exactly the same length. Now, there was just enough of the bombazine to make me my dress and leave over enough for alterations. But the muslin has never been made up. So I will take that to the shop and get a piece so large that one will just cover the other, when they are both spread out." "That will be a good deal of trouble," said Roger. "Yes, so it will," said Miss Sessions; "but what else can I do." "Why," said Roger, "you might take a stick, and hold the end of it against the corner of the muslin, and stretch the list along the stick, and hold your finger on the list where the second end of the stick comes, and then put the first end there and stretch more of the list along the stick, and count how many times you could do this before you came to the end of the muslin, and then carry the stick to the shop, and stretch that silk along the stick the same number of times. Then you would know you had just as much of that as of the other."

"Well, I will do that; and I happen to have a very good stick for the purpose." So the stick was used in [the] manner proposed; and it was found that the cloth was 12 times as long as the stick. The next day they all returned to the shop. "Well," asked the salesman, "have you found out how much you wanted?" "Yes," said Miss Sessions, "I want 12 times the length of this stick." "You mean you want 12 yards. But what should you bring the stick for?" "To show you how long it is." "Did you think I hadn't a yardstick, too? See, mine is just the length of yours. It is a yard." "Of course," said Eulalie, "Miss Sessions knew that, all along. But it was only a bit of her fun to pretend she never heard of measuring cloth,[1] [...]"

---

[1] Peirce's notes to himself are incorporated in the manuscript and read as follows:
Addition in Primary Arith.

In group-counting the child has already practised addition and knows the table to perfection. Nothing remains but to accustom him to add in first one number and then another, together with the word.

Introductory Example. Poor family without food. Each member contributed something. Put them down — Add them up. Find the sum total.

Describe the process carefully.

Family out walking finds little girl without shoes.

Miss Sarah Sessions had taken her school of boys and girls out for a ramble in the woods, and who should they find but a poor little girl with bare feet, seated on a style and crying softly. "What is the matter, my dear," said Eulalie, who first came up to her. "I have no shoes." "Miss Sessions," cried Eulalie, "here is a little girl without shoes; let us go and buy her a pair." "But have you the money?" "I have only eleven cents," said Eulalie. "I have 7," said Richard. "I have 2," said Amy. "I have 9," said Robert. "I will give 6," said Theodore. "And I 5," said Julia. "And I 8," said Emily. "And I 3," said George. "And I 3," said Gregory. "And I 4," said Hermann. "And I 4," said Louisa. "And I seven," said Helen. "Set down the amounts one under the other, Eulalie," said the teacher. So they were neatly written, thus:

Eulalie	11
Richard	7
Amy	2
Robert	9
Theodore	6

1893

Addition in Primary Arithmetic

Sheldon's Elementary Arithmetic begins with it. He sticks down $1 + 1 = 2$ right at the very first! Before introducing the number 4! This is madness!

Wentworth Primary Arithmetic introduces the thing but not the name before use of all the numbers. He puts off the use of the name very injudiciously.

Greenleaf's First Lessons does about the same.

Rickoff First Lessons in Arithmetic does the same.

The Franklin the same.

Ray's New Primary. Avoids this great mistake.

Robinson's New Primary partly avoids it.

Robinson's Progressive Primary wholly avoids it.

Teach one thing at a time, is what the most of them forget. But slight preparatory hints of what is coming without special teaching is permissible and recommendable.

Terminology of addition

Addition
Add, cast up, sum
Sum total
To carry

Subtraction

subtract, deduct, rebate
minuend
subtrahend
remainder, remainer
to borrow

Julia	5
Emily	8
George	3
Gregory	3
Hermann	4
Louisa	4
Helen	7

"Now who can cast up the amounts and find the sum total?" asked Miss Sessions. "Do you mean who can add them together, and find out how many cents there will be when they are all put together?" asked George. "Yes, that is the same thing." "I can do it," said George. "Let me see how you do it." "Eleven and seven are 18, and 2 are 20, and 9 are 29, and 6 are 35, and 5 are 40, and 8 are 48, and 3 are 51, and 3 are 54, and 4 are 58, and 4 are 62, and 7 are 69." "How much must I add, then, to make 75?" "Six cents," said George.

"That is right, and the whole addition is right," said Miss Sessions. "But you must learn to do addition, — that is to count numbers together, — in the easiest and quickest way; for every grown person has many sums to cast up every day, and it is tiresome if not done skillfully, and very bad to make mistakes. Whoever makes mistakes in arthmetic gets terribly punished in life." "How should I add?" asked George. "Point with a pencil at each number, just as you are about to add it in; and that the pencil may not hide what comes next, begin at the bottom. Say 7, and pointing at the 4, say 11. Only do not say this loud, but keep your mouth shut. Then move the pencil up, so as to point at the upper 4. Do not say 'And 4,' even to yourself. But *look at* the 4 and say to yourself, 15; keeping your lips firmly shut. If you stop to talk, you cannot add rapidly. Move your pencil up to the 3, and say to yourself 18. Move your pencil up to the upper 3, and say to yourself 21. Move your pencil up to the 8, and say to yourself, 29. Move your pencil up to the 5, and say to yourself, 34. Move your pencil up to the 6 and say to yourself, 40. Move your pencil up to the 9, and say to yourself 49. Move your pencil up to the 2, and say to yourself 51. Move your pencil up to the 7, and say to yourself, 58. Move your pencil up to the 11, and say to yourself 69. Draw a line under the column of figures and under it write 69. It is the sum total."

Some boys agreed to put their money together and buy a football. "I will give 7 cents," said Alfred; "and I 4," said Charley; "and I 2," said Ned; "and I 9," said George; "and I 6," said Ike; "and I 4," said Max; "and

I 1," said Nick; "and I 8," said Philip; "and I 6," said Dick; "and I 3," said Bob.

"How many cents will there be, altogether?" asked Alfred. "All put down their money, and we will count it," said Charley. "But I left mine at home," said Ned. "So did I," said Ike. "And so did I," said Nick. "Let us cut out papers," said Bob, "and pretend they are cents, and everybody give as many of those as he will give of cents; and then we will count the papers, and that will show how many cents, there will be." "It will be much easier to add the amounts," said George. "How do you do that?" said Max. "I will show you," said George. "You begin by writing the numbers one under the other so." Then he wrote:

Alfred	7
Charley	4
Ned	2
George	9
Ike	6
Max	4
Nick	1
Philip	8
Dick	6
Bob	3

"Now," he continued, "you say 7 and 4 make 11; and 2 makes 13; and 9 makes 22; and 6 makes 28; and 4 makes 32; and 1 makes 33; and 8 makes 41; and 6 makes 47; and 3 makes 50. So there will be 50 cents in all."

While George was explaining this, the school-mistress, Miss Sessions, came up; and when he had done, she said: "Yes, George, that is right. But did I hear you say you did this addition because it was quicker and easier than counting pieces of paper?" "Yes," he answered, "is not that so?" "Yes, indeed. Only, if you add because it is a quick and easy way of finding out what you want to know, then you want to do it in the quickest and easiest way. Now, your way is right; but here is a quicker and easier way.

"You write the numbers exactly under one another in as straight a column as you can. Then, you take a pencil and point at the lowest number, — in this case, 3 — and keeping your lips tight shut, — say silently to yourself, 3. Then, point to the number next higher, here 6, look at it, but do not say it to yourself; only say silently to yourself 9, which comes next after 3 in counting by 6s. Then point to the number next higher, — here 8, — look at it, and say silently to yourself 17, which comes next after 9 in counting by 8s. So you go on:

> Pointing at 1, say silently 18.
> Pointing at 4, say silently 22.
> Pointing at 6, say silently 28.
> Pointing at 9, say silently 37.
> Pointing at 2, say silently 39.
> Pointing at 4, say silently 43.
> Pointing at 7, say silently 50."

"Do you add in this way?" asked George. "No," said Miss Sessions, "I have a quicker way still; but the way I tell you is the best way for beginners."

"Say, Miss Sessions," said Alfred, "George has set me a sum that I cannot do." "What is it, Alfred?" "There is a hymn,

> Jesus shall reign where'er the sun
> Does his successive journeys run.

The first verse has 26 words, the second 25, the third 24, the fourth 25, the fifth 27, and the sixth 22. How many words, are there in all?" "Let us see," said Miss Sessions. "We write them down carefully." She wrote

1st Verse	26
2nd	25
3rd	24
4th	25
5th	27
6th	22

"Now let us not count the twenties, at first; but only the numbers over twenty. They make how many?" "What?" asked Alfred. "Why how much do the 6, 5, 4, 5, 7, 2 make, without the twenties?" "Oh, they make 29." "Right. Now set down the 9 and add in all the twenties. The 20 of the 29 and the 20 of the 22, make 40, do they not?" "I suppose 20 and 20 make 40," said Alfred. "Are you sure they don't make 37?" "Yes, I am sure they make 40." "Now the 20 of the 27 makes 60; and the 20 of the 25 makes 80; and the 20 of the 24 makes 100; and the 20 of the 25 makes 120; and the 20 of the 26, makes 140. Now, we had 9 set down. 140 and 9 make 149. But I will show you an easier way. You add up the last column, the 6, the 5, the 4, the 5, the 7, and the 2. We call this the column of units. The units are 29. We set that down, making the two very small, thus:

1st Verse	26
2nd	25
3rd	24
4th	25
5th	27
6th	22

2
9

We say this is 'carried.' That is, it is carried to the other column.

Now the other column is the column of tens. Twenty is the tens. Add these up as if they were units, not leaving out the 2 of the 29."

"Miss Sessions, if you please," said George, "there are 365 days in the year. Now January, the first month, has 31 days. At the end of January how many days remain before the end of the year?" "You must set down 365 and 31 under it, thus:

Whole year	365 days
January	31

Now you must ask, how many must be added to 1 to make 5, that is what goes before 5 in counting by 1s? What is the answer to that?" George said, "4." "Very well. Set that down below, thus:

365
31
____
4

Now ask how much must be added to 3 to make 6, that is, what goes before 6 in counting by 3s?" George said, "3." "Good. Set that down, thus:

365
31
____
34

Now nothing is taken away from the hundreds. So they remain 3. So the answer is

Whole year	365 days
January	31 days
Rest of year	334 days.

This work is called *subtraction*, which is taking away. 31 is subtracted from 365 and leaves 334. We call 365 the *minuend*, 31 the *subtrahend*, and 334 the *remainder* or *remainer*. You can also say *deduct*: 31 is deducted from 365. Also, you can say you *rebate* 31 from 365. You can call 334 the *remainder*, or you can call it the *balance*. To prove you have done the substraction right, add

$$\begin{array}{r} 334 \\ 31 \\ \hline 365 \end{array}$$

It gives the minuend."

George said, "The second month is February, and it has 28 days? How shall I subtract 28 from 334?"

Miss Sessions replied, "Set down the subtrahend under the minuend." George sets it down thus:

$$\begin{array}{r} 334 \\ 28 \end{array}$$

"No," said Miss Sessions, "that won't do. You must set down units under units and tens under tens, thus:

$$\begin{array}{r} 334 \\ 28 \end{array}\text{''}$$

"But " said George, "I cannot ask how much must be added to 8 to make 4, because 8 is more than 4."

"That is true," replied Miss Sessions, "so you must borrow ten from the 30. That is you must think of 334, not as 330 with 4 besides, but as 320 with 14 besides. Then, how much must be added to 8 to make 14? That is, what goes before 14 in counting by 8s?"

George replied, "6."

"Good, set down the 6 thus:

$$\begin{array}{r} 334 \\ 28 \\ \hline 6 \end{array}$$

Now you have to take 20 from 320 or 2 from 32, or say 2 from 2. How much is that, George?"

"In counting by 2s, there is no number which goes before 2."

"That is true. But if you put 2 marbles on the table, you can then take 2 marbles away, and how many are left?"

"None at all."

"Then put down, 0 which [is] nothing, naught, cipher, or zero."

"Then I get

$$334$$
$$28$$
$$306$$

Is that right?"

"Add the remainder to the subtrahend; and see if you get back the minuend."

George does the sum

$$306$$
$$28$$
$$334$$

"Yes, I do."

"Then, it is plainly right. Now, see here. There were in 1890, 62 622 250 persons in our country and 32 067 880 were men and boys. How many women and girls were there?

| People | 62 622 250 |
| Men | 32 067 880 |

Say, 0 from 0 is how many?"

George does not know.

"2 from 2 left none. Put 1 marble on the table and then take 1 away, and how many are left?"

George says, "None."

"Put no marbles at all on the table, and take none away, and how many are there?"

George says, "None. But then," added he, "that seems silly."

"It would be silly, if that was the whole of it; but it is not silly, when it helps you to subtract 32 067 880 from 62 622 250."

"No, that is true," said George.

"Very well: Put down the 0, thus

$$62 622 250$$
$$32 067 880$$
$$0$$

Now, 8 from 5 is how many?"

"I can't take 8 from 5," said George.

"That is true. Then, take 8 from 15, borrowing from the 2 to the left. That leaves how many?"

"In counting by 8s, before 15 comes 7 " said George.

"Good; then put down the 7, thus:

$$\begin{array}{r} 62\,622\,250 \\ 32\,067\,880 \\ \hline 70 \end{array}$$

Now, 8 from 1 leaves how many?"

"I can't," said George, "but borrowing 1, 8 from 11 leaves 3, because, in counting by 8s, 3 comes next before 11."

"Very good. We set that down

$$\begin{array}{r} 62\,622\,250 \\ 32\,067\,880 \\ \hline 370 \end{array}$$

Now 7 from 1 leaves how many?"

"I can't," said George, "but borrowing 1, 7 from 11 leaves 4, because, in counting by 7s, 4 comes next before 11."

"Good again. We set that down

$$\begin{array}{r} 62\,622\,250 \\ 32\,067\,880 \\ \hline 4\,370 \end{array}$$

Now 6 from 1 leaves how many?"

"I can't," said George, "but borrowing 1, 6 from 11 leaves 5, because, in counting by 6s, 5 comes next before 11."

"Right again. We set that down

$$\begin{array}{r} 62\,622\,250 \\ 32\,067\,880 \\ \hline 54\,370 \end{array}$$

Now 0 from 5 leaves how many?"

"I don't know how to count by naughts " said George; "but if I put 5 marbles on the table and take none away, 5 will remain."

"Excellent. We set that down

$$\begin{array}{r} 62\,622\,250 \\ 32\,067\,880 \\ \hline 554\,370 \end{array}$$

Now, 2 from 2 is how many?"

"Naught," said George.

"Right, we set that down

$$62\,622\,250$$
$$32\,067\,880$$
$$\overline{0\,554\,370}$$

Now, 3 from 6 is how many?"

"In counting by 3s, next before 6 comes 3 " said George.

"Right. We have then the answer complete

People	62 622 250
Men and boys	32 067 880
Women and girls	30 554 370.

Now I will ask you a question. If the 30 554 370 women and girls were each to be married to a man or boy, how many bachelors would be left over?"

George answered correctly.

"And if all these bachelors were to hire themselves out as servants to as many of the married couples, how many couples would remain without bachelor servants?"

"There were in the country that year 43 431 136 sheep. If they had all belonged to different people, how many people would remain without sheep?"

Eulalie said to Miss Sessions, "I am slow in doing subtraction; because though I can count by groups forward readily enough, I cannot count backwards so quickly." "There is another way of doing subtraction," said Miss Sessions, "which a few persons find advantageous. This method is called subtraction by addition. Suppose, for instance, you want to subtract a number written entirely with 9s. Subtract from 62 622 250 the number 999 999. The easiest way is to subtract 1 000 000 and then add 1:

$$62\,622\,250$$
$$999\,999$$
$$\overline{61\,622\,251}$$

But if the subtrahend is not all nines, you must call every 9 a 0,

every 8 a 1,
every 7 a 2,
every 6 a 3,
every 5 a 4,
every 4 a 5,
every 3 a 6,
every 2 a 7,

every 1 a 8,
every 0 a 9,

and add them in. Also add 1 and subtract 1 from the place next higher than the highest place of the subtrahend. Thus, to subtract 32067880 from 62622250 write them down and proceed as follows:

62622250
32067880

Say 0 and 9 (really 0) are 9 and 1 makes 10. Set down 0 and carry 1. 1 and 5 are 6, and 1 (really 8) makes 7; set it down. 2 and 1 (really 8) are 3: set it down. 2 and 2 (really 7) are 4: set it down. 2 and 3 (really 6) are 5: set it down. 6 and 9 (really 0) are 15: set down 5 and carry 1. 1 and 2 are 3; and 7 (really 2) are 10: set down 0, and carry 1. 1 and 6 are 7; and 6 (really 3) makes 13: set down 3 and carry one. From 1, subtract 1 leaving 0."

MULTIPLICATION

"George," asked Miss Sessions, "can you tell me how many points there are in this block without counting them, if I tell you that there are 7 in every row and 6 in every column?" and she showed him a paper with dots upon it, like this.

. . . .
. . . .
. . . .
. . . .
. . . .
. . . .

"I can say 6, 12, 18, 24, 30, 36, 42. There are 42," said George. "But can you not tell any quicker way?" George thought a minute. "It is a little quicker to tell 7, 14, 21, 28, 35, 42; because then I only have to count 6 numbers, instead of 7," said he. "Yes, but George," said Miss Sessions, "you must learn that the 6th number in counting by 7s, or 6 times 7, as we say, is 42, so that you will not have to stop to think. When you are grown up, it will happen every day that something important depends on how much 6 times 7 is, and you will be in such a hurry that you cannot stop to say 7, 14, 21, 28, 35, 42. You have to learn by heart that 6 times 7 is 42; so that you know it, the moment the question comes, like a flash."

"Of course," said George, "we have practised so much counting by 7s and other groups that I should know 6 times 7 made either 35 or 42 or 49; but I should have to count to see which it made."

"Well, now you must learn it by heart. And in learning it by heart this little cross will be an assistance." [Fig. 1]

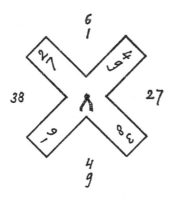

She gave him a little cross like this.[2] "How do you use it?" he asked.

"In the first place," she said, "you have to remember that all multiples of even numbers are even."

"What is a multiple?" asked George.

"Why the multiples of 6 are 12, 18, 24, 30, 36, 42, 48, 54, 60, and so forth. The multiples of 7 are 14, 21, 28, 35, 42, 49, 56, 63, 70, 77, 84, 91, 98, etc. Do you understand? The *multiple* of a number is a number of times that number. Now all multiples of even numbers are even: remember that. So 6 times 7 is an even number. Now bring either the 6 or the 7 on the cross to the top, by turning the cross; and look for the other number (say 6) outside the cross. Then on the cross opposite that number you find the last figure of the answer. In this case opposite 6 outside the cross, we find 2 and 7 on the cross. Therefore 6 times 7 ends either with a 2 or a 7. But it is an even number and therefore cannot end with a 7. So it ends with a 2; and since you have already learned all the multiples of 7, you will see it must be 42."

"That is curious," said George.

"Here is the multiplication table," said Miss Sessions, "which you have got to know just as well as you know the alphabet," said Miss Sessions.

---

[2]　This is a cut-out cardboard cross attached at its center to the page with a string like the calendrical wheels in medieval manuscripts.

1	2	3	4	5	6	7	8	9
2	4	6	8	10	12	14	16	18
3	6	9	12	15	18	21	24	27
4	8	12	16	20	24	28	32	36
5	10	15	20	25	30	35	40	45
6	12	18	24	30	36	42	48	54
7	14	21	28	35	42	49	56	63
8	16	24	32	40	48	56	64	72
9	18	27	36	45	54	63	72	81

"You begin by learning the multiples of 5; then those of 2; then those of 4; then those of 8. Then those of 9; then those of 3; then those of 6. Last those of 7. It is a big piece of work; but go at it industriously, and you will accomplish it, at last."

"All right: I will try hard," said George.

"Dear Miss Sessions, do give us something to help us a little in this terrible task of learning the multiplication table," said Thisbe.

"Learn in the first place the squares, or numbers down the dexter diagonal —"

"Oh, please," said Thisbe, "I beg pardon. What is a dexter diagonal?"

"A *diagonal* is a line from one corner to another, not next to it. The *dexter* diagonal of a square is the line from the upper left hand to lower right hand corner. The line from the upper right hand to lower left hand corner is called the sinister diagonal. You can learn first the numbers in the dexter diagonal. These are

0 time 0 is 0
1 time 1 is 1
2 times 2 are 4

etc. They are called the *squares*. Thus, 4 is the *square* of 2, and 9 is the *square* of 3. You then learn the products placed next to the diagonal." [...]³

"Oh," said Eulalie, "please give us something to help us in this work of learning the multiplication table. It is so very tiresome."

³ Another teaching comment is pertinent here. It states that "There is nothing more instructive for children in many ways than cards bearing the successive numbers from 1 to 100. Each number should be expressed in Arabic figures, below; and above should be that number of red spots. These dots may be arranged so as to show the factors of the number, or if it is a prime to show that it is one more or less than a multiple of 6. For if the arrangement should be remembered, which is not to be desired, it will, at least, recall a fact of value."

"Well, I will tell you something," said Miss Sessions. "Take two packs of arithmetic cards, one with red backs, the other with blue backs. Arrange each pack in order beginning at the back. Lay the red pack on the table face down. Remove card 101 from the blue pack. Hold the blue pack in your hand face down. Deal the cards out one by one into three packets face up. Take up the middle packet, put the first packet at the back of it and the last packet at the back of that. Take off the back card (which will be the 3) and lay it down face up as the first card of a new pile; and in place of it put the top card of the red pack.

"Again deal out the pack into three packets, as before. Take up the packets as before. Take off the back card (which will be the 9) and lay it down as the second card of the new pile.

"Do this a hundred times, and you will find you have only red cards in your hand, while the 100 blue cards will be in the new pile. Now spread this new pile out in ten rows of ten cards in a row. Here will be the arrangement.[4]

"Now, if you want to know how much 6 times 7 make, look for the places of the 6 and 7. The 6 is in the 30th place for it is the 3rd row 10th column. The 7 is in the 61st place, 7th row 1st column. Add together 30 and 61. The sum is 91. Therefore, in the 91st place you find 42, the product of 6 and 7. Suppose you want to find 5 times 2. The 5 is in the 96th place, the 2 in the 29th place. Add 96 and 29. The sum is 125. Strike off the 100 and in the 25th place you find 10, the product of 5 and 2.

"If the product of the two numbers taken is more than 100, what you will find is a number which must be added to 101, 202, 303, or some multiple of 101 to get the product. Thus, suppose we want the product of 19 and 41. This must be nearly 800; for that is 20 times 40. Now 19 is in the 84th place, and 41 is in the 5th place. The sum of 84 and 5 is 89. In the 89th place is 72. But the cross shows the real product ends with 9. This 72 ends with 2, which taken from 9 leaves 7. So we add 707 and find 779, which is the product of 19 and 41."

---

[4]   Peirce fails to indicate the arrangement in the manuscript.

C. S. PEIRCE'S VULGAR ARITHMETIC
ITS CHIEF FEATURES (178)[1]

It is a two-book arithmetic. The Primary Part is the one upon which the most labor has been bestowed.

I propose here to explain the leading features, beginning with the manner in which the operations are performed in both books, after which I shall explain my aim in the style etc. including the examples.

NUMERATION

A great point is made of the manner of writing the figures etc.

The figures must be very distinct, free from all fanciful forms, and so open, that, in case of error, a figure can have another written over it without becoming illegible

$$1 \quad 2 \quad 3 \quad 4 \quad 5 \quad 6 \quad 7 \quad 8 \quad 9 \quad 0$$

The figures must be written in clearly marked columns as evenly as may be.

In the Advanced book, the pupil is required to state his proceeding and write against each number what it is, and render the whole a perspicuous statement.

ADDITION

Addition is by very much the most indispensable part of arithmetic. If one is an accomplished adder, one can *à la rigueur* go without knowing

---

[1] MS. 177 on the other hand is called "The Practice of Vulgar Arithmetic," and duplicates much in 178. Materials that are different will be referred to in these footnotes.

even the multiplication table; and at any rate when addition is thoroughly mastered, it affords a master-key to all the other operations. It is also by far the most difficult of the operations of arithmetic. For all these reasons taken together, I bestow upon addition more time and exercise than upon all the other operations taken together, particularly in the primary book.

I hold that my way of teaching addition is the only really efficient way. It consists of teaching the children to count *rapidly* by ones, by nines, by fives, by twos, by eights, by fours, by sixes, by threes and by sevens *beginning from any number*. This is entirely on oral performance. The psychological image is at first *auditory*, but the appearance of the figures is associated with the sound from the first. For the simultaneous activity of two senses is a great advantage.

Packs of cards are provided, each card bearing a number, and these run up to 101 inclusive. The pack being arranged in order of increasing number from back to face is dealt out into piles. In counting by ones, — that is, 1, 2, 3, 4, etc. and by *nines*,

1,	10,	19,	28,	37,	46,	55,	64,	73,	82,	91,	100
2,	11,	20,	29,	38,	47,	56,	65,	74,	83,	92,	101
3,	12,	21,	30,	39,	48	etc.					

the cards are already shown. The dealing begins with dealing into five packs thus:

1	2	3	4	5
6	7	8	9	10
11	12	13	14	15
16	17	18	19	20
21	22	23	24	25
26	27	28	29	30
31	32	33	34	35
36	37	38	39	40
41	42	43	44	45
46	47	48	49	50
51	52	53	54	55
56	57	58	59	60
61	62	63	64	65
66	67	68	69	70
71	72	73	74	75
76	77	78	79	80
81	82	83	84	85
86	87	88	89	90
91	92	93	94	95
96	97	98	99	100
101				

These and all the other modes of counting must be drilled into them until these operations become easier and more sure than talking.

There will be also some drill, — not so much, — upon descending counts. Not much is necessary in order to render it perfectly easy.

This counting is the chief business of the primary arithmetic. The children are also to be taught games to play with the cards out of school, these games depending for success in being able quickly to tell what, after any dealing, is the number of the card in any place of any packet.

The children are also taught to gather up the cards in a particular way after they have been dealt out. Namely, the rule is (the cards lying face up with the higher card toward the faces of the packets) to take first the packet showing 101 at the top, and next, *at the back* of this packet, that one which is the *n*th to the left (the cards having been dealt, turning the face of each up, from left to right) of the packet last taken, where *n* is the number of packets there originally were to the right of the packet showing 101. Of course, there must always be at least one to the right, since 101 is a prime number. But if there are not enough packets to the left, continue the count of the packets round and round, counting the extreme right hand one as virtually next to the left of the extreme left hand one.

Another form of the rule of taking up the packets is to count the packets from left to right and always *skip* as many packets as there are at first to the *left* of the packet showing 101.

For example, after dealing into 8 packets, they will appear as here shown; and the numbers below show the order in which they are to be gathered up.

97	98	99	100	101	94	95	96
5th	2nd	7th	4th	1st	6th	3rd	8th

The extreme right hand one is always taken last.

The object of teaching this method of gathering, which may be omitted if the children are too dull, is that if, for example, after they have been dealt into eight packs, they are now dealt right out again, say into three packs, the cards will fall as follows:[2]

Packets	I.	II.	III.
	8	16	24
	32	40	48
	56	64	72
	80	88	96
$3 = 96 + 8 - 101$	3	11	19
	27	35	43
	51	59	67
	75	83	91
$99 + 8 - 101 = 6$	99	6	14
	22	30	38
	46	54	62
	70	78	86
$94 + 8 - 101 = 1$	94	1	9
	17	25	33
	41	49	57
	65	73	81
$97 + 8 - 101 = 4$	89	97	4
	12	20	28
		etc.,	etc.

Now there will be a game in which the child will want to be able to tell how the cards fall after two or three dealings. In that way he will not only insensibly learn the multiplication table ($3 \times 8 = 24$) and many other things about numbers, but he will also be taught to count by 24s etc. which is virtually adding two columns at once.

For this sort of thing a smaller pack (say of 41 cards, for the number should be prime) may be used to advantage.

After this counting with every interval up to ten has been *thoroughly* mastered, it will be time to begin the adding up of columns. The expression "adding *up*" describes the right way, which is to begin at the bottom; although the column should always be run down again as a check.

Suppose the column is this:

4
7
6
2
8
3
9
8
4
7
7
5

Holding some sort of pointer, place it on 5. Keep *the mouth shut all the time you are adding,* but mentally say "five." Point at the 7 and mentally say "twelve." *On no account say* "5 and 7 make 12" or anything but just 12. You look at the 7 and say "twelve" and the less you *think* about it the better, *though you must not think of anything else.* One of the great advantages of addition is the training it affords in keeping the mind from wandering. Point at the upper 7 and mentally say "nineteen" without a real sound and so on. When you get to the top of the column and find (in this case) the sum to be 70, set down the 0 below with a little 7 thus ₇0, so that if for any reason an error in this addition be subsequently expected, — each column may be gone over apart from the others. Having added *up,* now run down, and in doing so do not use the pointer but take bird's-eye views; thus:

I notice that the 4 in the first line and the 6 in the third make 10 and then 2 and 8 make 20 and a 3 combines with the 7 in the second line to make 30. Then the 9 and 8 make 47 and the 4 and 7 make 58 and 7 is 65 and 5 is 70, as before.

If your two additions do not agree, you may add the column ten times and take the mean of your results, just as if you thought a man had murdered a friend of yours, in case he really had been murdered, but you weren't quite sure that anything had happened to him, good sense would dictate your hanging the supposed murderer just a little, so as to about half execute him.

There should be plenty of practise in adding long columns, — say of 50 lines. It is not only a most useful art but is excellent exercise, not of *intellect,* surely, but of mental control.

SUBTRACTION

is a trifle less facile than addition, and there should be a certain amount of exercise in the use of the *arithmetical complement*. For in long division it appreciably relieves the fatigue.

MULTIPLICATION[3]

Of course, the Multiplication Table must be learned. Exhortation must be resorted to. The imagination must be excited by the most lurid accounts of the ruin and disasters of all kinds public and private due to mistake in multiplication.

At the same time, after thorough drill in counting, to say what 6 times 8 is is merely to say what is the sixth card of the right hand packet after dealing into eight packets.

Everything should be so presented as to stimulate mathematical imagination. Hence the multiplication table should be printed as on the opposite page.[4]

At this point the author of the text-book and the teach[er] have to put forth their most strenuous endeavors to make the subject interesting. To allow it to excite disgust is simply a crime against the soul of the pupil.

Anything that he seems to be interested in connected with the multiplication-table (and if his faculty of observation has been cultivated there will certainly be something) should be seized upon and developed.

For example, he may remark that no products in the multiplication table end in 1 except once each in the odd rows excluding the fifth. There only, there are terminal 5s; and there alone with the zero row there are terminal zeros.

Odd terminals occur only once each in the odd rows excluding the 5 rows. In each of these rows every terminal occurs just once.

---

[3]   In MS. 177 Peirce writes:

"Children should be taught to play games with the pack of 101 cards and these games should be so devised that success shall be made to depend on being able to say promptly what card in dealing into any given number of packs will be in any given place of any given pack.

When this is done, the child will know far more than the multiplication-table. It will be able to give an instantaneous answer to the question. How much is $U \cdot V + W$? whatever digits U, V, W may be.

To learn the multiplication-table is tolerably easy when one has learned to count by every digit. For it is only to be able to say what card is in each place of the *last pack* in every dealing."

[4]   It so appears in the notebook.

In the even rows only even terminals occur, and excluding the zero row, five occur in each and are repeated in the same order, so that in *every* even row

6 times an even digit ends in that digit

$$6 \times 0 = 0 \quad 6 \times 2 = 12 \quad 6 \times 4 = 24 \quad 6 \times 6 = 36 \quad 6 \times 8 = 48$$

7 times an even digit and twice that digit have the same terminal; thus:

$$2 \times 0 = 0 \quad 2 \times 2 = 4 \quad 4 \times 2 = 8 \quad 6 \times 2 = 12 \quad 8 \times 2 = 16$$
$$7 \times 0 = 0 \quad 2 \times 7 = 14 \quad 4 \times 7 = 28 \quad 6 \times 7 = 42 \quad 8 \times 7 = 56$$

8 times an even digit and 3 times that digit have the same terminal; thus:

$$3 \times 0 = 0 \quad 3 \times 2 = 6 \quad 3 \times 4 = 12 \quad 3 \times 6 = 18 \quad 3 \times 8 = 24$$
$$8 \times 0 = 0 \quad 8 \times 2 = 16 \quad 8 \times 4 = 32 \quad 8 \times 6 = 48 \quad 8 \times 8 = 64$$

9 times an even digit and 4 times that digit have the same terminal; thus:

$$4 \times 0 = 0 \quad 4 \times 2 = 8 \quad 4 \times 4 = 16 \quad 4 \times 6 = 24 \quad 4 \times 8 = 32$$
$$9 \times 0 = 0 \quad 9 \times 2 = 18 \quad 9 \times 4 = 36 \quad 9 \times 6 = 54 \quad 9 \times 8 = 72$$

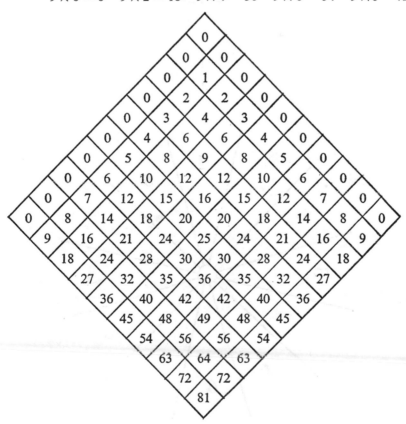

It is possible that a little instrument on the principle of the wheel on [this] page might aid to stimulate the pupils to think about the multiplication-table and so impress its items on their memories. To use this

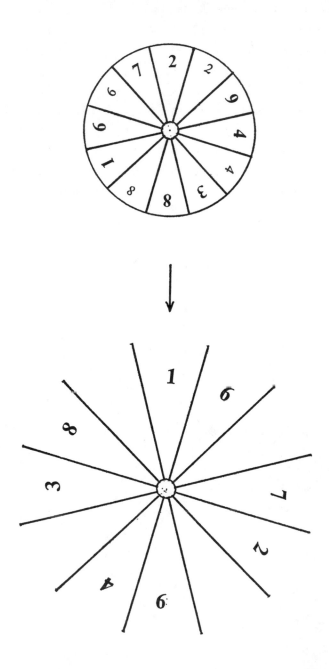

wheel bring under the arrow that *blue* [boldface] number on the wheel that is equal to the final figure of a multiplier.

Then opposite the final figure of the multiplicand outside the wheel will be found on the wheel the final figure of the product.[5]

The objection to inserting this would be that the teachers would not understand the mathematical principle on which it depends, and might therefore be exposed to embarrassing questions.

It would be easy to arrange the numbers in a block so that the last *two* figures should be given, by a similar measurement.

It is well to complete the learning of the multiplication-table by carrying it to 12×12, and the expert computer will be familiar with the following products.

$7 \times 13 = 91$	$7 \times 43 = 301$
$7 \times 17 = 119$	$17 \times 19 = 323$
$7 \times 19 = 133$	$7 \times 47 = 329$
$7 \times 23 = 161$	$7^3 = 343$
$7 \times 29 = 203$	$19^2 = 361$
$7 \times 31 = 217$	$7 \times 53 = 371$
$13 \times 17 = 221$	$13 \times 29 = 377$
$13 \times 19 = 247$	$17 \times 23 = 391$
$7 \times 37 = 259$	$13 \times 31 = 403$
$7 \times 41 = 287$	$7 \times 59 = 413$
$17^2 = 289$	$7 \times 61 = 427$
$13 \times 23 = 299$	$19 \times 23 = 437$
	$7 \times 67 = 469$
	$13 \times 37 = 481$
	$17 \times 29 = 493$
	$7 \times 71 = 497$

In multiplying in the head there are a variety of devices which should be taught; such as multiplying by factors of the whole multiplier and of certain figures of it.

Thus, if the multiplier is 2571, we can multiply by 41 and 60 successively and add to the product the product by 70.[6]

Of course to multiply by a power of 5 we divide by the same power of 2 and then multiply by [the same power of] 10.

---

[5] This is another version of the little cross in MS. 179 (I,2). The circular piece is a separate sheet of paper attached to the notebook at its center as indicated in the figure. The *blue* numbers on the wheel, reading clockwise, are 1, 6, 7, 2, 9, 4, 3, 8; on the page, under the wheel, the numbers appear in that order and are all blue.

[6] Peirce means 2571a = 41a + 60·41a + 70a.

If multiplier and multiplicand are one odd and the other even, the latter should be divided by two and the product remultiplied by 2. Both being odd or both even, their product is the square of their half sum less the square of their half difference. Thus $41 \times 19 = \left(\dfrac{41+19}{2}\right)^2 - \left(\dfrac{41-19}{2}\right)^2$

$= (30)^2 - (11)^2 = 900 - 121 = 779.$

This use of a table of quarter squares will be explained in small print in the higher arithmetic,[7] since this is designed to serve as a handbook as well as a text book.

Cross multiplication, which is indispensable in multiplying in the head, should also be taught.

Long multiplication ought to be performed without the use of the multiplication table; and the following method should be thoroughly practised.

Multiply 87183 and 366917

We begin by forming a table of the first nine multiples of 87183, as follows:

Set down the multiplier 87183

3 being the last figure, proceed to count by 3s setting down the last figure only of each count in a column under the 3 thus:

87183
    6
    9
    2
    5
    8
    1
    4
    7
    0

Any number in the column so written is for the most part greater than the number immediately above it. Where this is not so, put a dot called a "break" in the column next to the left, thus:

[7] Peirce never completed this. It was called advanced arithmetic on page 1.

87183
  6
  9
 .2
  5
  8
 .1
  4
  7
 .0

Next form the column next to the left. Since the breaks are where the change is from large to small and since 8 is at the head of the new column, count by 8s and set down only the last figure until you come to a break where set down the next higher figure and go on from that counting by 8s. The tenth figure should be the same as the number of breaks which is the number at the head of the column last formed. This will be a check. We shall thus get:

87183
 66
 49
 32
 15
 98
 81
 64
 47
 30

In the columns so formed the numbers generally diminish as we go down. Where they do not put "breaks" in the column next to the left, thus:

87183
 66
 49
 32
 15
.98
 81
 64
 47
 30

The number of breaks added to the number at the head of the column last formed should make 9, as we see it does. This is a check.

We now start the next column since 1 is at the head of it. We count by *twos* because the breaks are ascending breaks. We set down the last figure of each counted number till we reach a break where we set down 1 less and proceed from that counting by twos as before; thus:

87183
366
549
732
915
098
281
464
647
830

The tenths figure should be the same as that at the head of the last column.

Now the numbers written in the three columns mostly increase. Hence we insert *descending* breaks in the column next to the left; thus:

87183
366
549
732
915
.098
281
464
647
830

The number of descending breaks equals the number at the head of the last column as it should. Because the breaks are descending and 7 is at the head of the next column, we count from it by sevens, setting down only the last figure until we reach a break, where we set down the next higher figure and go on from that, thus:

```
87183
 4366
 1549
 8732
 5915
 3098
 0281
 7464
 4647
 1830
```

The tenth figure is the same as that at the head of the column last formed, as it should be.

The numbers now generally decrease and we therefore insert ascending breaks of which there should be $9 - 7 = 2$.

```
87183
 4366
 1549
.8732
 5015
 3098
 0281
.7464
 4647
 1830
```

Since the breaks are ascending and 8 is at the head of the next column we count by 9s except at the breaks, thus:

```
87183
74366
61549
48732
35915
23098
10281
97464
84647
71830
```

The tenth figure is the same as that at the head of the last column as it should be.

Since the numbers generally diminish we insert ascending breaks of which there should be $9 - 8 = 1$.

```
87183
74366
61549
48732
35915
23098
10281
.97464
84647
71830
```

Since the break is ascending and 0 is virtually at the head of the column we count from it by 1s except at the break:

```
 87183
174366
261549
348732
435915
523098
610281
697464
784647
871830
```

The tenth figure is the same as that at the head of the last column.

We have now formed the multiples and we proceed to number them:

```
 87183   1
174366   2
261549   3
348732   4
435915   5
523098   6
610281   7
697464   8
784647   9
871830
```

We now use this table instead of a multiplication table to multiply into 366917

$$
\begin{array}{r}
366917 \\
\hline
261549 \\
523098 \\
523098 \\
784647 \\
087183 \\
610281 \\
\hline
31988924811 \\
\end{array}
$$
01011331110

Nobody who is trained to perform long multiplication in this way will ever have the patience to perform it otherwise.[8] This process will be given in the little book.

The use of *Crelle's Rechentafeln* for multiplication should be explained in the large arithmetic.

Logarithms will be treated separately later.

DIVISION

Since addition is appreciably less fatiguing and quicker than subtraction, in performing long division the arithmetical complements of the nine multiples of the divisor should be used. NxAr.co.M = Ar.co.(NxM).

With division higher arithmetic naturally begins, and for the more advanced pupil it will be proper here to insert a short course on that subject. But in the arrangement of the book it will be better to place all theoretical matter together and to go on with Vulgar Arithmetic using such propositions of higher arithmetic as may be called for without attempting to prove or explain them. (Such for example is the proposition that a fraction whose denominator has other factors than 2 and 5 is expressible as a circulating decimal.)

It will have to be stated that the number of figures in the circulating decimal representing a fraction is equal to the totient of the denominator; that is, to the number of numbers less than that denominator and prime to it.

Therefore before decimal fractions can be studied it will be necessary to study the greatest common denominator and that algorithm must be practised.

---

[8] Peirce himself uses this multiplication procedure throughout his manuscripts.

That will lead to the study of remainders after division. The following rules will be given:

The remainder after division by 2 is the same as that of the last figure of the dividend.

The remainder after division by 3 is that of the sum of the figures of the dividend.

The remainder after division by 4 is that of the last figure *plus* twice the last but one.

The remainder after division by 5 is that of the last figure.

The remainder after division by 6 is that of the last figure diminished by twice the sum of the rest of the figures.

The remainder after division by 7 is equal to the sum of the units, millions, billions, trillions, etc. *less* the thousands, thousand millions, thousand billions, etc. *plus* twice the hundreds, hundred millions, etc. *less* twice the hundred thousands, hundred thousand millions, etc. *plus* thrice the tens, ten millions, etc. *less* thrice the ten thousands, ten thousand millions, etc.

Thus the remainder after dividing 365 by 7 is the same as that after dividing $5 + 2 \cdot 3 + 3 \cdot 6 = 29$ and this is the same as that of $9 + 3 \cdot 2 = 15$ and this is the same as that of $5 + 3 \cdot 1 = 8$. So there is one day more than a whole number of weeks in a year.

The remainder after division by 8 is the same as that of the units *plus* twice the tens *plus* four times the hundreds.

The remainder after division by 9 is that of the sum of the figures.

The remainder after division by 10 is that of the last figure.

The remainder after division by 11 is that of the units *plus hundreds plus ten thousands* plus *millions* etc. less that of the *tens, thousands, hundred thousands*, ten millions etc.

The remainder after division by 12 is that of the *units*, less twice the *tens*, plus four times the sum of all the other figures.

Thus 11111 divided by 12 leaves a remainder of 11.

The remainder after division by 13 is that of the units, plus millions, plus billions, etc. less thousands, thousand millions, etc. *plus* thrice the ten thousands, the ten thousand millions *minus* thrice the tens, the ten millions etc. *plus* four times the hundred thousands etc. *minus* four times the hundreds etc.

The remainder after division by 17 is the sum of the figures in the 1st (units) place and every 16th place to the left *minus* those in the 9th (hundred millions) place and every 16th place to the left,

    plus twice those in the 11th and every 16th place to the left

minus twice those in the 3rd and every 16th place to the left
plus thrice those in the 12th etc.
minus thrice those in the 4th etc.
plus four times those in the 13th etc.
minus four times those in the 5th etc.
plus five times those in the 16th etc.
minus five times those in the 8th etc.
plus six times those in the 6th etc.
minus six times those in the 14th etc.
plus seven times those in the 10th etc.
minus seven times those in the 2nd etc.
plus eight times those in the 15th etc.
minus eight times those in the 7th etc.

The remainder after division by 19 is that of the sum of units and every 18th place to the left

minus those in the 10th etc. places
plus twice those in the 18th etc. places
minus twice those in the 9th etc. places
plus 3 times those in the 6th etc. places

minus 3	15th
plus 4	17th
minus 4	8th
plus 5	3rd
minus 5	12th
plus 6	5th
minus 6	14th
plus 7	13th
minus 7	4th
plus 8	16th
minus 8	7th
plus 9	11th
minus 9	2nd

The remainder after division by 23 is the sum of units and every 22nd figure to the left minus 12th place etc.

plus 2 times 9th place etc.		− 20th
plus 3 times 21st place etc.		− 10th
plus 4	17th	− 6th
plus 5	16th	− 5th
plus 6	7th	− 18th
plus 7	22nd	− 11th

plus 8	3rd	– 14th
plus 9	19th	– 8th
plus 10	2nd	– 13th
plus 11	4th	– 15th

The calculation is the same as that of finding the reciprocal thus:

```
23    1    100
46    2    92———04
69    3    80————————3rd place + 8
92    4    69———003
115   5    110————————4th place + 11
138   6    92———0004
161   7    180————————5th place + 18 = – 5
184   8    161———00007
207   9    190————————6th place + 19 = – 4
230  10    184———000008
           6————————7th place + 6
```

$$[\text{Ans. } .043478 \quad \ldots\ldots\ldots = \tfrac{1}{23}]$$

In order to get the entire circulating decimal representing any vulgar fraction

1st   If the last significant figure of the denominator is 5 multiply numerator and denominator by 2 until this ceases to be the case; but if the last significant figure of the denominator is even, multiply numerator and denominator by 5 until this ceases to be the case.

2nd   That done, if the denominator ends in one or more zeros strike them out thus multiplying by a power of 10, and when the operation is complete divide by the same power by shifting the decimal point.

[3rd]   If in consequence of the suppression of zeros, or for other reason the fraction is not a proper one, convert it into a mixed quantity and consider only the proper fraction at first.

4th   Form two numbers to be called the "initial number" and the "current multiplier" as follows:

If the denominator ends in 9, strike this off and increase the denominator thus truncated by 1 for the "current multiplier." The numerator is the "initial number."

If the denominator ends in 7, strike this off and having multiplied the truncated residue by 7 add 5 to the product to make the current multiplier. 7 times the numerator is the initial number.

If the denominator ends in 3, strike this off and having multiplied the truncated residue by 3, add one to it for the current multiplier. The initial number is 3 times the numerator.

If the denominator ends in 1, strike this off and having multiplied the truncated residue by 9 add one to it for the current multiplier. The initial number is 9 times the numerator.

5th   Strike off the last figure of the initial number. Multiply this by the current multiplier and add to the truncated residue to get a new number to be treated in the same way. Continue this process until the initial number is reproduced as a number to be treated in the same way.

Then the succession of figures struck off in their reverse order from last to first are the circulating decimal.

Examples

To find the circulating decimal representing $\frac{2}{79}$. 8 is the current multiplier, 2 the initial number.

$$
\begin{array}{r}
1\ 6|2 \\ \hline
1|6 \\
4\ 8| \\ \hline
4|9 \\
7\ 2| \\ \hline
7|6 \\
4\ 8| \\ \hline
5|5 \\
4\ 0| \\ \hline
4|5 \\
4\ 0| \\ \hline
4|4 \\
3\ 2| \\ \hline
3|6 \\
4\ 8| \\ \hline
5|1 \\
8| \\ \hline
1|3 \\
2\ 4| \\ \hline
2|5 \\
4\ 0| \\ \hline
4|2 \\
1\ 6| \\ \hline
2|0 \\
0| \\ \hline
\end{array}
$$

Initial Number $=$ 2

$\frac{2}{79} = .\dot{0}25316455696\dot{2}$

Find the circulating decimal representing $\frac{17}{137}$.

13|7	17	96 is the current multiplier
7|	7	119 the initial number
91	119	
5		
96		

96	1		1 1|9
192	2		8 6 4|
288	3		8 7|5
384	4		4 8 0|
480	5		5 6|7
576	6		6 7 2|
672	7		7 2|8
768	8		7 6 8|
864	9		8 4|0
960			0|
			8|4
			3 8 4|
			3 9|2
			1 9 2|
			2 3|1
			9 6|

Initial Number =   1 1 9

$$\frac{17}{137} = .\overset{.}{1}2408759\overset{.}{}$$

Find $\frac{5}{353}$.

35|3	106 is the current multiplier
3|	15 the initial number
105	

106	1		1|5
212	2		5 3 0|
318	3		5 3|1
424	4		1 0 6|
530	5		1 5|9
636	6		9 5 4|
742	7		9 6|9
848	8		9 5 4|
954	9		1 0 5|0
1060			0|
			1 0|5

[repeated from previous page]

```
                                                    1 0|5
                                                    5 3 0|
                                                    ─────
                                                    5 4|0
                                                      0|
                                                    ─────
                                                      5|4

              1 0 0|5                               4 2 4|
              5 3 0|                                ─────
              ─────                                 4 2|9
              6 3|0                                 9 5 4|
                0|                                  ─────
              ─────                                 9 9|6
                6|3                                 6 3 6|
                3 1 8|                              ─────
                ─────                               7 3|5
                3 2|4                               5 3 0|
                  4 2 4|                            ─────
                  ─────                             6 0|3
                  4 5|6                               3 1 8|
                    6 3 6|                            ─────
                    ─────                             3 7|8
                    6 8|1                             8 4 8|
                    1 0 6|                            ─────
                    ─────                             8 8|5
                    1 7|4                             5 3 0|
                  4 2 4|                              ─────
                  ─────                               6 1|8
                  4 4|1                             8 4 8|
                1 0 6|                              ─────
                ─────                               9 0|9
                1 5|0                               9 5 4|
                  0|                                ─────
                ─────                               1 0 4|4
                1 5 = Initial number                4 2 4|
                                                    ─────
                                                    5 2|8
                                                  8 4 8|
                                                  ─────
                                                  9 0|0
                                                    0|
                                                  ─────
                                                    9|0
                                                    0|
                                                  ─────
                                                    |9
                                                9 5 4|
                                                ─────
                                                9 5|4
                                                4 2 4|
                                                ─────
                                                5 1|9
                                                9 5 4|
                                                ─────
                                                1 0 0 5
```

$\frac{5}{353}$ = .01416430594900849858356940509915 (with dots over)

Find $\frac{121}{351}$.

35|1	121	316 is the current multiplier
9|	121	1089 is the initial number
315	1089	

316	1
0632	2
0948	3
1264	4
1580	5
1896	6
2212	7
2528	8
2844	9
3160	

```
             1 0 8|9
             2 8 4 4|
             2 9 5|2
             6 3 2|
             9 2|7
           2 2 1 2|
           2 3 0|4
           1 2 6 4|
           1 4 9|4
           1 2 6 4|
           1 4 1|3
           9 4 8|
           1 0 8 9 = Initial number
```

$\frac{121}{351} = .\overset{.}{3}4472\overset{.}{9}$

It will be seen that this is exceedingly rapid and secure. But the entire circulating decimal is rarely wanted.

INVOLUTION

Of course, the ordinary explanations will be given. Throughout this account I omit referring to this.

Involution by differences is [to be given].

Thus required the fifth power of 63.[9]

IDEAS OF NUMBER

Throughout both books number will be treated as essentially ordinal. Cardinal numbers are nothing but ordinal numbers in a special application, to the order of multitudes. It is a very pretty application but outside pure arithmetic and will therefore be introduced later.

One advantage of considering numbers as ordinal is that after explain-

---

[9] The page of numerical work is tentative and incomplete.

ing subtraction and exercising the pupil in it, it becomes perfectly easy to explain *negative* numbers.

The signs $= < > + - \cdot$ (for $\times$) and $/$ will be freely used and even letters will be used to denote numbers. In fact, the pupil will be seduced into algebra before he knows it.

Until after division nothing whatever will be said about fractional quantity, and it may be supposed impossible to treat this kind of quantity properly while preserving the strictly ordinal conception of number; but this is a mistake.

In the advanced book the ordinal relation will be explained as follows:

Suppose that school-boys were of such a nature that if we compare any two, say M and N (Matthew and Nicholas, or Maurice and Napoleon, or whatever their names may be) either N knows everything that M knows, or else he doesn't know anything that M does not know.

Or suppose that all liquids were of such a nature that taking any two whatever, say L and R, either L will dissolve everything that R dissolves or else L will fail to dissolve everything that R fails to dissolve.

Or suppose solid matter is of such a nature that taking any two masses whatever, O and P, either O will outweigh everything that P will outweigh or else O will fail to outweigh everything that P fails to outweigh.

Or suppose that novels were of such a nature that, taking any two whatever, A and B, either A is liked by everybody that likes B or else A is not liked by anybody that does not like B.

In any of these cases we have an *ordinal* relationship.[10]

---

[10]   MS. 177 has a section on *The Rule of False* and solving an algebraic equation.

To solve an algebraic numerical equation

If there are several possible solutions all on a par, no general rule can lead to any one solution rather than another. Therefore the equation had better be put into such a form that one solution is *smaller* than any other; and *that* solution is sought. For example, if the equation is $x^2 = 10$, that is, if we seek the square root of 10, there are two equal values, one positive the other negative. Let us, however, seek the positive value. It is near 3. Let us therefore write

$$x = 3 + y, (3 + y)^2 = 10, \text{ or } y^2 + 6y + 9 = 10, y^2 + 6y = 1$$

When this is done and the equation is brought to the form

$$Ay^n + By^{n-1} + Cy^{n-2} + \dots \text{ etc.} + My + N = 0$$

divide by -N and so bring it to the form

$$1 = -\frac{A}{N}y^n - \frac{B}{N}y^{n-1} + \dots \text{ etc.}$$

or say

$$1 = ay^n + by^{n-1} + \dots \text{ etc.}$$

Now change this equation

$$1 = ay^n + by^{n-1} + \dots \text{ etc.}$$

to the following:

$$y_{m+n} = ay_m + by_{m+1} + \ldots \text{ etc.}$$

for instance $1 = y^2 + by$ will be changed to $y_{m+2} = y_m + by_{m+1}$.

The m, $m+1$, $m+2$ are to be regarded as ordinal numbers, or numbers of places in a row, and y_m, y_{m+1} etc. as quantities in those places of which the first n are given almost any values we like. I prefer to make them all zero except the last which I make 1. Then use the equation

$$y_{m+n} = ay_m + by_{m+1} + \ldots \text{ etc.}$$

to calculate successively new values. In example take the equation $y_{m+2} = y_m + by_{m+1}$. First make $m = 0$, $y_0 = 0$, $y_1 = 1$.

Then by the equation

$$y_2 = 0 + 6 \cdot 1 = 6$$
$$y_3 = 1 + 6 \cdot 6 = 37$$
$$y_4 = 6 + 6 \cdot 37 = 228$$
$$y_5 = 37 + 6 \cdot 228 = 1405 \quad \text{etc.}$$

Then the successive approximation to y will be

$$\tfrac{1}{6} \quad \tfrac{6}{37} \quad \tfrac{37}{228} \quad \tfrac{225}{1405}$$

and the successive approximations to $\sqrt{10}$ will be 3 more than that. Thus:

$$(3 + \tfrac{1}{6})^2 = 9 + 2 \cdot \tfrac{3}{6} + \tfrac{1}{36} = 10 \tfrac{1}{36}$$
$$(3 + \tfrac{6}{37})^2 = 9 + 2 \cdot \tfrac{18}{37} + \tfrac{36}{1069} = 10 - \tfrac{}{1069}$$
$$(3 + \tfrac{37}{228})^2 = 9 + \tfrac{228}{222} + \tfrac{37^2}{228^2} = 10 \tfrac{1}{228^2} \quad \text{etc.}$$

In this way square roots, cube roots, etc., and many other quantities are easily found.

The Rule of False

There are cases in which this rule won't work. But it always discovers itself that it won't work; and those cases are rare.

Let us measure two quantities, one known, say n, and the other unknown, say x, along two directions at right angles; say x horizontally from a fixed point toward the right and n upwards from x. Then the conditions of the problem are such that we can tell what n *would be* for each value of x. And what we want to know is what value x has for the *actual* value of n.

It is assumed that if we take two false values of x, one too small, the other too great, all the intermediate values will be such that the different values of n will lie on a curve... [Fig. 1]. If the values of x are pretty close to the truth there won't be room between them for any waves to speak of, and the curve will be pretty nearly a straight line. The Rule is to assume it is a straight line and so calculate a value of x which may be wrong but which will be much nearer the truth; and then we can use this as one of the values for a new approximation. But the rule won't work if for example the curve is like this [in Fig. 2], because that is not a straight line and the result of the rule will be a value much worse than those originally assumed. This however we find out when we proceed to make a new approximation.

I will first show how to work the ordinary "rule of false" or "Rule of Double Position" and then I will give a rule of Fivefold Position which defeats the fallacy of the ordinary rule when there is one.

We assume two values of x, one too large, the other too small, and calculate from each what some known quantity would be [Fig. 3]. For instance I want $\sqrt{10}$. I assume it to be 3. Then the square would be 9. I assume it to be 4. Then the square would be 16. The error in one case is -1, in the other $+6$. Then a difference of 1 in x makes a difference of 7 in the square. But I only want to change the square by 1 from 9. Therefore I will change that value of x by $\tfrac{1}{7}$ and assume as a first approximation $\sqrt{10} = 3\tfrac{1}{7} = \tfrac{22}{7}$. But the square of this is $\tfrac{484}{49}$. That is, its error is about $-.1$. Then a difference of x of $\tfrac{6}{7}$ between $3\tfrac{1}{7}$ and 4 has made a difference in the square of

6.1. But I only want to increase the square by .1 or say $\frac{1}{61}$ part of that difference and therefore I only want to change the value $3\frac{1}{7}$ by $\frac{1}{61}$ of $\frac{6}{7}$ or $\frac{1}{71}$, making about $3\frac{78}{497}$. $3\frac{78}{498}$ is nearly $3\frac{78\frac{1}{2}}{500}$ or 3.157.

$$3^2 = 9$$
$$30^2 = 900$$
$$(31)^2 = 961$$
$$(310)^2 = 96100$$
$$(315)^2 = 96125 + 3100 = 99225$$
$$(316)^2 = 99226 + 630 = 99856$$
$$(3160)^2 = 9985600$$
$$(3157)^2 = 9985609 - 6 \times 3160 = 9966649$$

But we see that $(3.16)^2 = 9.9856$ and is therefore not quite enough.

$$(317)^2 = 99857 + 632 = 100489.$$

Thus $(3.16)^2$ is .0144 too little
$(3.17)^2$ is .0489 too much
.01 makes a difference of .0633

633	1	144	(.00227
1266	2	1266	
1899	3	174	
2532	4	1266	
3165	5	474	
3798	6		
4431	7		
5064	8		
5697	9	Then $\sqrt{10} = 3.16227$ nearly.	
6330			

I will now consider a case in which the rule does not work. I will suppose that I have the means of ascertaining the value of the tangent of an arc of any given number of minutes, and I want the value of the arc whose tangent is 10.

I know tan 5000′ $= 8\frac{5}{9}$
tan 6000′ $= -5.6713$

Then a difference of 1000′ seems to make a difference in the tangent of 14.2269 or about 70.3′ for every unit and since I wish to change the tangent by 1.44 units, I get 4900′ for a first approximation. But the tangent of 4900′ is 6.827. This is very bad. Still, if I persevere I shall do better.

tan 4900′ $= 6.827$
tan 5000′ $= 8.556$

Difference 100′ makes 1.729 or 58′ for 1 and since I wish to produce $1\frac{4}{9}$, 5084′ should be about right.

tan 5084′ $= 10.848$

and further approximation would bring me right.

Fig. 1

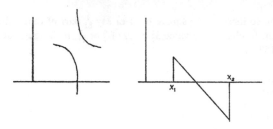

Fig. 2   Fig. 3

PRACTICAL ARITHMETIC   (168 with examples from 167)[1]

CHAPTER I. INTRODUCTION

Arithmetic is the knowledge of numbers. Practical arithmetic is the knowledge of how to use numbers.

In this practice, two qualities are to be aimed at, — accuracy first, and then dispatch. The necessity of accuracy in the use of numbers is plain: the man who only claims ten dollars when a hundred are due him will soon come to grief, while he [who] claims a hundred when only ten are due is in greater danger, still. The advantage of being able to make calculations rapidly can only be appreciated by experience. Time must often be taken by the forelock; opportunities occur which must be seized promptly or not at all; and upon these the success of life often depends. But wise decision calls for calculation, and rapid decision calls for rapid calculation. Many special rules for attaining these ends, — accuracy and dispatch, — will be found in this book, and a few general maxims may be given at the outset.

I.   Do not make too much exertion; or rather, exert yourself easily and composedly.

II.   Think of what you are about, and keep all wandering thoughts out of your mind.

III. Never trust to a result being right at the first calculation; but perform the computation a second time, and in a second way, if possible. Or else, retrace the work from the last step to the first, or otherwise assure yourself that no mistake has been committed; for the best arithmeticians sometimes commit errors, though it be but rarely.

IV. Try to view every problem from a practical standpoint: imagine yourself in a situation in which you can immediately see, if not exactly, at least approximately, what the result will be.

V.   Write your work in such a form that everybody can immediately

---

[1]   MS. 168 is a typewritten copy. MS. 167 is in handscript.

see what you have done, can see that the right operation has been performed, and that you have rightly performed it.

CHAPTER II. NUMERATION

The *cardinal numbers, numerals*, or *count-words*, are a series of words
used to count with. They are, *one, two, three, four, five, six, seven,
eight, nine, ten, eleven, twelve*, etc.

What is counting? The pupil can already count: he has only to notice
what it is that he does when he counts. To *count* a collection, or lot, of
things is to take the things singly, and to give a count-word to each,
using the count-words in their regular sequence, beginning with *one*.
For example, we may point to the things one after another calling a
number at each as we point: and we must call off the numbers in their
regular order, *one, two, three*, etc. During this process, each thing, as
soon as it receives a count-word, is said to be counted, and when all
the things have received count-words, the whole lot is said to be counted.
The last count-word used is the *number of things in the collection*.

The word *number* has four different meanings. 1st, a number expresses
the fact that the count of a collection ends with a certain count-word;
as when we say that there is the same number of cents in a dollar as of
years in a century. 2nd, we sometimes speak of a number, meaning a
countword; though it would be more proper to say "numeral." 3rd, a
series of written figures equivalent to a count-word is called a number.
4th, any collection of things is called a number; as when we say, a school
is composed of a "number" of young persons under a teacher or a "number" of teachers.

That branch of arithmetic which teaches the art of forming numerals,
or names of numbers is called *Numeration*. The first count-words are
given at the beginning of this chapter. To form the higher ones we form
groups of tens. Thus, we count as follows:

One:	Eleven:	Twenty-one:	Thirty-one:	Forty-one:
Two:	Twelve:	Twenty-two:	Thirty-two:	Forty-two:
Three:	Thirteen:	Twenty-three:	Thirty-three:	Forty-three:
Four:	Fourteen:	Twenty-four:	Thirty-four:	Forty-four:
Five:	Fifteen:	Twenty-five:	Thirty-five:	Forty-five:
Six:	Sixteen:	Twenty-six:	Thirty-six:	Forty-six:
Seven:	Seventeen:	Twenty-seven:	Thirty-seven:	Forty-seven:
Eight:	Eighteen:	Twenty-eight:	Thirty-eight:	Forty-eight:
Nine:	Nineteen:	Twenty-nine:	Thirty-nine:	Forty-nine:

Fifty-one:	Sixty-one:	Seventy-one:	Eighty-one:	Ninety-one:
Fifty-two:	Sixty-two:	Seventy-two:	Eighty-two:	Ninety-two:
Fifty-three:	Sixty-three:	Seventy-three:	Eighty-three:	

Words Relating to Numeration

ARITHMETIC is a modification of the Latin word *arithmetica*. Latin was the language of the ancient Romans; but afterward it became the learned language of Europe; that is, all educated could write and speak it, and used it for all learned writings. To the ancient Romans, Greek was the learned language; since most men of learning were Greeks. The Latin *arithmetica* is borrowed from the Greek word *arithmetike*, which means "about number" or "what we know about number," from *arithmos* number. An ARITHMETICIAN is a person skilled in arithmetic.

ALGORITHM, called in old times AUGRIM, a pretty word, and now by some pedants ALGORISM (as if there were not enough isms, without this), formerly meant practical arithmetic; but now it is used for any arithmetical process. This word is the corruption of the name of the Arabian author of a work on arithmetic. The man's real name was Abu Ja'far Mohammed ben Musa; but he was called al *Khowarazmi*, which means a citizen of Khiva.[2] When the book was translated into Latin it was called the book of Algorithm, which was meant for the name of the author, but was understood as the name of the art it taught.

NUMERAL, from Latin *numerale*, relating to a number, from *numerus*, number, is properly a name of a number. NUMERATION is telling the names of numbers.

Our grandfathers used to call counting aloud "telling," and the word TALE is still used to mean "saying how many."

> Money being the common scale
> Of things by measure, weight, and tale.   *Hudibras.*

DECIMAL (Latin, *decimale*, from *decem*, ten) means going by tens. All our counting is "decimal."

UNIT is simply a "one," a single thing counted. It seemed awkward to speak of "ones" in the plural, because someone might say, "if there

---

[2]   Peirce identified the famous ninth-century Arab mathematician in this way in the *Century Dictionary* under the term *algorism*. The transliteration of the name is usually given as Mohammed ibn Musa Al-Khwarizmi and Peirce uses that spelling also in many manuscripts (see I,6).

are more than one, why call them one?" Consequently, the word *unit* was taken. ...

Ten is called a *dicker*, a *decad*, a *decade* (especially of days, and of years), the *tetractys*, the *quarternary number*. But the last two are not cardinal numbers.

A *hundred* is called a *century* (especially of years).

A *thousand* is called a *chiliad*.

Ten thousand is called a *myriad*, and a *sum* (of nails).

A *hundred thousand* is called a *lac* (of rupees, etc.), and a *plum* (of pounds sterling).

A *thousand million* is called a *milliard*.

The first exercise in arithmetic should be to count beans, slips of paper, etc. (always repeating the count as a check), until the pupil has learned to count with great rapidity and perfect accuracy.

ADDITIONAL EXERCISE. Each pupil in the class is to be provided with a cup of beans, a slip of paper, and a pencil. Each counts out about a thousand beans, without telling how many, sets down the number at the head of his slip, and folds it down, so as to hide it. When all have made their counts, each hands his beans to the next on his right, to be counted again. Having made their counts, they all set down this number, each on his own paper, and again fold it down. So they go on, till every lot of beans has been counted from three to five times. Each one then unfolds his paper. The first begins and gives the number at the head of his paper; the second one gives his second number, which should be the same as the first on the first paper, and so they go on. Those who have made no errors in counting, win the game. Instead of setting down the numbers themselves, they may go up and tell them privately to the teacher.

Numbers are employed not only in counting, but also in measuring. Measurement is the precise numerical comparison of things. In order to show the purpose of measurement and all that is required to make it fulfill its purpose, I will imagine an instance. A country is invaded by a hostile army: the officers of justice are killed, the ablest men driven away, ruffians are without restraint, and everybody knows that his life and property are in the utmost danger. Now, one of the inhabitants has in his house a large amount of silver plate, a precious collection of medals, and other valuables of the sort which can neither be left in the house with safety nor carried out of the country. He determines to bury the things in a field and flee. It may, however, be years before he returns, even if he escapes with his life. The burial must be deep, so that the treasure may remain concealed. How, then, shall he or his heirs contrive to find it again? He must make a written description of the spot so precise as to enable anybody to find and recognize it, and that, although the houses may be burnt and the forests destroyed by the operations of war; the streams diverted from their channels and the whole face of the country changed. But he reflects that though the house be burnt down, its foundation will always remain, and can be identified. He, therefore, draws up his directions for finding the cache in this way: the searcher is first to find the north-east corner of the house, and from that he is to proceed in a certain direction for a certain distance. To determine the direction, there is the line of the wall of the house; it is only necessary to say how much the direction to be taken is to deviate to the right or left from that. This requires the determination of an angle, which he can represent upon the paper, by drawing two lines with a bend precisely like that between the wall of the house and the line from the corner to the pit. It only remains to measure the distance. It so happens that he has no tape-measure or yard-stick, and the shops are all shut. Nothing is to be had; but there is the side of the house; that will remain, and cannot change its length. He, therefore, takes a piece of tape, and makes a mark upon it near one end; this he causes to be held down against the corner of the foundation, stretches the tape along the wall, and marks upon it the point which comes against the other corner.

The first end of the tape being still held against the corner of the house, he carries the other end out as far as possible in the direction of the pit. A pole being set up over this, the man at the back end of the tape can always sight along and see that the forward end is always kept in the line. Just at the point where the mark at the second end of the tape comes, a stake is stuck in the ground. The first end of the tape is then brought forward and the mark upon it brought exactly to the nail. The second end is carried forward until it is stretched, it is moved to one side or the other, until it is in the line to the pit, and another stake is put into the ground as before. They go on in this way, counting the stakes as they go, until the distance from the last stake to the pole over the center of the pit is less than the length of the string. To take account of this remaining distance, he folds the tape up, say into ten equal lengths, called *tenths* of it, and counts the number of tenths which cover the distance. If he thinks this is not precise enough, he folds one of the tenths up into ten equal lengths, tenths of a tenth, or *hundredths*; or he might fold one of these hundredths up into ten equal parts, called *thousandths*; or one of these into ten equal parts called each *one ten thousandth*, etc.

This instance illustrates the following general principles of measurement.

The principle use of measurement is to make a precise description of something, to be preserved, so that it may be recognized later.

To measure anything, we must have (a) at the starting point, something which will remain there and be recognizable until the purpose of the measurement is fulfilled; like the foundation corner. We must, also, have (b) something permanent and recognizable which shall serve to show the direction of the measurement; like the line of the wall. We must also have (c) a standard of length which shall not stretch nor shrink, and which shall remain accessible; like the line of the wall. Furthermore, we must have (d) a bar or tape, which we can carry about, and which shall have two marks or ends which shall not change their distances during the process of measurement. We must also be able to divide, and sub-divide this into equal parts.

To express the measure, or result of measurement, we require words enabling us to describe the direction. As the words in use are not decimals, i.e. do not proceed by tens, they will be explained in another chapter. I will only mention here that if we are speaking of a good many measures from the same point in one direction, say west, so that we have, say, *four feet*, *twenty feet*, *one hundred feet*, all west, and if we come to a measure which is to be taken in the opposite direction, instead of saying, for example, *three feet east*, we may say, *minus three feet*, or *three feet reversed*, or *the negative of three feet*. To express the measure we require, secondly, to give the number of units, each equal to the standard. And thirdly, we require to express the *fraction* or part of a unit as so many *tenths*, *hundredths*, *thousandths*, etc., these being equal.

I will now explain these systems of units of measure which are decimal.

MEASURES OF LENGTH. The *Metre* is the length which is marked off, by means of two very fine lines, upon a certain bar made of platin-iridium, a very inalterable metal, and guarded with the greatest care, at the joint expense of the chief governments of the world in the cellar of a building called the Pavillion of Breteuil, in Sèvres, near Paris, in France. This bar, like everything else, changes its length according as it is warmer or cooler; but the *metre* is the length of it at the temperature of melting ice. Officials at Breteuil, by means of the most delicate instruments, compare with this "prototype" metre, other similar bars, which are distributed to the different governments; and these governments send copies of these, to their officials whose duty it is to see that nobody uses

false measures. A metre is about three yards three inches and three eighths;
or more accurately thirty-nine and thirty-seven hundredths inches; or
still more accurately two hundred and fifty-four ten thousandths of a
metre is one inch. Lengths of ten, a hundred, a thousand, and ten
thousand metres, have special names.

A *decametre* is ten metres.

A *hectometre* is a hundred metres.

A *kilometre* is a thousand metres, being 19 feet 2 inches less than $\frac{5}{8}$
of a statute mile.

A *myriametre* is ten thousand metres.

Ten million metres is twenty-five metres less than the shortest distance
along the sea-level from the north pole to the equator. (A. R. Clarke in
Encyclopedia Britannica, vol. vii, p. 607.)

There are also names for one tenth, one hundredth, one thousandth,
and one millionth of a metre.

A *decimetre* is one tenth of a metre.

A *centimetre* is one hundredth of a metre.

A *millimetre* is one thousandth of a metre, and twenty-five and four
tenths millimetres make an inch.

A *micron* is a millionth of a metre, a miscroscopic length.

The pupil should be provided with a folding metre measure divided
into centimetres and millimetres; and during his leisure hours he should
practice the following exercises.

1.   Measure all kinds of things in the house, trying first to guess their
lengths.

2.   Mark a decimetre, a centimetre, a millimetre, from memory; and
practice this until you can be sure your error will be less than one tenth
of the distance.

3.   Make a tape line of ten metres, and measure the widths of streets,
the lengths of blocks, or the sides of fields, trying to guess as before.

MEASURES OF MASS. *Mass*, or as it is ordinarily called *weight*, is
the quantity of matter. The pupil will learn more clearly what it is in
the book of Natural Philosophy or Physics. Suffice it to say, here, that it
is that which is measured in the operation of weighing, provided the
proper small allowance is made for the circumstance that the air buoys
things up a little. Water, for example, weighs about one eight hundredth
part less in air than it would in empty space. The one thousandth part
of the mass, of a certain platinum weight which is kept in the Pavillion
of Breteuil is called a *gramme* or *gram*. It is about one twenty-eighth

part of an ounce averdupois. It is very nearly one centimetre cube of water, at 39° Fahrenheit at which temperature water is at its heaviest. The multiples of a *gram* have names, like those of the multiples of a metre, as follows:

A *decagram* is ten grams.

A *hectogram* is one hundred grams.

A *kilogram* or *kilo* is a thousand grams, or about two and two tenths pounds averdupois.

A *myriagram* is ten thousand grams.

A *metric ton* is a million grams, or about a long ton.

The submultiples of a gram also have names like those of the metre as follows:

A *decigram* is one tenth of a gram.

A *centigram* is one hundredth of a gram.

A *milligram* is one thousandth of a gram. Sixty-four and eight tenths milligrams are about a grain Troy.

MEASURES OF AREA. The size of a square piece of land measuring ten metres on each side, being about one fortieth of an acre is called an *are*. Its multiples and submultiples are

A *myriare*, ten thousand ares, being about thirty-nine square miles.

A *kilare*, a thousand ares.

A *hectare*, a hundred ares, about two and a half acres.

A *decare*, ten ares.

A *deciare*, one tenth of an are.

A *centiare*, one hundredth of an are, being about ten and three quarters square feet.

A *milliare*, one thousandth of an are.

MEASURES OF VOLUME. The bulk of a cube of which every edge measures one metre, is called a *stere*. The bulk of one *kilo* of pure water, when the Fahrenheit thermometer in it marks about 39°, this being the temperature at which its bulk is the least, or, as we say at its maximum density, is called a *litre*. A thousand litres are for all practical purposes equal to a *stere*. The multiples and submultiples of these measures are as follows:

A *myriastere*, ten thousand steres.

A *kilostere*, a thousand steres.

A *hectostere*, a hundred steres.

A *decastere*, ten steres, equal to a *myrialitre*, ten thousand litres.

A *stere*, equal to a *kilolitre*, a thousand litres.

A *decistere*, a tenth of a stere, equal to a *hectolitre*, a hundred litres.

A *centistere*, a hundredth of a stere, equal to a *decalitre*, ten litres.

A *millistere*, a thousandth of a stere, equal to a *litre*.

A *decilitre*, a tenth of a litre.

A *centilitre*, a hundredth of a litre.

A *millilitre*, a thousandth of a litre, equal to a *centimetre cube*.

MONEY.[3] Dollar is a word having three meanings in this country. There is a gold piece called a *dollar* coined in the United States mint, one thousand five hundred and four and two thirds milligrams of fine gold. There is also a silver piece called a *dollar*, coined in the United States mint from twenty-four and six hundredths grams of fine silver. In law, these two coins are considered to be of equal value, and a *dollar* is, in the third place, the name of any money which may legally be paid instead of one of the coins so called. One hundredth of a dollar, in the last sense, is a *cent*; one thousandth is a *mill*. An *eagle* is a gold coin having the value of ten dollars. A *dime* is a silver coin having the value of a tenth of a dollar. The same system of money is used in Canada, and Liberia.

The unit of money equal in value to nineteen and three tenths cents is used in Belgium, France, and Switzerland under the name of a *franc*, in Greece under the name of a *drachma*, in Italy under the name of a *lira*, in Spain under the name of a *peseta*, and in Venezuela under the name of a *Bolivar*. The hundredth part of it is called in France, Belgium, and Switzerland a *centime*, in Greece a *lepta*, in Italy and Spain a *centesimo*.

In Germany, a *mark* is a money of the value of twenty-three and eight tenths cents. Its hundredth part is called a *pfennig*.

In Holland, a *florin* or *guilder* is a money of the value of forty and two tenths of our cents. Its hundredth part is called a *cent*.

In Portugal, the unit of money is a *re*. One thousand *reis* are called one *milreis*, one thousand *milreis* a *conto* and one thousand *contos* a *conto of contos*. A *milreis* has the value of one dollar and eight cents.

In Russia, a *rouble* worth fifty-eight and two tenths cents ($0.582) is divided into a hundred *copecks*.

In Denmark, Norway, and Sweden, the unit is a *krone* of the value of twenty-six and eight tenths cents ($0.268) divided in one hundred *ore*.

In Turkey, the unit is a *piastre*, of which one hundredth is an *aspre*,

---

[3] No attempt has been made to modernize these conversions. Peirce's statements are of historic interest.

and a hundred make a *lira*. The value of the piastre is four and four tenths cents ($0.044).

In British India, the unit is the *rupee*, worth thirty-four and six tenths cents ($0.346). In some places, it is divided into one hundred *cents*.

CHAPTER III. THE ARABIC NOTATION

The following is an example of a number written in the Arabic notation

453·59

The dot after the 3 is called the *decimal point*. It is sometimes written on the line; but we write it above the line after Sir Isaac Newton.[4] When it comes after all the figures, it is not written; and when a number has no decimal point, it must be imagined to have one immediately after the last figure.

A figure written immediately before the decimal point signifies one of the first nine numbers; namely,

1, one,   .
2, two,   :
3, three,   ∴
4, four,   ∴.
5, five,   ::
6, six,   ⋰⋰·
7, seven   ::
8, eight,   ::
9, nine,   ·⋰⋰·

The figure 0 is called the cipher, or zero. It only serves to remove the other figures from the decimal point, but itself signifies no other number. The effect of removing any figure one place to the right is to make its value ten times as great; the effect of every remove to the left is to make its value only one tenth as great as it was before. Thus,

1 is one,	2 is two,	3 is three;
10 is ten,	20 is twenty,	30 is thirty;
100 is a hundred,	200 is two hundred,	300 is three hundred;
1000 is a thousand,	2000 is two thousand,	300 is three thousand;

---

[4] In this MS., which Peirce had typed, the decimal point is written on the line, as he usually did elsewhere. However, in MS. 167, of which 168 is a typewritten copy, the dot is placed above the line, and it is so placed throughout MS. 167.

10000 is ten thousand;
100000 is a hundred thousand;
1000000 is a million;
10000000 is ten million, etc.

So on the other side of the decimal point,

0.1 is one tenth,   0.2 is two tenths,
0.01 is one hundredth,   0.02 is two hundredths,
0.001 is one thousandth,   0.002 is two thousandths,
0.0001 is one ten-thousandth,   0.0002 is two ten-thousandths,

0.3 is three tenths;
0.03 is three hundredths;
0.003 is three thousandths,
etc.

The different figures in one written number are all intended to be written together. Thus,

21 is twenty and one or twenty-one,
201 is two hundred and one,
2001 is two thousand and one,
20001 is twenty thousand and one,
200001 is two hundred thousand and one,
2000001 is two million and one.

In order to read a number we count up the places beginning to the left of the decimal point, thus: — units, tens, hundreds, thousands, tens of thousands, hundreds of thousands, millions, etc. We then name the first figure, and then its place, then the second figure and its place. Thus, 453·59 reads

four hundred,
and fif -ty,
three units
and five tenths,
nine hundredths.

Many persons, however, would read it

four, five, three, point, five, nine;

and this is perhaps easier to understand.

CHAPTER IV. THE ARABIC NOTATION (continued)

The following apparatus is required for this chapter. An arithmetical frame made as follows: A frame with a handle, so that it can be held up high, has 12 horizontal wires, on each of which nine balls run; the color of all nine balls on each wire is the same; but the fifth ball is of an oblate form, so as to bulge out more; and so facilitate counting. The colors of the balls on the different wires, beginning at the lowest one are as follows: black: blue: red: green: yellow: white: black: blue: red: green: yellow: white.

A number of sheets ruled in oblongs, of the right size and shape to put a number in each (see the sample) and with columns headed, successively, milliaids: lacs of millions: myriads of millions: thousands of millions: hundreds of millions: tens of millions: millions: lacs: myriads: thousands: hundreds: tens: units: tenths: hundredths: thousandths. Blackboards ruled the same way. Copy-books for each pupil tastefully ruled in the same oblongs, but without the headings.

The arithmetical frame used with the book is constructed on the same principle as your counters, each ball represents one of the counters. When they are not wanted they are pushed to one side of the frame, and when they are intended to have a meaning, they are brought to the other side. The balls have no names upon them, but in place of that each kind runs on a distinct wire, and these wires are placed in regular order, units: tens: hundreds: etc. These fixed places of the wires make the frame a far clearer way of indicating a number than your counters are. (The teacher will explain the use of the frame with sample.)

Exercise. Express the following numbers, first with your counters, and then on the frame. The following are the heights of some of the principle mountains above the level of the sea in metres:

Gowrlsankar, Asia	8840
Dapsang, Asia	8821
Kinonin-Jinga, Asia	8580
Aconcagua, South America	8834
Illampou, South America	8560
Chimborazo, South America	8253
Kilima-Njaro, Africa	5705
Elbrouz, Europe	5847
Demauend, Asia	5665
Popocatapetl, North America	5410
Wocho, Africa	5060
Ararat, Asia	4912
Klioochew, Asia	4900
Brown, North America	4876
Mont Blanc, Europe	4810

St. Elias, North America	4568
Finster-aar-horn, Europe	4275
Okhir, Oceanica	4222
Mauna-kea, Oceanica	4197
Kinabaloo, Oceanica	4172
Viso, Europe	3845
Mulanacen, Europe	3554
Miltsin, Africa	3475
Pic d'Aneto, Europe	3405

(From the *Annuaire des Longitudes*, 1888)

The abacus blanks provided for the pupil are ruled in columns part of which are headed Units, Tens, Hundreds, Thousands, Myriads, Lacs, Millions, etc. These numbers are called *articles*, from the Latin *articulus*, a joint, because they were anciently counted on the joints of the fingers.

The spaces are called decimal places. There are also columns headed tenths, hundredths, thousandths. These spaces are also called decimal places. These columns correspond precisely to the wires of the arithmetical frame; but in place of using balls, we write in the columns certain figures, called the *Arabic figures*. There are ten of these, as follows:

1	+	One
2	++	Two
3	+++	Three
4	++++	Four
5	++++ +	Five
6	++++ + +	Six
7	++++ + ++	Seven
8	++++ + +++	Eight
9	++++ + ++++	Nine
0		Nothing

The first nine numbers are called digits, from the Latin *digitus* a finger, because they were anciently counted on the fingers; and the figures for these numbers have the same name. The tenth figure, which is only used to fill up a space, when there is no digit to be written in it, is called the *cipher* or *zero*. It is also called naught. These figures are to be written in the columns of the Abacus-blank precisely as the balls are used in the arithmetical frame, except that we must carefully observe that something has to be written in every column; and if nothing else belongs in it, a zero must be written. The following example shows several numbers written in words, and in figures on the abacus-blank.[5]

---

[5] No figure was given by Peirce.

The numbers will be equally intelligible written without any abacus-blank. Only then we must take pains in writing several of them, to place them accurately in vertical columns, the units under units, the tens under tens, etc. The following are examples.

the number of feet in a yard is   3
the number of inches in a foot is   12
the number of links in a chain is   100
the number of feet in a mile is   5280

EXAMPLES [From Ms. 167]

Read the following:

Mercury revolves round the sun in   87.9693 days.
Venus revolves   in   224.7008 days.
The Earth   in   365.2564 days.
Mars   in   686.9797 days.
Jupiter   in   4332.5848 days.
Saturn   in 10759.2198 days.
Uranus   in 30686.8208 days.
Neptune   in 60126.7200 days.

One grain Troy is equal to 0.06479895 grammes.

The length of the year is 365 days 5 hours 48 minutes 45.69 seconds.

The equatorial diameter of the earth is 20926202 feet.

The polar diameter is 20854895 feet.

The Absolute cold is −273.1 degrees Centigrade. (The line before the number is read *minus*, and signifies that it is so many degrees below zero instead of above.)

According to the census of 1880, the population of the United States was 50155783, of which 25518820 were male, 43475840 were native, 43402970 were white, and 36761607 were ten years old and over. Those engaged in agriculture were 76704393; those engaged in professional and personal services were 4074238; those engaged in trade and transportation were 1810256; and those engaged in manufactures and mechanical and mining industries were 3837112.

The circumference of a circle is
3.141592 653589 793238 462643 383279 502884 197169 399375 105820 974944 592307 816406 286208 998628 034825 342117 067982 148086 513282 306647 ...

times its diameter. This may be read: three and one hundred and forty one thousand five hundred and ninety-two millionths six hundred and fifty three thousand five hundred and eighty-nine billionths etc.

FACTOTAL AUGRIM (169)

INTRODUCTION

"Augrim" is a charming old English name for a very familiar thing for which no other word in our language is exclusively appropriated, namely, the art of using the so-called "Arabic" figures. The cause of the disuse of the word "augrim" seems to have been that the learned Robert Recorde, the author of the first treatise on the subject in the English language, declared therein that "augrim" was a "corrupt" word (as, in fact, all words are), and that it must be called "algorism." Naturally, rather than use such a word as that (itself, by the way, a "corruption"of *Al-Kwarizmi*), people preferred to call the art *'rithm'tic*, and have done with it, although the word *arithmetic* is needed in its proper sense of the mathematics of numbers. It is true that the name "Vulgar Arithmetic" designates augrim unmistakably; but the word "vulgar" has itself come, with the unlearned, to imply an objectionable fashion, and what is worse, the name is far too long, with its six syllables, to serve as the name of so familiar an art. "Practical arithmetic" is still longer. "Ciphering" is a good word for the *practice* of the art, but not for the art itself. *Algorithm*, a more agreeable and less pedantic form of "algorism," is in common use among mathematicians to denote a form of working a process of augrim on paper, especially when the form is peculiar. It will be so used in this book.

A book, like a person, in addition to its family name, needs an adjectival name to distinguish the individuals from others of the same family. I christen this book Factotal Augrim, because I mean it to teach an augrim which will serve as a *factotum*, performing on demand and without giving trouble every office for which the Arabic figures can, with any advantage be employed; as, for example, in so numbering objects not serially arranged, such as the faces, summits, and edges of polyhedra, as to aid one in making out their relations.

This textbook has three Divisions. The first called Elementary Augrim deals with those elementary operations of which all other arithmetical and algorithmic operations are compounded. The second called Composite Augrim treats of operations compounded of those treated in the first division. The third, called Applied Augrim, shows how to select the most convenient methods with view to avoiding needless labour, with a view to the lucidity of the record, etc.

The First Division, on Elementary Augrim, has three Parts, devoted respectively to Integers, or whole numbers, Fractions and the like, and Surds.

The First Part of the First Division has three Books, treating respectively of Unlimited Numeration, Cyclical Numeration, and Singular Numeration, where the march of the numbers branches at certain places, or halts.

The First Book has three Chapters, the first concerning the nature of integers, the second concerning the systems of counting, and the third concerning the elementary arithmetical operations.

FIRST DIVISION. ELEMENTARY AUGRIM.

PART ONE. OF INTEGERS.

BOOK I. UNLIMITED NUMBER.

CHAPTER THE FIRST. WHAT IS NUMBER?

All our thinking is performed upon signs of some kind or other, either imagined or actually perceived. The best thinking, especially on mathematical subjects, is done by experimenting in the imagination upon a diagram or other *scheme*,[1] and it facilitates the thought to have it before one's eyes. But the only point I just now wish to make is that a thought being always a sign, if one wishes to consider such a question as what the concept of number is, external signs answer every purpose, and there is no need at all of considering what passes in one's mind, which is a question that nobody is fit to discuss who has not been through a long, arduous and absorbing course of reading, experimentation, and meditation about the difficult science of psychology, and not even then, unless he happens

---

[1] There is no note in the manuscript although Peirce indicates that a note is given.

to have a special aptitude for the subject. Not only is nothing gained by trying to make out what passes in the mind, but this irrelevant question imposes an onerous handicap upon the logical inquirer, as is shown by the fact that psychologists usually quite miss the point when they undertake to discuss logical questions, such as this. The reason is the simplest in the world: when you want to consider anything, you had best turn your thoughts to that, and not to something quite different; especially if that quite different thing be connected with your problem in inessential ways. I mean for example that when you want to know what number is, you should not allow your energy to be wasted and your thoughts diverted by the entrancing interest of all the anthropologists have to tell you about how different men think of number, nor by what the psychologists have to tell about how all men alike think of it. For what should engage your attention is just the questions what number is, what it does, how it can influence a rational being, etc. I even dread the effect upon your thought of the little squint at the mind that this paragraph may have invited; and in case you do not quite understand what I have been saying, pray desist from attempting to do so but go on at once to what I am about to say now.

Every language that is adapted to the purposes of civilized people needs, and actually has, more than one series of words called *numerals*, and that which the different numerals of one series do or might distinguish is called this or that kind of *number*. There are three kinds of number which it is specially important clearly to understand, and which we shall call the three *primary series of numbers*.

Before explaining the first of these, I shall have to prepare your minds by calling attention to certain ways of speaking and thinking. The word "population," being a common noun in the singular number, if it denotes anything that really exists, denotes some single object of the kind which it describes. Such an object is one whose being consists in there being, in the place and at the time to which the population belongs, such inhabitants as there happen there and then to be, and to be without others. For example, the population of Robinson Crusoe's island after Friday came, was just what it was by virtue of the three facts that Robinson lived there, that Friday lived there, and that nobody else lived there. If any one of those three facts had been otherwise, the island whould have had another population. This kind of population would be described in a census as "a population of 2." Before Friday came, the population was just what it was by virtue of the two facts, that Robinson Crusoe lived there, and that nobody else lived there. A census would describe it as

"a population of 1." Before Robinson's own arrival a census would have
set down the island as having "a population of 0." To be sure, we should
ordinarily say that an uninhabited [island] has no population whatever.
But that is because we ordinarily prefer to take the word "population"
in a slightly different sense from that which is most convenient for the
purposes of augrim. In augrim we mean by the "population," the answer
to the question, "What inhabitants, and no others, had the given place
at the given time?" The answer for an uninhabited island is "none."
"*Population*" is a so-called *collective noun*, that is, it names a single object
as considered to be at once single and to have a being consisting in the
being of objects which might be denoted by a noun in the plural. Almost
any object *does* consist of such parts; but a noun in the plural calls attention to this and neglects the fact that the object is, nevertheless, single;
while the collective noun draws attention at once to the singleness and
the plurality.

An "object" means that which one speaks or thinks of. Therefore, if
I say, or even think, that a star, a caterpillar, and a blot of ink can be
seen from where I sit, the star, the caterpillar, and the blot of ink forth-
with make up a single object. Every noun in the plural is the name of a
single object; but we call the object, after the noun, a *plural* when it is
not our purpose to draw attention to its being an object. If we do intend
to draw attention to that circumstance and to its plurality, as well, we
call the object a *collection*.* The difference between a plural and a collection is very trifling.

(*In these days, when young men have for half a century gone to Germany to acquire every sort of knowledge, excepting that of their mother
tongue, which they seem disposed to "reform," without much understanding of it, I find there are many people, well-educated in other matters,
who seem to imagine that it is not strictly accurate to speak of a "collection" of objects, unless they have, in some way, really been brought together. If it were of the propriety of the French language that they were
speaking, influenced as that has been by ignorant grammarians and
rhetoricians, I think they would be right. But in respect to English, which
has been influenced in regard to logical words far more by the Latin,
most by scholastic Latin, but also by the ancient language, very much
more than by the French or by any etymological considerations, they
are certainly wrong. The very earliest known instance of the occurrence
of the word *as a known English word* (for I leave out of account a case
in which Trevisa, about 1390, translates "festa collectionis" by "feast of
the collection," and then, because this word "collection" was not then

English, and the verb "coil," which has since taken the form "cull," and certainly implies a real bringing together, though usually only on paper, thinks himself obliged to add the English equivalent "gathering") is in the phrase "collection and discourse of reason." Nor has there been any period since the date of that passage, 1529, when "collection," in the severest formality of English writing, implied any physical culling. It could not be so; because English has followed much the scholastic usage, which was decidedly against that limitation. Those who were inclined to rebel against the dominion of the scholastics would go back to Cicero, or perhaps even to Plautus. But in every age of Latin speech it was the same; in the majority of instances "collectio" refers to a merely mental collation. If we go a step further, and inquire into the original meaning of the verb *lego*, λέγω, we find, indeed, that the comparative philologists give "gather," as its original meaning. But that idea is simply an inheritance from the great scholars who founded the science of comparative linguistics, and who having passed their lives in such villages and little towns of Germany, as harboured universities, knew nothing at all about primitive man except that they supposed he differed from themselves as the German artisans or peasants did, only still more so. By that comparison, they were led to imagine that every root must have originally signified some physical action. But since those great men have passed away, a genuine science of anthropology has arisen, especially under the tutelage of that remarkably genuine man, the late Major Powell. Young Americans have gone and become so thoroughly naturalized among primitive peoples, that the latter enthusiastically endorsed them as their spokesmen, and even wished to acknowledge them for their chiefs. We must suppose that such men understand primitive man. If they do not, who does? Now these men tell us, quite as unanimously as unhesitatingly, that there is no other kind of man who is so perpetually thinking of himself and his feelings as is the primitive man. Admitting that, then, there is one sort of experience which must have made itself peculiarly prominent to the man who, when speech was something new, was trying to describe his experiences through this novel medium. That experience must have been of the effort required to bring together, in his intended utterance, the different intelligible sounds which would render his meaning plain. Surely, if that man was in the least like the presumably far less "subjective," or emotional, Amerindians with whom the young, and first really scientific, anthropologists have become acquainted, he must have had *some* linguistic root that originally expressed the action of his mind in choosing its medium of expression. Now what root can that have been but the *leg, log* to which the facts on the whole tend to assign this meaning, nothing opposing this suggestion but modern notions imbibed, in some way, by men of the most ignorant class that exist, the students?

At any rate, there is nothing in etymology, any more than in the usage of speech, to support the idea that before a plural can strictly be called in English a "collection," its members must have been actually and really brought together. Every class of facts points, on the contrary, the other way.)

I proceed now to state the requisite properties of any series of numerals which is to be adapted to counting every possible collection. In this statement, I avoid using any such expression as that one numeral comes *after*, or *later*, than another, for two reasons; first, that should anybody ask me precisely what I mean by "after" or "later" in the series, I should be obliged to give substantially the same statement which I prefer to give at once; but secondly also, — and this is the more important reason, — I wish to place before the attention of the student every feature of the structure of the series of numerals, so as to enable him to see just how it comes about that it possesses any property that it does possess.

I shall allow myself, however, in this statement, the use of one abridged expression, because it will render the statement decidedly clearer and easier to comprehend. Namely, I shall speak of one numeral, call it N, "*supposing*" another, which we may call M, which will be an abbreviated form of words employed in place of saying that "the *use* of N, in counting, supposes the *use* of M;" that is to say, there could not possibly be a count in which N should be used but M not be used, for the reason that N comes later in the series than M, and therefore, in counting, is not used until after M has been used. But the best explanation of my phrase "N supposes M" is that it means, "take whatever possible count you may, and if N is used in it, so is M."

The relationship between the different numerals of one series, in respect to the operation of counting, from which their whole significance is derived, is as follows:

1st, Given any two numerals of one series, there might be a count in which one of them would be used, and the other not.

2nd, Among any numerals of one class or group, there will always be one which is used in every count in which any of them are used.

3rd. Given any intelligible description of a numeral, which description we may call D, it will be of one or other of three kinds, to wit: First, D may be such that there is no numeral to which it applies. Second, D may be such that given any numeral, N, whatever this N may be, there will be some numeral, I, to which the description D applies, such that in some possible count N would be used, but I would not be used. (Of course, if a different numeral, say N', be taken in place of N, then it may be necessary to find a different numeral, I', to take the place of I. Suppose, for example, the description, D, were that the numeral should end with four, as twenty-four, thirty-four, etc. If then one hundred were taken as N, we might take one hundred and forty-four for I, but if one hundred and fifty were taken for N' we should have to take some number beyond that, say one hundred and fifty-four, or one million and fifty-four for I'.)

Thirdly, if D has neither of the two properties already described, then there will be some numeral, U, to which the description D applies which is used only in counts in which every numeral of the description D is used, and there must, moreover, be some numeral, V, to which the description D does not apply which will be used in some possible counts in which U is used and not in others.

The above three statements taken together signify, either explicitly or implicitly, every fact which is true of every complete series of numerals, without regard to anything else. Those things are signified *explicitly* which are stated in so many words. Those things are signified *implicitly* which, though not stated explicitly, can be seen to be true of any state of things of which what is explicitly stated is true. I will now restate these important propositions in less simple but more familiar and compendious language. For this purpose, I will say that one numeral, call it P, comes *earlier* in any count than another, say Q, if, and only if, P is used although Q is not used. Applying the second of the above statements to that class or group of numerals that consists in the pair, P and Q, we learn that there is one of the two which is used in *every* count in which either is used. Since, then, P is used in some count and Q not, it follows that P must be used in *every* count in which Q is used, although Q is not used in every one in which P is used. We thus see that that one of two numerals which comes earlier than the other in *any* count comes earlier in *every* count, that is, if only one is used, it is always that one.

Our three propositions, then, may be expressed as follows: 1st, Of any two numerals one is earlier than the other. 2nd, Of any plural of numerals some one is the earliest. 3rd, If a numeral to which a given description would apply be called a *d*, then one of three things is the case. Namely either

1st, There is no *d*; or

2nd, Every numeral comes earlier than some *d*; or

3rd, There is a *d* than which all other *d*s come earlier, and this latest *d* is earlier than some numeral that is not a *d*.

FACTOTAL AUGRIM

FIRST DIVISION.   ELEMENTARY AUGRIM.

PART ONE.   OF INTEGERS.

BOOK II.   CYCLICAL NUMBERS.

CHAPTER THE FIRST.   WHAT IS CYCLICAL NUMERATION?

Any Wednesday is the fourth day of its week; that is, it is the fourth day after the last day of the previous week; or, there have been four days as early in its own week as Wednesday.

Suppose we should wish to know on what day of the week will fall a day that is 5 days later than a Wednesday. How shall we proceed to do this sum? We have seen that in any row the Nth place after the Mth place is the $(M+N)$th place. Therefore, the 5th day after the 4th day must be the $(4+5)$th day, or the 9th day. But there are only 7 days in a week; and the 8th day, or next day after the 7th day, is the first day, Sunday. We count round and round, as the figure shows. The 8th day is the same as the 1st day, if we do not care what week it may be in, but only want to know the day of the week; and 9th day will be the 2nd day. Therefore, the 5th day after the 4th day will be the 9th day, which is the 2nd day, or Monday.

Here is another question· If the 1st day of January falls on Thursday, on what day does the 1st day of February fall? Now there are 31 days of January; so that the first of February is 31 days later than the first of January. Consequently, since the first of January is Thursday, the 5th day of the week, the first of February will be the $(5+31)$th, or the 36th day. Subtract from 36 the largest multiple of 7 that is not greater than 36. That will be 35; for $7 \times 5 = 35$. Then subtracting 35 from 36, the remainder is 1; and therefore, the first of February will be the 1st day, or Sunday. By the phrase "cyclical numeration" is meant counting round and round. The number of places in a round, or "period," is called the "modulus" (i.e. the measurelet). Thus, in counting days of the week, regardless of the difference of one week and another, the "modulus" is 7. Two numbers which fall in the same place and which are, therefore, the same, so far as the cyclical numeration considers them, are said to be not *equal*, exactly, but "congruent," each to the other, *"for that modulus."*

The modulus, for example, is congruent to 0 for that modulus. 9 is congruent to 16 for modulus 7. We write this thus:

$$9 \equiv 16 \text{ (mod. 7)},$$

or, in general,

$$(a\,m + c) \equiv (b\,m + c) \text{ (mod. m)}$$

The result of subtracting from any positive number that multiple of the modulus that comes nearest to, without being greater than, that number is called the *residue* of that number for that modulus. (Germans call it the *rest*.) Thus, the residue of 20 for the modulus 7 is 6, while the residue of 21 is 0. The residue has a meaning only when we pass from one system of numeration to another. As long as we are counting with one modulus, all congruent numbers are the same. Monday is Monday, and Tuesday is Tuesday, and nothing else, so long as we have not to do with the distinction between one week and [another].

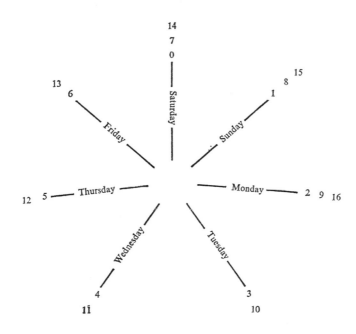

FAMILIAR LETTERS
ABOUT
THE ART OF REASONING (186)

Stagira, May 15, 1890.

My dear Barbara:

The University of Cracow once conferred upon a very good fellow a degree for having taught the philosophical faculty to play cards. I cannot tell you in what year this happened, — perhaps it was 1499. The graduate was Thomas Murmer, of whose writings Lessing said that they illustrated all the qualities of the German language; and so they do if those qualities are energy, rudeness, indecency, and a wealth of words suited to unbridled satire and unmannered invective. The diploma of the university is given in his book called *Chartiludium*, one of the numerous illustrations to which is copied to form the title page of the second book of a renowned encyclopaedia, the *Margarita Philosophica*. (Published at Heidelberg in 1496, at Freiberg in 1503, in Strassburg by Grüninger in 1504, in Strassburg by Schott in 1504, in Basle in 1508, etc.) Murmer's pack contained 51 cards. There were seven unequal suits; 3 hearts, 4 clubs (or acorns), 8 diamonds (or bells), 8 crowns, 7 scorpions, 8 fish, 6 crabs. The remaining seven cards were jokers, or unattached to suits; for such cards formed a feature of all old packs. The object of Murmer's cards was to teach the *art of reasoning*, and a very successful pedagogical instrument they no doubt proved.

If you will provide yourself, my dear Barbara, with a complete pack of cards with a joker, 53 in all, I will make a little lesson in mathematics go down like castor-oil in milk. Take, if you will be so kind, the 1, 2, 3, 4, 5, 6, 7, 8, 9, 10 of spades, and arrange these ten cards in their proper order. I mean by this that the ace, or 1, is to be at the back of the pack, the 2 next, and so on, the ten alone showing its face. I call this the "proper order," because I propose always to begin the count of cards in a pack at the back, so that, in the pack of ten cards you have just been so obliging as to arrange, every card is in its proper place, that is the number it bears on its face is equal to the number of its place from the back of the pack. The face-value of the 2nd card is 2, that of the 3rd card, 3, and so on.

Now let us add 3 to the face value of each card in the pack. How shall we do that without a printing-press? Why, by simply taking three cards from the back of the pack of ten and carrying them to the face. The face-value of card number 1 is now $3+1$, or 4; that of card 2 is 5, and so on up to card 7 which is 10. Card 8 is 1; but 1 and 11 are the same for us. Since we have only ten cards to distinguish, ten different numbers are enough. We, therefore, treat 1, 11, 21, 31, as equal, because we count round and round the ten, thus:

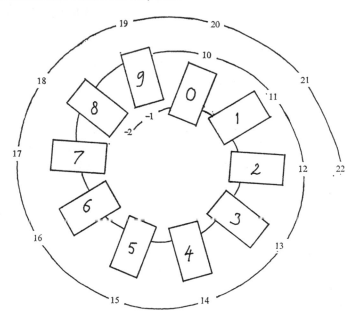

We say 13 and 23 are equal, meaning their remainders after division by ten are equal. This sort of equality of remainders after division is called *congruence* by mathematicians and they write it with three lines, thus

$$13 \equiv 23 \ (\text{mod. } 10)$$

The number 10 is said to be the *modulus*, that is, the divisor, or the smallest number congruent to zero, or the number of numbers in the cycle.

Instead of ten cards you may take the whole suit of 13, and then, imagining a system of numeration in which the base is thirteen and in which we count

1 2 3 4 5 6 7 8 9 10 Jack Queen King

we have a similar result. Fourteen, or king-ace is congruent with 1; fifteen, or king-two, with 2, etc.

It makes no difference how many cards there are in a pack. To cut it, when arranged in its proper order, and transpose the two parts, is to add a constant amount to the face-value of every card. So much for *addition*.

Now how shall we *multiply*? Suppose we have the pack of ten in its proper order, and wish to multiply the face value of the cards by 3. We deal out the cards one by one from first to last, into 3 piles laying them face up upon the table. We first take up the pile the ten, or zero, falls upon, then the next pile, last the third, putting each pile after the first at the back of that last taken. We now find in place 1 card 3, or 3 times 1;

in place 2 card 6, or 3 times 2;
in place 3 card 9, or 3 times 3;
in place 4 card 2, congruent to 3 times 4;
in place 5 card 5, congruent to 3 times 5;
in place 6 card 8, congruent to 3 times 6;
in place 7 card 1, congruent to 3 times 7;
in place 8 card 4, congruent to 3 times 8;
in place 9 card 7, congruent to 3 times 9;
in place 10 card 0, congruent to 3 times 10.

Take this pack and multiply again by 3. Multiplying by 3 twice is multiplying by 9. But $9 \equiv -1$. Accordingly we shall now find

In place 1 card -1 or 9,
In place 2 card -2 or 8,
In place 3 card -3 or 7,
etc.

Multiply again by 3, and since $3 \times 9 \equiv 7$, we shall find

in place 1 card $7 \times 1 \equiv 7$,
in place 2 card $7 \times 2 \equiv 4$,
in place 3 card $7 \times 3 \equiv 1$,
in place 4 card $7 \times 4 \equiv 8$,
in place 5 card $7 \times 5 \equiv 5$,
in place 6 card $7 \times 6 \equiv 2$,
etc.

Take a pack of 11 cards. We shall now have

$$11 \equiv 0$$
$$12 \equiv 1$$
$$23 \equiv 1$$

and, in short, to find what any card will be, having performed the necessary arithmetical operation, we subtract the number in the tens place from the number in the units place, and repay anything we borrow in the addition. Thus, suppose we deal into 5 piles and take up the piles from left to right putting each one at the back of the pile that was at the left of it. We shall now have

in place 1, since $5 \times 1 = 5$, card 5;

in place 2, since $5 \times 2 = 10$, card 10;

in place 3, since $5 \times 3 = 15$ and 1 from 5 leaves 4, card 4;

in place 4, since $5 \times 4 = 20$ and 2 from 10 leaves 8, and repaying 1 borrowed we have 9, card 9;

in place 5, since $5 \times 5 = 25$ and 2 from 5 leaves 3, card 3;

in place 6, since $5 \times 6 = 30$ and 3 from 10 leaves 7, and repaying 1, we get 8, card 8;

in place 7, since $5 \times 7 = 35$ and 3 from 5 leaves 2, card 2;

in place 8, since $5 \times 8 = 40$ and 4 from 10 leaves 6, and repaying 1 we get 7, card 7;

in place 9, since $5 \times 9 = 45$ and 4 from 5 leaves 1, card 1;

in place 10, since $5 \times 10 = 50$ and 5 from 10 leaves 5, and repaying 1 we get 6, card 6;

in place 11, since $5 \times 11 = 55$ and 5 from 15 leaves 10, and repaying 1 we get 11, card 11 ($\equiv$ 0).

Suppose we now deal again into 9 piles. Now, the last card falls on the 2nd pile. How are we to take up the piles? Answer: After the cards are exhausted, go on dealing in rotation upon the piles to the right of the last single card dealt no longer single cards but whole piles always taking the extreme left hand one. Thus, in the present case, after the piles are all dealt out, put the left hand pile upon the pile to the right of the Jack, the last single card dealt; that is, put the pile headed by the 6 on that headed by the 4. Then, on the pile one further to the right, that headed by the 9, put the extreme left one headed by the Jack. Next, on the one headed by the 3 put the one headed by the 6, and so on until the piles are reduced to one. You will then find the proper order restored. Why? Because you have multiplied by 5 and by 9, that is, by 45, and 4 from 5 leaves 1, so that you have multiplied the cards in their proper order by 1, which leaves them in their proper order.

I now beg you, my dear Barbara, to take the full pack of 53 cards, and arrange them in their proper order, first the spades, second the diamonds, third the clubs, and fourth the hearts, each suit in its proper order,

1   2   3   4   5   6   7   8   9   X   J   Q   K

with the Joker at the face. Deal them out into twelve piles and take up the piles according to the rule. Namely, denoting the Joker by O,

place the pile headed by the X on the pile headed by the 3;
then place the pile headed by the J on the pile headed by the 4;
then place the pile headed by the Q on the pile headed by the 5;

K	6;
O	7;
X	8;
J	9;
Q	X;
K	J;
O	Q;

then place the pile headed by the O on the pile headed by the K.

Next deal the cards out again into 31 piles, and take up the piles according to the rule. Namely,

first, place the pile headed by the K♠ on the pile headed by the J ♠;
then, place the pile headed by the Q♦ on the pile headed by the X ♦;
then, place the pile headed by the J ♣ on the pile headed by the 9 ♣;

X♥	8 ♥;
8 ♠	6 ♠;
7 ♦	5 ♦;
6 ♣	4 ♣;
5 ♥	3 ♥;
3 ♠	1 ♠;
2 ♦	K♠;
1 ♣	Q♦;
K♣	J ♣;
Q♥	X♥;
X♠	8 ♠;
9 ♦	7 ♦;
8 ♣	6 ♣;
7 ♥	5 ♥;
5 ♠	3 ♠;
4 ♦	2 ♦;
3 ♣	1 ♣;
2 ♥	K♣;

then, place the pile headed by the O on the pile headed by the Q♥;

$$
\begin{array}{ll}
4\ \blacklozenge & \text{X}\ \spadesuit; \\
3\ \clubsuit & 9\ \blacklozenge; \\
2\ \heartsuit & 8\ \clubsuit; \\
\text{O} & 7\ \heartsuit; \\
4\ \blacklozenge & 5\ \spadesuit; \\
3\ \clubsuit & 4\ \blacklozenge; \\
2\ \heartsuit & 3\ \clubsuit;
\end{array}
$$

then, place the pile headed by the O on the pile headed by the 2 ♥.

This restores the original order because $12 \times 31 = 372$, and 53 into 372 goes 7 times and 1 over; so that

$$12 \times 31 \equiv 1 \ (\mathrm{mod}\ 53);$$

that is, the two dealings are equivalent to multiplying by 1; that is, they leave the cards in their original order.

You, Barbara, come from an ancient and a proud family. Conscious of being raised above the necessity of using ideas, you scorn them in your own exalted circle, while excusing them in common heads. Your cousins Baroco and Bocardo were always looked upon askance in the family, because they were suspected of harboring ideas, — a quite baseless suspicion, I am sure. But do you know that the unremitting study of years has tempted me to favor a belief subversive of your kindred's supremacy, and of those principles of logic that are accepted upon all hands, I mean a belief that one secret of the art of reasoning is to *think*? In this matter of card-multiplication, instead of conceiving the dealing out into piles as one operation and the gathering in as another, I would prefer a general formula which shall describe both processes as one. At the outset, the cards being in no matter what order, we may conceive them as spread out into a row of 53 piles of one card each. If the cards are in their proper order, the last card is the Joker. In any case, you will permit me to call any pile that it may head the *Ultima*. The dealing out of the cards may be conceived to begin by our taking piles (single cards, at first) from the beginning of the row and putting them down in successive places following the *ultima*, until we reach the pile which we propose to make the final one, and which is destined to receive all the cards. When in this proceeding, we have reached the final pile, let us say that we have completed the first "round." Thereupon we go back to the pile after the ultima as the next one upon which we will deposit a pile. We may complete a number of rounds each ending with placing a pile (a single card) on the final pile. We make as many as [the] number of cards in the pack will permit, and we will call these the rounds of the "first set." It will be found useful, by the way, to note their number. Having completed them, we go on just as if we were beginning another; but when we have moved the ultima, let us say that we have completed the first round of the second set. Every round of the first set ends by placing a pile on the final pile. Let us call such a round "a round of the *odd* kind." Every round of the second set ends by moving the ultima. Let us call such a round a round of the even kind. We make as many rounds of this kind as the whole number of places after the ultima enables us to complete. We call these the rounds of the second set. We then return to making rounds of the odd kind and make as many as the number of piles before the ultima enables us to make. So we go alternating sets of rounds of the odd and the even kind, until finally the ultima is placed upon the final pile; and then the multiplication process is finished.

I will now explain to you the object of counting the rounds. But first let me remark that the last round, which consists in placing the ultima upon the final pile, should always be considered as a round of the odd kind. When you dealt into twelve piles and gathered them up, with the first 48 cards you performed 4 rounds of 12 cards each, and had 5 cards left over. These five you dealt out, making the first round of the second set; and then you transferred these five piles over to the tops of the second five, making another round of the second set. Then from these five piles you dealt to the other two piles twice, making two rounds of the third set. Next the ultima was placed upon the next pile, making a round of the fourth set. Finally the ultima was placed on the last pile which, being a round of an odd set, belonged to the fifth set. So the numbers of rounds were

$$4, \quad 2, \quad 2, \quad 1, \quad 1.$$

From this row of numbers, which we will call the Ms, we make a second row, which we will call the Ns. The first two Ns are 0, 1, the rest are formed by multiplying the last by the first M not already used and adding to the product the last N but one. Then the Ns are

$$0, \quad 1, \quad 4, \quad 9, \quad 22, \quad 31, \quad 53.$$

The last N is 53. It will always be the number of cards in the pack. Reversing the order of the Ms

$$1, \quad 1, \quad 2, \quad 2, \quad 4$$

will make no difference in the last N. Thus, the Ns will be

$$0, \quad 1, \quad 1, \quad 2, \quad 5, \quad 12, \quad 53.$$

Leave off the first M, and the last N will be the number of piles. Thus from

$$2, \quad 2, \quad 1, \quad 1$$

we get

0,   1,   2,   5,   7,   12.

Leaving off the last, will give the number of piles into which you must deal to restore the order. Thus from

4,   2,   2,   1

we get

0,   1,   4,   9,   22,   31.

If you deal 53 cards into 37 piles, the numbers of rounds will be

1,   2,   3,   4,   1.

If you deal into 34 piles the numbers will be

1,   1,   1,   3,   1,   2,   1.

If you deal into 33 piles, the numbers will be

1,   1,   1,   1,   1,   5,   1.

If you deal into 32 piles, the numbers will be

1,   1,   1,   1,   10,   1.

If you deal into 30 piles, the number will be

1,   1,   3,   3,   2.

You perceive that the object of counting the rounds is [to] find out how many piles you must deal into to restore the proper order, and consequently by multiplication how many piles you must deal into to make any given card the first.

Going back to 10 cards, if we were to deal them into 5 piles or 2 piles, the piles could not be taken up so as to conform to the rule. The reason is that 5 and 2 exactly divide 10; so that the last card falls on the last pile, and there is no pile to the right of the last card upon which to pile the others. To avoid that inconvenience, we had best deal only with packs having a prime number of cards, or one less than a prime number; for, in the last case, we can imagine an additional last card which remains in the zero place, as long as there is only multiplication, no addition; that is as long as the pack is not cut.

If we deal a pack of 10 cards into 3 piles twice or into 7 piles twice, we multiply by -1; for $3 \times 3 = 9$ and $7 \times 7 = 9$, and 9 is one less than 0 or 10. Suppose, then, starting with ten cards in their proper order we deal them into 3 piles (or 7 piles) and taking them up according to the rule next lay them down, backs up in a circle, thus:

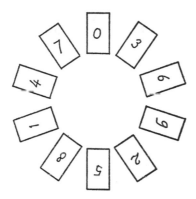

Then, my dear Barbara, you can say to your little friend Celarent, who is so fond of denying everything, "Celarent, what number do you want to find?" Suppose she says 6. Then, you count six places from the 0, say in the righthanded direction. You turn up the 6th card, which is the 8; and you say: "If the 8 is in the 6th place clockwise, then the 6 is in the 8th place counterclockwise." Thereupon, you count 8 places from the zero to the left and turn up the 8th card, and lo, it is the 6. Or you might have counted, at first, 6 places to the left and turning up the 6th card, have found the 2. Then you would say "If the 2 is in the 6th place counterclockwise, then the 6 is in the 2nd place clockwise." And counting two places from the 0 to the right, you would again find the 6. The same would hold good if Celarent were to call for any other number.

If you want to do this little trick with 13 cards, you must deal them into 5 or 8 piles. You might begin by asking Celarent how many piles she would like the cards dealt into. If she says 2 (or 11), deal them as she commands, and having done so, ask her whether she would now like them dealt into 4 or 9 piles. If she makes you first deal them into 3 or 10 piles, give her her choice afterward between 6 and 7 piles. If she makes you first deal into 4 or 9 piles, give her then a choice between 2 and 11. If she makes you first deal into 6 or 7 piles, give her her choice afterwards between 3 and 10 piles. If she makes you deal them into 5 or 8 piles, lay them down in a circle at once. In doing so let all be face down except the King, which you place face up. The order will be [as in the figure].

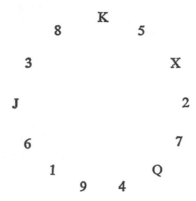

You ask, "What spade would you like to find?" If she says, "The Knave," reply, "Then we count to the Knave place." You count and turn up the 3. Then you say, "If the 3 is in the place of the Jack counting clockwise, then the Jack is in the place of the 3 counting counterclockwise." You can then count round to this place clockwise, and find it is the 10th. So you continue: "And if the Jack is in the place of the ten counting clockwise, then the ten is in the place of the Jack counting counterclockwise." You count, turn up and find it so. Then you count up to this card clockwise, and go on, "And if the ten is in the place of the 2 counting clockwise, then the 2 is in the place of the 10, counting counterclockwise."

The same thing can be done with a full pack of 52 or 53 cards.

We have thus far considered addition and multiplication separately. Now let us study them combined. Take a pack of 11 cards in their proper order. Cut it so as to carry three cards from back to face of the pack. That adds 3 to the face-value of the card in any given place. Now deal them into five piles and gather up the piles according to rule. This by itself would multiply the face value of the card in any given place by 5. But acting after the other operation, if x be the place and y the face-value (or original place) we have

$$y = 5x + 3$$

On the other hand, starting again with the cards in their proper order, if we first deal into 5 piles and then carry 3 cards from back to face, we have

$$y = 5(x + 3).$$

In short, the order in which the operations are to be taken in the calculation of the face-values is just the reverse of that of their actual performance. The reason is too obvious to require explanation.

It is easy to see that before dealing the cards out in the little trick I proposed your showing Celarent you can perfec'ly well allow her to cut the pack first, provided that after the dealing, or at any time, you recut so as to bring the zero card to the face of the pack. This will annul the effect of the cutting.

I want to call your attention, Barbara, to the fact that there is another way of effecting multiplication besides dealing out into piles and gathering in. Suppose for instance you hold in your hand the first eleven spades in their proper order while the first eleven diamonds in their proper order are lying in a pack face down upon the table. We will now effect upon the spades the operation

$$5x + 3$$

and simultaneously upon the diamonds the inverse operation

$$\tfrac{1}{5}(y - 3).$$

For this purpose begin by bringing three spades from the back to the face of the pack. Then bring 5 spades from back to face, lay the face card down on the table face up and in its place put the top diamond. Bring 5 more spades from back of pack to its face, lay the face card down face up upon the other card lying on the table face up, and replace it by the top card in the pile of diamonds. Repeat this process until it can be repeated no more owing to the exhaustion of the pile of diamonds. You will now hold all the diamonds in your hand. Carry three cards from the face of the pile to the back, and the whole double operation will be complete.

You can now say, "If the 7 of diamonds is the 5th card in the pack of diamonds, then the 5 of spades is the 7th card in the pack of spades," and, in short, each pack serves as an index to the other.

From the point of view of this proceeding, multiplication appears as a continually repeated addition. Now let us ask what will result from continually repeating multiplication. As before lay the 11 diamonds in their proper order face down on the table, and take the 11 spades in their proper order in your hand. Deal the spades into two piles and gather them up. Put the back card, the 2, down on the table and replace it by the top diamond. Again deal the cards in your hand into 2 piles and gather them up, and put the back card (the 4) upon the one lying face up, and replace it by the top diamond. Proceed in this way until you have laid down all your spades except the Knave which you never can get rid of in this way. You will now find that the spades run in geometrical progression, each the double of the preceding

2   4   8   5($\equiv 16$)   10   9($\equiv 20$)   7($\equiv 18$)   3($\equiv 14$)   6   1($\equiv 12$).

In fact, if, as before, x be the place, y the face value

$$y = 2^x$$

Then, in the other pack we ought to have

$$x = \log y \,/ \log 2.$$

In fact, for these the face value is increased by one when the place is doubled. For the order is

10	1	8	2	4	9	7	3	6	5

Double 2 the number of the place of 1 and you get 4 the place of 2

4	2	8	3
8	3	$16 \equiv 5$	4
5	4	10	5
10	5	$20 \equiv 9$	6
9	6	$18 \equiv 7$	7
7	7	$14 \equiv 3$	8
3	8	6	9
6	9	$12 \equiv 1$	10

Double 1 the number of the place of 10 and you get 2 the place of 1.

You may now do this surprising trick. Ask Celarent to cut the pack of diamonds (with the Knave of spades but without the Knave of diamonds). Then, ask how many piles she would like to have the diamonds dealt into. Suppose, to fix our ideas, she says 5. You obey and gather up the cards according to rule. You then cut so as to bring the Knave of spades to the face; and in doing so you notice the face value of the card is carried to the back. In the case supposed it will be 4. Then carry as many cards (i.e. in this case, 4) from the face to the back of the pile of spades. Then ask Celarent what diamond she would like to find. Suppose she says the 3. Count to the 3rd card in the pack of spades. It will be the 6. Then say, "If the 6 of spades is the 3rd card, then the 3 of diamonds is the 6th card," and so it will be found to be.[1]

I have not given any reason for anything, my Barbara, in this letter. In your family you are very high in reasons and in principles. But if you think I have said anything not true, it will be a nice exercise in the art of reasoning to make sure whether it is true or not.

---

[1] Peirce's interest and skill in games of chance — chess, backgammon, and card games — is reflected in the many card tricks in the manuscripts. One recalls his reviews for *The Nation* of Rouge et Noir's *The Gambling World* and of John Ashton's *The History of Gambling in England.*

8

SECUNDALS

A. SECUNDAL NUMERICAL NOTATION (61)

By *Secundals*, or a Secundal Numerical Notation, I mean a system of written signs (originated by Leibniz) by which any rational number can be denoted to the exclusion of all others, the distinguishing characteristics of any such system being these four.

1st, The number denoted is represented as a sum of different powers of 2 (although this sum may degenerate into a single power of 2). To avoid confusing repetitions of the phrase "power of two" it will be convenient to substitute the expression "2-power."

2nd, This sum is represented, not by exhibiting signs of the different summand 2-powers, each marked with an indication of its exponent, but by exhibiting all the 2-powers within certain limits, and marking each as present in or absent from the sum. Consequently, the representation of any number will contain an individual character to refer to each 2-power within limits; and only two incomplex numerical legisigns, or sign-types, will be needed, the one to signify the presence in, the other the absence from, the sum of that 2-power to which the individual character embodying the one or other sign-type refers.

3rd, It is essential to the system that the different 2-powers to which the different individual characters that compose the sign denoting any number refer are not marked by conventional symbols, but are shown by the exhibition of their succession, which is an icon of the succession of the different 2-powers. For this purpose, all these individual characters are arranged in a row (although this may degenerate to a single character) in which every character (with the exception of at least one, and at most two *limiting characters*) has two others reciprocally next to it. It is, therefore, further necessary that there should be some legisign, or generally employed type of sign, which is applied to show which of the two limiting characters represents the highest and which the lowest of the 2-powers referred to. The former is considered as the first character of the row, the latter the last. Moreover, another legisign must be adopted whose application shall show which of the characters, conveniently designable as the *origin* of the row, shall refer to the zero 2-power, or unity. Then the exponent of the two-power to which any other character refers is $\begin{Bmatrix} \text{greater} \\ \text{less} \end{Bmatrix}$ by one than the exponent of the 2-power to which the character next $\begin{Bmatrix} \text{later} \\ \text{earlier} \end{Bmatrix}$ than it in the row refers.

4th, Because we cannot write an endless series of characters, it will be necessary to have a legisign by means of which any regular endless series of characters that can represent the last and endless part of an endless sum of different powers of two, so long as that sum is a rational number. For this it suffices that there be a type of mark of which a replica can be attached to any series of characters forming the last part of a row and signifying that this series is to be conceived as followed in every case, in the number represented, by a repetition of itself. This type of mark may be called the *repetifex*, and the series of numbers the *repetite* or *repetend*, according as it has the repetifex attached to it or only is to have it attached.

I will now describe the particular form of secundals which I propose here to employ. The two numerical legisigns shall be α or A importing the presence and o or O importing the absence from the sum of 2-powers of that 2-power to which each individual replica of one or other of these types refers. The row of characters shall be horizontal beginning at the left and ending at the right; and the origin, or character that shows the presence or absence of 2^0 in the sum of 2-powers shall be marked by the use of the tall forms, A and O, of the two legisigns in that place, while in all other places the short forms, α and o, shall be used.[1] The repetifex shall consist of a heavy horizontal line drawn over all the characters of the repetend and over no others. Moreover, a repetend is apt to be excessively long, containing in the representation of a fraction with a prime denominator usually but one character less than the number of that

---

[1]   Peirce's disapproval of the use of a dot to separate the successive positive powers of the base (including the zero power) from the successive negative powers is apparent throughout his secundal writings.

In MS. 61, A or O are used to designate units' place; otherwise α or o.

In MSS. 687 and 1, ȯ or Ȯ are used to designate units' place; otherwise ● or o.

In MS. 54, 1 or ● are used to designate units' place; otherwise 1 or .

In MS. 57, ⊹ or ⊖ are used to designate units' place; otherwise 1 or 0.

Also see footnote 1 to MS. 213 (I,9,d).

denominator. But in such case the last half of the repetend is just like the first half except that, α or o, everywhere replace each other. Thus one nineteenth is

$$\frac{A}{\alpha o o \alpha A} = O \overline{o o o o o \alpha \alpha o \alpha o \alpha \alpha \alpha \alpha o o \alpha o \alpha}$$

Accordingly, instead of writing the whole, it will suffice to write the first half with a wavy line over it, called the *semirepetifex*.

$$\frac{A}{\alpha o o \alpha A} = O \overset{\sim\sim\sim\sim\sim}{o o o o o \alpha \alpha o \alpha o}$$

It must never be forgotten that $O\bar{\alpha} = A\bar{o}$

It is evident that in place of any repetite may be substituted any desired number of repetitions of it. Thus, one seventh is

$$\frac{A}{\alpha \alpha A} = O \overline{o o \alpha} = O \overline{o o \alpha o o \alpha} = O \overline{o o \alpha o o \alpha o o \alpha} = \text{etc.}$$

It is also evident that any repetite may be extended one place (and therefore any number of places) further to the right by repeating its first character after its last and shoving forward the repetifex. Thus

$$\frac{A}{\alpha \alpha A} = O \overline{o o \alpha} = O o \overline{o \alpha o} = O o \overline{o \alpha o o} = \text{etc.}$$

By the application of these two principles, any two (and therefore any number) of signs of numbers may be made to end at the same place of secundals in repetites of equal length.

RULE FOR ADDITION

1st, Make all the summands end at the same place in repetites of equal length.

2nd, Write the summands, so treated, under one another so that the different characters which refer to the same 2-power shall be in one vertical column. In this rule, we will suppose, for the sake of clearness, that the repetites are added separately from the rest of the numbers. Accordingly, the repetites are first to be all removed.

3rd, Begin at the last column that contains more than one α (or more than one A, for, in this 3rd step, α and A are not distinguished from each other). Draw a line at once joining and cancelling two αs in this column and continue it to the left cancelling with it one α in each column until a column is reached which contains no α, where an α is to be inserted.

4th, Repeat the third step until there remains no column containing more than one α.

5th, Add the repetites in the same manner except that when a cancelling line is continued beyond the repetites, and α is to be inserted in the column to the left of the repetites, and another α is to be inserted in the last column of the repetites. The αs so inserted to the left of the repetites have to be added to the other numbers according to the rule. In practice, this 5th step will be performed in combination with the third and fourth.

6th, Write for the result an α below each column containing an α and a o in each of the other columns.

Examples in Addition.

(For the sake of clearness the cancelling lines are drawn in colors.)[2]

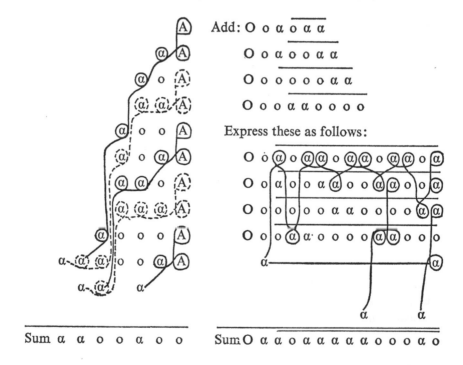

Add: O o α o α α

O o α o o α α

O o o o o o α α

O o o α α o o o o

Express these as follows:

Sum α α o o α o o   Sum O α α o α α α α α o o o α o

RULE FOR SUBTRACTION

1st, Express the minuend and subtrahend so that they end with repetites beginning and ending in the same two secundal places, i.e. with characters referring to the same 2-powers.

2nd, Write the subtrahend under the minuend, each character directly under a character referring to the same 2-power, prefixing os to the subtrahend to give it the same extent as the minuend.

3rd, Beginning at the extreme right hand examine successively each vertical couple of characters. From the left hand of the first α under an o draw a line under the subtrahend as far as the left hand of the first o under an α which is toward the left from the point where the line began, and there let the line stop. Continue toward the left until another $\overset{o}{\alpha}$ is met with where commence repeating the whole operation including this repetition. The operation stops when the whole pair of rows has been gone through.

4th, If an $\overset{o}{\alpha}$ from which a line is to be drawn according to clause 3rd occurs within the repetite and there is no $\overset{\alpha}{o}$ within the repetite to the left of it, the line must not only be continued beyond the repetite but another branch of it must start at the extreme right of the repetites, and be continued to the left of a $\overset{\alpha}{o}$ or, if there be none such before the line has run through the whole repetite it must remain under the whole; for a line once drawn according to the rule should never be erased or rendered ineffective.

[5th] The remainder is now to be written by writing below the subtrahend, in every column through which no line is drawn, 0 under $\overset{o}{o}$ and under $\overset{\alpha}{\alpha}$ and α under $\overset{\alpha}{o}$ and $\overset{o}{\alpha}$; but in columns through which a line is drawn, α under $\overset{o}{o}$ and $\overset{\alpha}{\alpha}$ and o under $\overset{\alpha}{o}$ and $\overset{o}{\alpha}$, the repetite having the same extent as before.

Examples in subtraction

For clearness the subsidiary line is drawn brown

Minuend   αooooooooαooαaaaαoooαaαooαoooαoαoαA
Subtrahend oooooαaoαaoαaooooooαaaaaαoαoαaoooαO

Remainder oαaaαooαaαoooαaoαaaaaαooαaoαaaaαooA

Minuend   Oαaaαoαo   Minuend   Aαoαaa   Minuend   Aαoo
Subtrahend Ooαoαaaα   Subtrahend Oαaαoα   Subtrahend Oαaο

Remainder Oαooαoαa   Remainder Oαaooα   Remainder Oαoα

MULTIPLICATION

Long multiplication, the only kind there is, is very simple when there
are not two repetites to be multiplied. In that case, if the result is not
too complicated to permit of its being written down, the readiest way is
to repeat the repetites sufficiently to observe the regularity of sequence
in the product. There are, however, special cases when the product can
be readily written directly, and other cases that are facilitated by the
operation of division. In short, the repetites have in general to be treated
just as circulating decimals are.

DIVISION

Of course, long division is perfectly simple.

Besides that operation, there is another leading to processes by which
any multiplication or division may be performed (when I say "may be,"
I mean supposing human life to last long enough, but then, of course,
this whole business of secundals flutters upon the butterfly wings of the
"theoretically"). The immediate object of this rule is to divide one number
expressible as a finite sum of different powers of two by another such
number.

1st, Multiply the dividend by such a two-power, 2^d, that the product
shall be an odd whole number; and multiply the divisor by such a 2-
power, 2^t, that the product shall be an odd whole number.

2nd, Strike off the last α from the divisor and add it to what remains,
treated as a whole number. (In other words, you add one to the divisor
and divide by 2.) Call the result the applicand.

3rd, Call the dividend the operand. Strike off its last character and to what remains, treated as a whole number you add the product of that last figure that has been struck off into the applicand. (In other words, you subtract from the operand whatever power of 2 not having a negative exponent is necessary [that] will leave it divisible by 2, and then divide the remainder by the highest power of 2 that will divide it, and to the quotient add the applicand.) The result is to be treated as a new applicand in the same way.

4th, This process is to be repeated until you reach the first applicand that is equal to a previous applicand. You strike nothing off this. You now bring all the characters that have been struck off from the applicands vertically down into a horizontal row. (That is you write them in a row in the reverse order of their being struck off.)

5th, Then if the dividend was less than the divisor, you place the repetifex over this series and prefix 0, which makes the quotient.

But if the dividend was greater than the divisor beneath this row you are to write another consisting of all the characters struck off down to the operand that has reappeared, inclusively, and repeat this indefinitely to the left and from this the row above considered as a whole number having been subtracted, the remainder is the quotient required.

This operation is much simpler in practice than in description.

Examples

Divide A by αoαA.

αoα|A
A
———
α α o = Applicand

Proof by long Division

A   (oooαoαααoα
αoαα—— | ||| |
—————
ooαoα ||| |
  αoαα ———||| |
  ————
   αooα || |
    αoαα———| | |
    ————
     ααα | |
     αoαα———| |
     ————
      αα |
      αoαα ———|
      ————
       α Same as dividend

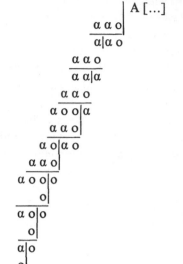

A [...]
α α o
———
α|α o

α α o
———
α α|α

α α o
α o o|α
α α o
———
α o|α o
α α o
———
α o o|o
   o|
α o|o
   o|
α|o
o|

α = Same as 1st operand,
      i.e. the Dividend
————————————
Oooοαoαααoα = Quotient

Divide αO by αoαA

Applicand as before ααo

|A o
α α o
———
α|α o
α α o
———
α α|α
α α o|
α o o|α
α α o
———
α o,α o
α α o|
α o o|o
   o|
⌈α o|o
   o|
 ———
 α o = Dividend⌉

Quotient = O ————————————
                 ooαoαααoαo

[From the previous page] the last [is] repeated with more room and quite fully

$$\begin{array}{r} \alpha | o \\ o | \\ | \alpha \\ \alpha\, \alpha\, o | \\ \alpha\, \alpha | o \\ o | \\ \alpha | \alpha \\ \alpha\, \alpha\, o | \\ \alpha\, \alpha | \alpha \\ \alpha\, \alpha\, o | \\ \overline{u\, o\, o | \alpha} \\ \alpha\, \alpha\, o | \\ \alpha\, o\, \alpha | o \\ \overline{o |} \\ \alpha\, o | \alpha \\ \alpha\, \alpha\, o | \\ \overline{\alpha\, o\, o | o} \\ o | \\ \overline{\alpha\, o | o} \\ o | \\ \overline{\alpha\, o} = \text{Dividend} \end{array}$$

Divide $\alpha\,\alpha\,o\,A$ by $\alpha\,o\,\alpha\,A$

The applicand, as before, is $\alpha\,\alpha\,O$

$$\begin{array}{r} \alpha\, \alpha\, o | \alpha \\ \alpha\, \alpha\, o | \\ \overline{\alpha\, \alpha\, o | o} \\ o | \\ \overline{\alpha\, \alpha | o} \\ o \\ \overline{\alpha | \alpha} \\ \alpha\, \alpha\, o | \\ \overline{\alpha\, \alpha | \alpha} \\ o | \\ \overline{\alpha\, o\, o | \alpha} \\ \alpha\, \alpha\, o | \\ \alpha\, o\, \alpha | o \\ \overline{o |} \\ \alpha\, o | \alpha \\ \alpha\, \alpha\, o | \\ \overline{\alpha\, o\, o | o} \\ o | \\ \overline{\alpha\, o | o} \\ o | \\ \overline{\alpha | o} \\ o | \\ \overline{| \alpha} \\ \alpha\, \alpha\, o | \\ \overline{\alpha\, \alpha\, o} = \text{Same as } 3^{\text{rd}} \end{array}$$

Quotient $= O\,\overline{o\,o\,\alpha\,o\,\alpha\,\alpha\,\alpha\,o\,\alpha\,o}$

$= O\ \overset{\thicksim\thicksim\thicksim}{o\,o\,\alpha\,o\,\alpha}$

	Operand
	$\alpha\,o\,o\,o\,\alpha\,o\,\alpha\,\alpha\,\alpha\,o | o\,\alpha$
	$\alpha\,o\,o\,o\,\alpha\,o\,\alpha\,\alpha\,\alpha\,o | \alpha\,o\,o\,o\,\alpha\,o\,\alpha\,\alpha\,\alpha\,o\,\alpha\,o\,o\,o\,\alpha\,o\,\alpha\,\alpha\,\alpha\,o$
	$A\,\overset{\thicksim\thicksim\thicksim}{o\,o\,\alpha\,o\,\alpha}$

Divide α O by αA

$$\frac{\alpha \big| A}{A \big|}$$

$\overline{\alpha o}$ = applicand

$$\frac{\alpha \big| o}{o \big|}$$
$$\frac{\big| \alpha}{\alpha o \big|}$$
$\overline{\alpha o}$ = same as Dividend

Quotient = $O\overline{\alpha o}$ = $O\widehat{\alpha}$

Divide α oA by αA
Applicand α o

$$\frac{\alpha \; o \big| \alpha}{\alpha \; o \big|}$$
$$\frac{\alpha \; o \big| o}{o \big|}$$
$$\frac{\alpha \big| o}{o \big|}$$
$$\frac{\big| \alpha}{\alpha \; o \big|}$$
$\overline{\alpha \; o}$ = | Same as 3rd operand

$$\frac{\alpha o \big| o\alpha}{\alpha o \big| \alpha o \alpha o}$$
Quotient = | $A\overline{\alpha o}$

Divide α ooO by αA
Applicand as before α O

$$\frac{\alpha \; o \; o \big| O}{o \big|}$$
$$\frac{\alpha \; o \big| o}{o \big|}$$
$$\frac{\overline{\alpha} \big| o}{o \big|}$$
$$\frac{\big| \alpha}{\alpha \; o \big|}$$
$\overline{\alpha \; o}$ = |Same as 3rd operand

$$\frac{\alpha o \big| o \; O}{\alpha o \big| \alpha O \alpha o \alpha o}$$

Quotient = $\alpha O\overline{\alpha o \alpha o}$

Divide α α A by α A

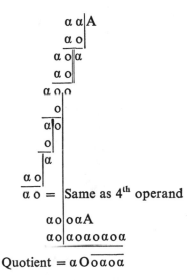

Quotient = α O̅o̅a̅o̅α

Divide A by α o o A

Applicand   α o α

Quotient O̅o̅o̅o̅a̅a̅α
= Ȯo͂o͂o͂

Divide A by α o A

Applicand = α α

Quotient O̅o̅o̅a̅α
= Ȯo͂o͂

Divide A by $\alpha\alpha$A

$$\begin{array}{c|} \alpha\alpha\,|A \\ A \\ \hline \end{array}$$
Applicand αoo

$$\begin{array}{c|} |A \\ \alpha o o \\ \hline \alpha o o \end{array}$$

Quotient $= \overline{O o o}\alpha$

Required to multiply $\overline{O o}\alpha$ by $\overline{O o o}\alpha$

$$\overline{O o}\alpha = \frac{1}{2^2 - 1} = \frac{A}{\alpha A}$$

$$\overline{O o o}\alpha = \frac{1}{2^3 - 1} = \frac{A}{\alpha\alpha A}$$

$$\frac{A}{\alpha A} \times \frac{A}{\alpha\alpha A} = \frac{A}{\alpha o\alpha o A}$$

$$\begin{array}{c|} \alpha\alpha A \\ \alpha\alpha\alpha \\ \hline \alpha o\alpha o A \end{array} \qquad \begin{array}{c|} |A \\ \alpha o\alpha o \\ \hline \end{array}$$
Applicand $\alpha o\alpha\alpha$

$$\begin{array}{c|} & & |A \\ \alpha\ o\ \alpha\ \alpha \\ \alpha\ o\ \alpha\,|\alpha \\ \alpha\ o\ \alpha\ \alpha \\ \hline \alpha\ o\ o\ o\ o \end{array}$$

$$\left.\begin{array}{r}\text{Product}\\ \text{required}\end{array}\right\} = \overline{O\ o\ o\ o\ o}\,\alpha\ \alpha$$

The same by long multiplication [see bottom of page 157].

To extract the rth root of a number A, let $x^r = A$

Let a be an approximate value of x and put $x = a + y$

Then $(y + a)^r = y^r + ra\,y^{r-1} + \dfrac{r(r-1)}{2}a^2 y^{r-2} + \text{etc} + a^r = A$

and whatever be the value of m

$$\frac{y^m + ra\,y^{-(m+1)} + \dfrac{r(r-1)}{2}a^2 y^{-(m+2)} + \text{etc} + a^{r-1}\,y^{-(m+r-1)}}{A - a^r} = y^{-(m+r)}$$

Instead of this use the equations

$$\frac{u_m + ra\,u_{m+1} + \dfrac{r(r-1)}{2}a^2\,u_{m+2} + \text{etc} + ra^{r-1}\,u_{m+r-1}}{A - a^r} = u_{m+r}$$

Assume any values arbitrarily for $u_0, u_1, u_2, \text{---}\ u_{r-1}$
and by this equation calculate $u_r, u_{r+1}, u_{r+2} + \text{etc}$.

Then if n is large $y = \dfrac{u_n}{u_{n+1}}$ nearly.

Examples

Find $\sqrt{3}$ assume $a = 2$

Then $(2 - y)^2 = 3$

or $1 = 4y - y^2$

Assume $1 = 4u_{m+1} - u_m$

$u_0 = $ o

$u_1 = $ A

$u_2 = \alpha$o O

$u_3 = \quad \alpha\alpha\alpha$A

$u_4 = \quad \alpha\alpha\alpha$oo O

$u_5 = \quad \alpha\alpha$oαooo A

$u_6 = \quad \alpha\alpha$oooo$\alpha\alpha$o O

$u_7 = \quad \alpha$o$\alpha\alpha$oαo$\alpha\alpha\alpha\alpha$A

$\therefore \sqrt{\alpha A} = \alpha O - \dfrac{\alpha\alpha\text{oooo}\alpha\alpha\text{o O}}{\alpha\text{o}\alpha\alpha\text{o}\alpha\text{o}\alpha\alpha\alpha\alpha A} = A + \dfrac{\alpha\text{ooooo}\alpha\text{o}\alpha\text{ooo}\alpha A}{\alpha\text{o}\alpha\alpha\text{o}\alpha\text{o}\alpha\alpha\alpha\alpha A}$ nearly

The square of this is $\alpha A + \dfrac{A}{\alpha\text{ooooo}\alpha\text{o}\alpha\text{o}\alpha\alpha\text{oo}\alpha\text{o}\alpha\text{ooooooo}A}$

[From middle of page 156.]

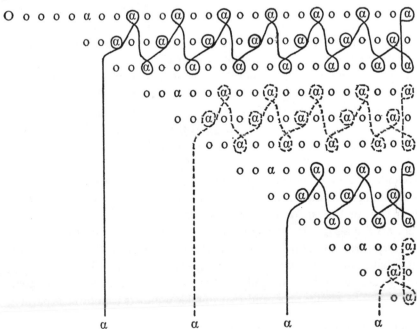

B. [A SYSTEM OF SECUNDALS] (687 and 1)

So you not only lament the decimal numeration, but really think the abolition of it a rational object of endeavour? Then, you have your choice between taking 6 as a base,[1] which is the best for counting on the fingers, and which makes division by 3 easy (which is desirable if, for example, in weighing, the weights are to be put either in the one pan or in the other) and which also facilitates division and other operations owing to the fact that every prime number, except 2 or 3, would end either in 1 or 5 (seven becoming 11, eleven 15, thirteen 21, seventeen 25, nineteen 31, twenty-three 35, twenty-nine 45, thirty-one 51, thirty-seven 101, forty-one 105, forty-three 111, forty-seven 115, fifty-three 125, etc.) thus greatly facilitating the finding of remainders after division, or of adopting 2 as the base of numeration, giving the *secundal* system, which is far the most elegant of all. I will give a few explanations about this. It might be supposed that the names of numbers must be very long in this system. Just to show that this is not so, I suggest the following method of naming (which no doubt could be much improved if the system should ever be seriously considered).[2] The first letters of the name shall show how many secundal places of figures there are to the left of the units' place; *a* (Continental Pronunciation, always) for *one*, as for *two*, s for three, *sa* for four, *sat* for five, *st* for six, *ast* for seven, *at* for eight, *t* for nine, *ta* for ten, *tas* for eleven, *ts* for twelve, *tsa* for thirteen, *tsan* for fourteen, *naj* for fifty-three, the principle being that *a* is 1, *s* is 3, *t* is 9, *n* is 27, *j* is 81, and that a smaller number following a greater one adds to it but preceding the greater diminishes it, and smaller numbers are always to be combined before greater ones, and two smaller numbers cannot be separated

---

[1] In MS. 67 Peirce gives an extended theoretical explanation of sextal numeration.
[2] MS. 1250 (p. 13-16) displays two additional schemes for naming the number. In that manuscript Peirce uses the more popular 1,0 notation for number representation.

by a larger one. The remainder of the letters describe the figures in the descending order of the places, *y* or *i* meaning 1 unit, *l* or *e* 3 successive units (*il* or *ye* two successive units, *li*, or *ey* four successive units), *k* 9 successive units (*lik* five, *ek* six, *yek* seven, *ik* eight), *ng* 27 successive units (*ki* ten, *kil* eleven, *ke* twelve, *kli* or *key* thirteen, etc. *kang* 18, the *a* being inserted for euphony, etc.), *w* or *u* a zero, *r* or *o* 3 successive zeros, *p* 9 successive zeros, *m* 27 successive zeros. Zeros after all the units need not be noticed.

I give some examples:

Arabic Notation	Secundal Notation	Proposed Names
0	o	u
1	.	i
2	.o	ay
3	. .	ayé or ail
4	.oo	asi
5	.o.	asiwi
6	. .o	asil
7	. . .	asé
8	.ooo	si
9	.oo.	siwoy or syuri
10	.o.o	siwi
11	.o..	ιiwil
12	. .oo	sil
13	. .o.	silwi
14	. . .o	sé
15	. . . .	slĭ
16	.oooo	say
17	.ooo.	sayoy
18	.oo.o	sayurĭ
19	.oo..	sayuril
24	. .ooo	sayl
25	. .oo.	saylwoy or saylurĭ
28	. . .oo	sal
29	. . .o.	salwĭ
30	. . . .o	sali
31	. . . . .	salιk
32	.ooooo	satĭ
33	.oooo.	satyowĭ

Arabic Notation	Secundal Notation	Proposed Names
47	.o....	satyulĭ
48	..oooo	saté
49	..ooo.	saterĭ
62	.....o	satlik
63	......	satek
64	.oooooo	sty
65	.ooooo.	stirupi
100³	..oo.oo	stilurĭ
365	.o..o..o.	astiwilwiluy
1000	.....o.ooo	teykuy
1904	...o...oooo	talul
10000	.oo...ooo.oooo	tsayurerĭ
100000	..ooo..o.o.ooooo	tsniloyluyuy
1000000	....o.oooo.oo.oooooo	atneywiruywoy

1234567890 .oo.oo..oo.o..ooooooo.o..o.oo.o nsyury urilury wilurpiur
uyuri nsyury urilury wilur piwilu yuri

This (though doubtless susceptible of improvement) is hardly worse than our present name "one thousand two hundred and thirty-four million five hundred and sixty-seven thousand eight hundred and ninety."

The arithmetical operations with the secundal notation leave hardly any room for errors. The rule for addition is as follows: The numbers having been written under one another with the different powers of .o (2) in clearly distinct columns, beginning in the right-hand-most of those columns which contain more than one . (a unit or y) each draw a line enclosing the two uppermost .s in that column in loops and continue the line to the left looping the uppermost y (or ., or unit) in each column until you come to a column containing no y, where end the line with a new y; and the looped ys are to be considered as no longer ys. Repeat this process until there remains no column containing more than one y. Then draw a horizontal line under all the numbers and beneath it, enter a y in each column that contains a y above the line, and enter a u (or o, or zero) in each column that contains no y; and the number so written is the sum required.

I give an example. I will mark the lines I successively draw in red, brown, green, blue, and pencil.

---

³ MS. 1 begins here.

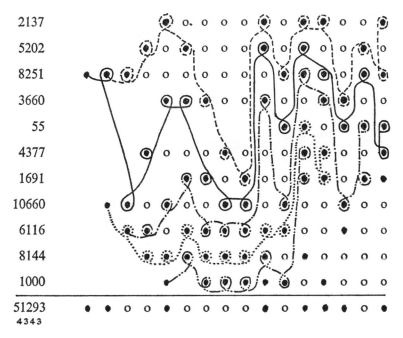

| 2137 |
| 5202 |
| 8251 |
| 3660 |
| 55 |
| 4377 |
| 1691 |
| 10660 |
| 6116 |
| 8144 |
| 1000 |
| 51293 |
| 4343 |

There may, perhaps, be more expeditious ways of adding; but in this way a mistake will not often occur and is sure to be detected by glancing over the work.

Subtraction can be performed in two ways, at least. The first rule I shall give is for simultaneously adding some numbers while subtracting any number of others. The rule is as follows:

Write all the addends and subtrahends under one another in a distinct colonnade, as in addition. Extend each of the subtrahends to the left, by prefixing us (os, or zeros) so that it shall begin at least as far to the left as the sum of the addends would begin or as any other subtrahend (after extension) begins. By shading, or otherwise, mark the subtrahends unmistakably. Treat every u (or zero) in a subtrahend as a y (or ., or unit) and every y as a u. So treating them add all the addends and subtrahends. To the sum add the number of subtrahends, and strike off from the extreme left of the sum this same succession of figures. The result is the required number.

In the following example, the three subtrahends are shaded:

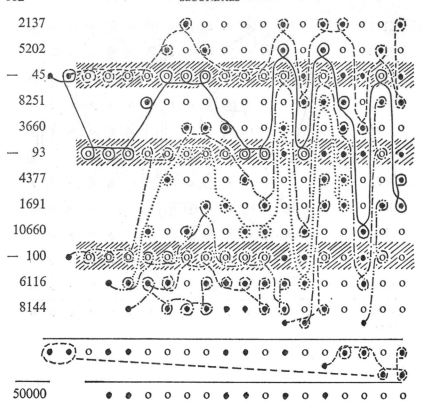

2137	
5202	
— 45	
8251	
3660	
— 93	
4377	
1691	
10660	
— 100	
6116	
8144	

50000

Since this process is by no means exempt from liability to mistakes (reversals of what is before one's eyes, especially when multiple, being the point where mistakes in computation are most to be feared), I give an easier rule for simple subtraction, as follows:

Write the subtrahend columnarly under the minuend and draw a horizontal line under them. Start at the right-hand-most case of a *y* under a *u*, drawing a line which in that column shall be below the horizontal line and thence being continued toward the left shall be above the horizontal line as long as there is a *y* in each column which it shall loop (looping preferably a *y* in the subtrahend) but passing below the horizontal line in every column that contains no *y* above it. And as soon as this line has looped a *y* in the minuend it shall there stop and go no further. Then pass to the right to the next case of a *y* below a *u* and proceed as before; and repeat the process as often as possible. Then, below the horizontal line put a *y* wherever a drawn line is below the horizontal line and wherever there is an unlooped *y* in the minuend without an unlooped *y* below it. In other columns put *us* and the number so written below the horizontal line is the remainder desired.

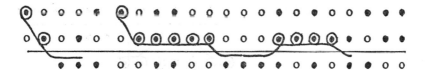

It would certainly be a comfort to children to have that awful multiplication table reduced to [•] , or "once one is one." A good rule of multiplication shall be given. I may here mention that if any number contains a *secundal fraction* (the analogue of a decimal) instead of a point, the units' place ought to be marked by a little curve like that over a short vowel upside down. This is a reform that ought to be introduced into our present notation for numbers, so that $\frac{1}{10}$ should be $\breve{0}1$, etc., and the product of two numbers having *r* and *r'* figures to the right and *l* and *l'* figures to the left of the units' place should (barring what there may be to carry) have $r+r'$ figures to the right and $l+l'$ figures to the left of the units' place, $\breve{4} \times \breve{5}$ being $\breve{0}$ with 2 to carry, etc.

The rule of multiplication is as follows:

Of two numbers to be multiplied, it will generally be convenient to call that the multiplicand which has the fewer *y*s in its expression. Write the multiplier with a *u* prefixed under the multiplicand column-wise with a horizontal line below them. Copy the multiplicand repeatedly, so that in one copy its units' place shall be under each *y* (or .) of the multiplier that has not a *y* (or .) immediately to the right of it, but has more than one *y* in immediate succession to the left of it in the multiplier. These are to be marked by shading or otherwise as subtractive; and the subtractive numbers should be extended by zeros so as to *begin* and *end* in the same columns. Further, copy the multiplicand so as to give one copy having the units' place under each *y* of the multiplier that has no *y* to the right and not more than one *y* to the left, and under each y that has one *y* to the right and none to the left, and under each *u* that has more than two *y*s to the right. All these copies are to be treated as additive. These copies are then to be combined by the first rule of subtraction with addition, and the result is the product required.

Example No. 1.

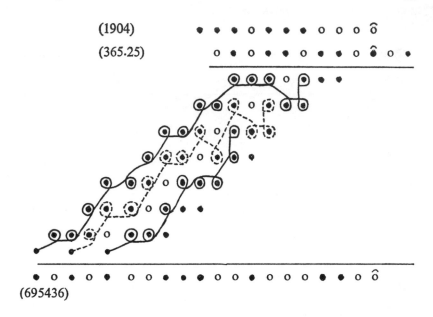

Example No. 2.

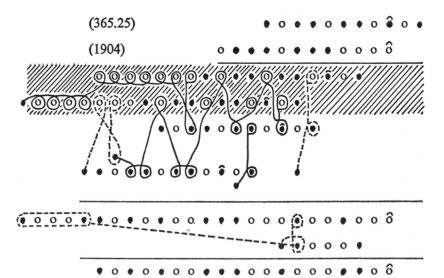

N.B. I have in this procedure departed from the rule by allowing the second copy to begin and end four places to the right of the first. More regularly, I should have had the following

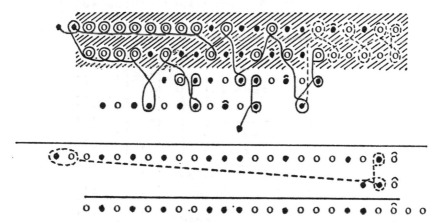

Long division is so obvious a proceeding that the rule need not be given. I will however give an example. To express a second as a decimal of an hour. First, divide one by sixty, or ....oô.

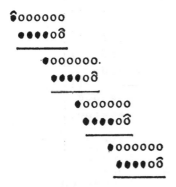

The quotient to be again divided by ....oô is

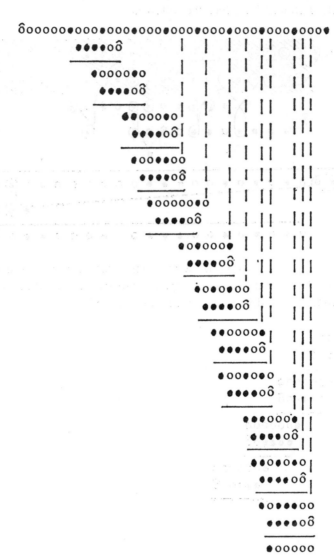

The answer is ôooooooooooo●oo●oooo●●o●ooo●o●o●●●oo●●● etc.

If the whole of the *circulating secundal* is desired, the best way is to begin by finding the reciprocal. The rule (the number being odd, of course) is as follows:

1st. Write the number whose reciprocal is required. Strike off its final . and consider what is left as the expression of a number. Add to it the . struck off; and call the result "the regular addend."

2nd. Write down . for the first "sum found."

3rd. Put a parenthesis mark (at the left of the right-hand-most . of the last "sum found." Considering what remains at the left of the parenthesis as the entire expression of a number, add to it "the regular addend." The sum will be the next "sum found."

4th. Repeat the third operation until you get a "sum found" consisting of a single . followed, or not, by os. Then these os, if there be any, followed by all the numbers to the right of the parenthesis marks, from last to first, constitute the circulating secundal of the reciprocal. Example: Find the reciprocal of 27, or ..o..

To get "the regular addend" ..o. .

Regular addend ...o

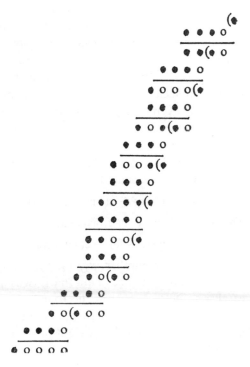

The reciprocal is ○̂ ○̇ o o o o ● o o ● o ● ● ● ● ● o ● ● o ○̇

Proof   ● ● o ● ●

[The] circulating decimal [in the answer], composed entirely of .s, differs from ○̇ by less than any finite number.

The secundal notation has also a mathematical interest. It expresses a number virtually in the form

$$a + 2b + 2^2c + 2^3d + 2^4e + \text{ etc.}$$

where a, b, c, d, e, etc. are such quantities that $a^2 = a$, $b^2 = b$, $c^2 = c$, $d^2 = d$, $e^2 = e$, etc., these quadratic equations expressing that they are each either 1 or 0. Let us use $\sim$ to represent the operation of taking the difference between two such quantities. So that if $x^2 = x$ and $y^2 = y$ $(x \sim y) = (x - y)^2$. This is also a quantity having the same property. Let us call such a quantity a *dyadic* quantity. The sum of two dyadics, x and y, is expressed in the secundal notation as $(x \sim y) + 2xy$. For xy is also a dyadic. The operation of taking the difference between dyadics is associative. That is $(x \sim y) \sim z = x \sim (y \sim z)$. Hence we may write $x \sim y \sim z$, without parentheses. The sum of three dyadics, x, y, z, is expressed in the secundal notation as

$$(x \sim y \sim z) + 2(xy \sim yz \sim zx)$$

The sum of four, x, y, z, w is expressed as

$$(x \sim y \sim z \sim w) + 2(xy \sim xz \sim xw \sim yz \sim yw \sim zw) + 2^2xyzw.$$

The sum of any number, x_1, x_2, x_3, x_4, x_5, etc. has in the units' place the continued difference of all; in the twos' place, the continued difference of all products of two; in the fours' place, the continued difference of all products of four of the dyadics; in the eights' place, the continued difference of all products of eight of the dyadics; and so on. Hence, the sum of

$a + 2b + 2^2c + 2^3d + 2^4e +$ etc. and
$a + 2\beta + 2^2\gamma + 2^3\delta + 2^4\varepsilon +$ etc. is
$(a \sim a) + 2(aa \sim b \sim \beta) + 2^2(aab \sim aa\beta \sim b\beta \sim c \sim \gamma)$
$+ 2^3(aab\beta \sim aabc \sim aab\gamma \sim aa\beta c \sim aa\beta\gamma \sim b\beta c \sim b\beta\gamma \sim c\gamma \sim d \sim \delta)$

+ the next term is quite complicated, though formed in an obvious way. The product of $a + 2b + 2^2c +$ etc. and $a + 2\beta \mid 2^2\gamma +$ etc. will be expressed in the secundal notation thus:

$aa + 2(a\beta \sim ab) + 2^2(a\gamma \sim ac \sim b\beta) + 2^3(a\beta ab \sim a\gamma ac$
$\sim a\delta \sim ad \sim b\gamma \sim \beta c) + 2^4(a\varepsilon \sim ae \sim b\delta \sim \beta d \sim c\gamma \sim aad\delta$
$\sim a\beta c\delta \sim ab\gamma d) +$ etc.

This sign $\sim$ has interesting relations to the algebra of logic where we write $a \curlyvee b$ for $(a + b) - ab$ but now $a \sim b$ is $(a \curlyvee b) - ab$. It is expressed in our usual notation for logical algebra, as $a\bar{b} + \bar{a}b$ or $(a \curlyvee b)(\bar{a} \curlyvee \bar{b})$.

I have written all this to show that I fully appreciate all the merits of secundal numeration, its simplicity and its educative value. But I do not think any propaganda would ever move the world, because there is nothing in secundal numeration to excite the emotional nature ....

C. SECUNDAL COMPUTATION
RULES (54)

Notation. *One* is denoted by a short vertical line called a "unit"; *zero* by a dot on the horizontal line on which that vertical line would stand.

Every number is represented by a horizontal row of such units and dots placed at successive horizontal intervals equal to the height of a unit; and if any unit were placed by one such interval further to the left the value it would represent would be doubled. Each unit thus represents an integer power of two; and the whole row denotes the sum of such powers. In the notation of any number, the "unit" or zero in the "*zeroth*" place, as it will best be termed, i.e. the place of the coefficient of B^0 (where B is the base of numeration, here *two*), is to be made heavy, thus: **1** or **.** and every place from the highest positive that is occupied by a unit to the highest negative that is so occupied must contain either a unit or a dot.

In the somewhat rare contingency of its being desired to express secundally the exact value of a rational fraction whose denominator has another prime factor than two, the circulant should be enclosed by a brace placed underneath the secundal expression of it; because [this] will enable one at once to see whether or not the half last of the circulant is the arithmetical complement of the first half, etc. For instance, one will thus be shown that. ●**.11.1..1** equals $\frac{11\ 1}{1\ldots1}$; since it evidently denotes a fraction whose denominator is $2^{4\times 2}-1$, i.e. $(2^4-1)(2^4+1)$, while its numerator is also divisible by (2^4-1), with **111** as the quotient.

Addition. First: Write the different numbers to be added together, according to the rule for Notation, one under another, and so all coefficients of the same power of two shall appear unmistakably in the same vertical column.

Secondly: Examine the right-hand-most column (of those whose examination has not yet been completed); and do this again and again, until you come upon a column that contains more than one uncancelled unit; and there cancel units to the exact number of any positive integral power of *two* you please (but preferably to the highest possible). Thence, *n* being the exponent of that power of *two*, skip to the *n*th column to the left of the one where you have just cancelled the $(1.)^n$ units, and cancel a single unit in it if there be one there. Now cancel a single unit in the column next to the left of the one where you last cancelled a single unit. But wherever the rule would require you to cancel a single unit if there were one but where you find there is none, there insert a single unit, at the foot of the column but forming a part of it, and returning to the column where you last cancelled more than one unit, and repeat the whole of this second operation, until it can no longer be repeated.

Thirdly: When there is no longer any column containing more than one unit, draw a horizontal line under the addends (or summands) and bring the units in the columns where they are, to express the sum required.

Subtraction. Having written the minuend and subtrahend, either over the other, place by place, secundally,

(2nd), bring your pen, lifted a bit above the paper, over a horizontal line imagined to be drawn below one of the two numbers just written, but above the other; and beginning at the right of all their units, pass, very attentively, to the left of them all, while scrupulously observing the following two rules:

Rule I. Whenever the pen is off the paper, let it remain so until it has *just passed* a secundal place where there is a unit in the subtrahend, without any in the minuend, when instantly depress the pen so as to make it begin to actualize the imaginary line.

Rule II. Whenever the pen is *on* the paper, it must continue to actualize the imaginary line until it has *just passed* a place where there is a unit in the minuend but none in the subtrahend, when instantly let the pen be raised and cease to mark.

(3rd). That done, pass over all the places occupied (more conveniently from left to right) and in whatever place the number, vertical and horizontal together, is *odd* (i.e. one or three), write a unit in the remainder; but wherever that number is even (none or two), mark a dot in the remainder.

Multiplication is, in general, best performed by long multiplication rather than by cross-multiplication. There are, however, many cases in which the operation can be abridged. Thus, where one of the factors contains in its secundal expression three or more units in succession, one can by a subtraction somewhat abridge the work. But, of course, a table of antilogarithms to base 1. is desirable.

Division, too, is, in general, best performed by long division or by logarithms, though the reciprocals of most low primes are very simply expressed.

Any *Root* of any Algebraic Equation is easily evaluated in the form of a rational fraction to a high degree of precision, as soon as a value has been obtained whose modulus differs less from that of the root required than from that of any other root. For it can then be put into the form $1 = \sum_1^m a_i x_i^{m-i}$; and then assuming any rough approximations to the first $m - 1$ positive powers of x, by calculating, according to the formula, the successive negative powers of x, after a considerable number of such easy calculations, x^{-n+1}/x^{-n} will be found to be very near to the true value. One should however avoid allowing any of the a_is to vanish.

Extraction of Square Roots. Of course, the practical way to extract a root is by a Table of Antilogarithms. With a view to making a definite test of the secundal notation, I have begun the computation of such a table;[1] but since such computations are founded on extractions of square roots, I here give the rule that I have used for the purpose.

I do this work on paper of letter-size ruled in squares, all the ruled lines being alike. They are ruled wider than 2 to the centimetre, but closer than 5 to the inch. Two secundal places go [into] the square, the

---

[1] Fragments of this labor are still extant. Peirce worked on logarithms, anti-logarithms, and square roots in secundals. Many details are found in manuscripts 218, 56, 58, 59, 60, and 65 where he computed $\sqrt{1.} = (10)^{.01} = \sqrt{2}$; $(10)^{.01} = \sqrt{\sqrt{2}}$; $(10)^{-.01} = \dfrac{1}{\sqrt{\sqrt{2}}}$; $10^{\frac{1}{11}} = 2^{\frac{1}{3}} = \sqrt[3]{2}$; $10^{.0001} = 2^{\frac{1}{8}} = \sqrt{\sqrt{\sqrt{2}}}$.

The following statement is found in MS. 65.

"*The Binary System of Numerical Notation*

This is a system of written signs by which every rational number can be denoted to the exclusion of all others, the essential characteristics of the system being as follows:

1st, The number denoted is represented either as an integral power of 2 or as the sum of different integral powers of two.

2nd, Only two incomplex numerical legisigns, or sign-types, are employed, one of which signifies the presence, the other the absence of that particular power to which any individual character of that type refers.

3rd, The sign of denoting a number consists of a row of individual characters each of one or other of those two types (though it may happen that the row reduces to a single such character), and by some mark or indication one

even places on the ruled lines. Each unit is half the height of a square. The numbers are written along the breadth of the paper, where there is room for fully 80 secundal places, which are equivalent to 24 decimal places. (For most *other* purposes, 3 secundal places go to a square; and sometimes 4.) But if one does not carry out one's figures beyond the *plus* 80th place (i.e. not beyond $\bullet 1^{1 \cdot 1 \cdots} \bullet$), there will remain a blank triangular area in the upper right hand corner of the paper, amply sufficient for carrying the root well beyond plus sixty-four places of secundals equivalent to 19 of decimals. (I postpone to a later page a proposal for a secundal *nomenclature* of numbers.)

I find it advantageous to use three colours of ink in rotation (perfectly regular after the first round); *black* for the minuends, obtained, after the first, as remainders, and for the horizontal lines below them required according to the rule for subtraction; *green* or *blue* (pale enough to show unmistakably as colored) for the part of any that may be derived from the approximation last already found and recorded for the root; and bright *red* for every [part] in the line appropriated to the root, as well as for the final figure of each subtrahend.

---

of those two characters in the row that have each but one next to it is distinguished, as its beginning, from the other limit as end. Furthermore, some one individual character in the row that denotes a number is distinguished by some kind of a mark put upon it from all the other characters of the same row as being that one which refers to the zero power of two, and then the power of two to which any other character of the row refers is known from one or other of two rules, namely.

Any character near the beginning of the row [other] than that character which refers to the zero power of two, refers to a power of two whose exponent may be ascertained by the rule that every character of the row except the last refers to a power of two whose exponent is greater by one than that power of two referred to by the character next to it in the row toward the end of the row.

The exponent of the power of two referred to by any character of the row that is nearer the end of the row than is that character that refers to the zero power of two may be known by applying the rule that every character in the row except the first refers to a power of two whose exponent is one less than the exponent of the power of two referred to by the character of character of the row that is next to this character but more toward the beginning of the row.

4th, Because an endless series of characters cannot be written, it follows that in order to represent in this system a number which is equal to the sum of an endless series of different powers of two, it is necessary to have some mark to show that a certain part of [a] row at the end of it is to be conceived as endlessly repeated, without the intervention of any other characters; and therefore that must be such a *mark of circulation*, if every rational number is to be distinguishable from every other."

Certain words in this rule have to be understood in somewhat special senses, which had better be explained at once. By a "*figure*" will be meant any arbitrary scribable sign that *may permissibly be understood* to denote a number. But since the term "arbitrary scribable sign" is applicable to two different categories of objects, namely, before it is actually written, to a general and always more or less indefinite *shape*, whose only real being is that of a habit of the imagination and of the nervous organization, and after it has been written, to each single instance of such writing that has ever been created, it follows that the definition of the word "figure" allows it to be used in these two senses, in one of which the secundal notation employs but two "figures," viz: 1, which shall be called the "*ace*," and ., which shall be called the "*dot*," while in the other sense (in the other "*acception*" is the more precise expression in such a case of a variation of meaning to which all the words of a broad logical class are alike is subject. Only, do not confuse "acception" with "acceptation") there will be as many secundal "figures" as there will have been written of "aces" and "dots" taken together. It is further to be observed that, according to the above definition of the word "figure," to say that the ace and the dot are "the only two 'figures' of the secundal notation" by no means implies that they *ought to* be, but only that they *could be*, regarded as denoting numerical quantities. In point of fact, a much truer conception of the system will result from regarding the ace as the affirmation and the dot as the denial of the presence of that power of .1, or a half, which is denoted in no other way than image-wise, in its exponent, by the succession of marked intervals from the place of a heavily marked figure, — that is, from the "*start*," or zero-place of the exponent of .1, to the place where the mark of assertion is, the exponent increasing by one at each additional interval toward the right, and *vice versa*. That this is the proper way of conceiving the Secundal Notation is a truth that will be forcibly brought home to us by analyzing, on the one hand, the conceptions of the different kinds of numbers, and on the other hand, the properties of the Secundal System. Numbers, as not being objects brought to light through sensation, but inventions imposed by the arts of reasoning, ought primarily to be recognized as having their very being in a classification, like all other products of reason. Now just as, not merely the arts of geometry, but the very objects are primarily: 1st, such as have in themselves no other characters than those involved in extension and in dimension, namely, Listing's numbers, which I call Chorisy, Cyclosy, Periphraxy, Apeirisy, *et cetera ad infinitum*, together with the different kinds of Singularities, or exceptional places, such as Terminations and Nodes (but not cusps and other merely projective singularities), and together also with such complications of the characters mentioned as we meet with, for example, in the theory of map-coloring; 2nd, such as if two coincide through any part of their extension coincide everywhere, as rays, unbounded planes, etc. which are the only objects that Projective Geometry *never* leaves out of view; and 3rd, the objects of Metrical Geometry, such as proportionality of lengths on rays, areas and angles on planes, volumes, spherical areas, etc. in flat solids (i.e. such as have their apeirisy zero); just as there are, I repeat, these three types of Geometrical Objects, because such objects are creatures of human instinct, i.e. of what we call Reason (!) (because we cannot discern its bounds), so we derive from the same origin, which seems to have decided tendency to trichotomy, a three-fold division of studies of numbers. This requires some explanation. Beginning with the idea of a particle, or of a dot, suppose we conceive [it] to be changed into a multitude of dots whether by some or all of the dots breaking, one into several, or by new dots coming into existence, and when this is endlessly repeated, the result is an "*infinite*" collection of dots, the characteristic of which is that it has parts each of which is equal to the whole, that is the dots of the whole can be conceived to be paired each with a dot of the part. No addition to, or multiplication by, itself could increase the infinite multitude; [...][2]

---

[2] In MS. 60 Peirce writes of the computation of $10^{\frac{1}{10}} = 2^{\frac{1}{2}}$. "There are two methods. The first is one of my own invention, which, in this particular case, reduces to the method of continued fractions (substantially). That is, we have to solve the equation $(1+x)^{10} = 10$ or $x^{10} + 10x = 1$. We start with any two numbers a, regarded as an approx. to x^{10} (though we will make it 0) and b, regarded as an approx. to x (though we will assume it to be 1). With these by means of the equation $x^{10} + 10x = 1$ we calculate an approx. to 1. Then since $x:1 = x^{10}:x$ we treat the approx. x and 1 as approx. to x^{10} and x, and proceed in that way as far as we please, finally dividing the last but one by the last to get the final value of x. Since we want it to be about forty or fifty secundal places, we work until the last two approx. to 1 have about 20 to 25 places each." A second method is given in MS. 56.

PREFACE

Secundal augrim is a tool of minor utility in mathematical reasoning, but still of very decided utility. It has a charm of simplicity.

CHAPTER FIRST. The Notation

In this system, a number is in general denoted by a horizontal row of figures, each of which is either a 0 or a 1. One of the figures has a bar through it, thus: θ or $\overline{1}$. The last (or righthand most) figure and one of the others may have dots over them. If so, this part of the row is called the *circulate* while the part to the left of it is called the *serious*.

The places of figures in the row are called the *secundal places*. Each has an ordinal number one greater than that of the place next to the right, the place of the barred figure being the zeroth.

Let l be the ordinal of the place of the last dotted figure in any row denoting a number and let k be the ordinal of the place of the other dotted figure. Let n_i be the value of the figure in the ith place (the value of 1 being unity and 0 not having any value). Then x being any arbitrarily chosen positive integer, the number denoted by the row is

$$(0) \qquad \sum_{k+1-x}^{\infty} n_i 2^i + \frac{1}{1-2^{l-k-1}} \sum_{l-x}^{k-x} n_i 2^i$$

Whatever positive integer x may be we may remove the first dot from the kth place to the $(k-x)^{th}$ place, provided we affix additional figures to the right of the lth place making $n_{l-j} = n_{k+1-j}$ for each positive value of j, and provided we remove the last dot from the lth place to the $(k-x+yl-yk)^{th}$ place, y being any positive integer we choose, and the number denoted will remain the same, by the formula (0).

CHAPTER THE SECOND.   Of Addition

The most convenient rule is as follows:

1st, Write the secundal expressions of the augend and its successive addends in *additory array*, that is, so that figures in the same secundal place are in the same vertical column.

2nd, Change the places of the dots so that they are over the same secundal places in all the numerical expressions, by making the k of each agree with the smallest k and $k + 1 - l$ for each the least common multiple of the $k + 1 - l$ of all as given.

3rd, Call the following operation the *Staple Process*, viz:

i. Scrutinize the right hand most column of the array, and if need be the column next to the left of the column last scrutinized, until you find a column containing more 1s than one. Cancel these two.

ii. If the column next to the left of a column in which one or more 1s have just been cancelled contains a 1, cancel one 1 in that column.

But if that column does not contain a 1 insert a 1 in it and thereby bring the Staple Process to an end.

Perform the staple process upon the circulate of the array again and again as long as any column contains more than one 1; and in doing this, if the rule requires a 1 to be inserted in a column to the left of the k column, and therefore in the serious, the 1 is not only to be inserted in that column of the serious but also in the column of the circulate that is $k + 1 - l$ places to the right of that column. If the final result is that there is one 1 in every column of the circulate, all these 1s are to be cancelled and a 1 is to be inserted in the last column of the serious.

4th, Perform the staple process upon the serious of the array, modified as it may be by insertions of 1s by the third operation. This operation [and] the third will in practice be performed as one.

5th, Draw a horizontal line under the array, and bring down into a row beneath it the 1s remaining in the array, without altering their secundal places, and filling with 0s the vacant places between them and in the last places, if there be any vacant to the right of all the 1s. Mark the same places as barred and dotted. The result is the sum required.

Example. Add the first sixteen odd numbers after attaching iȯ to the 1st, 5th, 9th, and 13th, ioi to those next following, ȯi to those next following, and ȯiȯ to the rest. I set down these numbers in black, enlarge the circulates with lead pencil, connect the cancellings with lines and use *brown, blue, red, green*, ink in cyclical order, so that it shall be easy to see what has been done.[1]

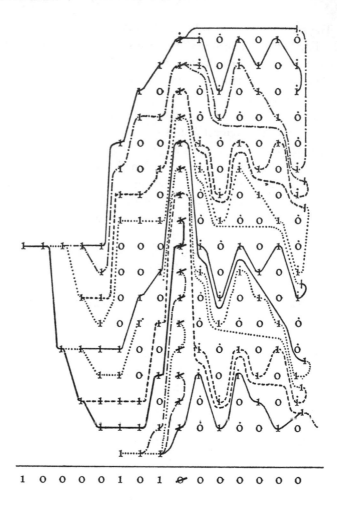

1 0 0 0 0 1 0 1 𝒐 0 0 0 0 0 0

CHAPTER THE THIRD.   Subtraction

The safest and best rule I know is the following:

1st, Write down the subtrahend and write the figures of the minuend under the collocated figures of the subtrahend, and extend the circulates so as to give k and l the same values in subtrahend and minuend.

These colors appear in the MS.

2nd, See whether the circulate of the subtrahend is greater than that of the minuend or not. If it be so, begin at the last place and draw a horizontal line between subtrahend and minuend and extend it until it has passed to the left of a place in which the figure in the subtrahend is 0 and that in the minuend is 1. If it be not so no horizontal line is to be between the last figures of subtrahend and minuend. In either case now pass a point along toward the left between subtrahend and minuend, until this point has passed a secundal place where the figure of the subtrahend is 1 and that of the minuend is 0 when a horizontal mark must immediately commence between subtrahend and minuend. And every time the point passes a secundal place on the line where the subtrahend has 0 and the minuend has 1, the line must immediately thereafter stop; while every time the point passes a secundal place where there is no line but subtrahend has 1 and minuend has 0, immediately thereafter the line must recommence. There must be no line at the beginning; for if there is, the subtrahend exceeds the minuend and subtraction becomes absurd.

3rd, Now begin at the extreme right hand place and write under each figure of the minuend the figure of the remainder for that secundal place, by means of this rule. Where there is no line between subtrahend and minuend, a 0 in the subtrahend shows that the figure in the minuend is to be copied in the same secundal place of the remainder; and where there is a line a 1 in the subtrahend shows the same. But where there is no line a 1 in the subtrahend or where there is a line a 0 in the subtrahend shows that the figure in the minuend must be changed from 0 to 1 or from 1 to 0 to give the figure in the remainder.

Example. Subtract $42097\frac{3}{7}$ from $61894\frac{20}{31}$. I write the subtrahend and minuend in black in the most compact form. I then perform the first operation in brown, the second in red, and the third in blue. The black dots must be imagined to be erased in the first operation.

Subtrahend i 0 1 0 0 1 0 0 0 1 1 1 0 0 1 ꓭ 0 1 1 0 1 1 0 1 1 0 1 1 0 i

Minuend   1 1 1 1 0 0 0 1 1 1 0 0 0 1 1 ꓭ 1 0 1 0 0 1 0 1 0 0 1 0 1 0

Remainder   0 1 0 0 1 1 0 1 0 1 0 1 0 0 1 ꓭ 0 0 1 1 0 1 1 1 0 1 1 1 0 0

CHAPTER THE FOURTH. Multiplication

This is the multiplication table

    1 0

    0 0

All multiplication will be ordinary long multiplication and calls for no example, except for the treatment of circulates. The proper way of treating these will be considered later. Meantime they *can* be managed as in the following example.

Example. Multiply $1\frac{3}{7}$ by $1\frac{2}{3}$. ....

That is $\dot{1}\dot{0}1\dot{1} \times \dot{1}\dot{1}\dot{0}$

This is $\dot{1} + \varnothing\dot{0}1\dot{1} + \varnothing\dot{1}\dot{0} + (11\varnothing \times \varnothing\dot{0}0\dot{1} \times \varnothing 0\dot{1})$

To multiply $\varnothing\dot{0}0\dot{1}$ by $\varnothing\dot{0}\dot{1}$ or $\varnothing\dot{0}1010\dot{1}$ by $\varnothing\dot{0}0100\dot{1}$

We have · $\varnothing\dot{0}\,0\,0\,0\,0\,1\,0\,\dot{1}\,0\,\dot{1}\,0\,\dot{1}\,\dot{0}$

which equals $\varnothing\dot{0}\,0\,0\,0\,1\,\dot{1}$

which we multiply by 11∅

                          $\varnothing\dot{0}\,0\,1\,1\,0\,\dot{0}$

                                1 1 0.

$11\varnothing \times \varnothing\dot{0}0\dot{1} \times \varnothing\dot{0}\dot{1} =$
              $\varnothing\dot{0}\,0\,0\,\dot{0}$

              $\varnothing\dot{1}\,0\,0\,\dot{0}$

         .. $\varnothing\dot{0}\,1\,1\,0\,\dot{1}$

Answer which is $2\frac{8}{21}$ $1\varnothing\dot{0}\,1\,1\,0\,0\,\dot{0}$

CHAPTER THE FIFTH. Division

Besides ordinary long division, I know of two easier ways of finding the circulate that represents the reciprocal of a given integer. One of these is about as easy as the other. I think that in decimals the less obvious of the two is a trifle the easier and in secundals the other. I will first give an example in decimal arithmetic of all three ways, because my way of doing long division merits attention. Required, then, the reciprocal of 351. I first begin a table of multiples as shown in A. I calculate a column at a time [and] having got it I run it down with my eye and where a figure is less than the one above, I put a dot in the column to the [left] to show that there is one to carry. There is a check. Namely, the last figure of each column must be the same as the first of the previously found column. So I next bring the table to the state B. Then to state C last to state D. This table greatly facilitates long division.[2]

A		B		C		D		$.00284\dot{8}\dot{9}$
1	0351	1	0351	1	0351	1	0351	0702
2	2	2	.02	2	702	2	0702	298
3	3	3	53	3	.053	3	1053	2808
4	4	4	.04	4	404	4	1404	172
5	5	5	55	5	755	5	1755	1404
6	6	6	.06	6	.106	6	2106	316
7	7	7	57	7	457	7	2457	3159
8	8	8	.08	8	808	8	2808	001
9	9	9	59	9	.159	9	3159	
	.0		.10		510		3510	

Second Way

```
        351
          9
       315|9
         1|
  1  0316
  2  0632
  3  0948
  4  1264
  5  1580
  6  1896
  7  2212
  8  2528
  9  2844
     3160
```

```
              (9
      2 8 4|4
      1 2 6 4
      1 5 4,8
      2 5 2 8
      2 6 8,2
    0 6 3 2
    0 9 0 0

    .0 0 2 8 4 9
```

Third Way

```
   000351
        3159
        1404
     2808
    0702


    002849
    000351
```

$$\tfrac{1}{2849}=.0003\dot{5}\dot{1} \qquad \tfrac{1}{351}=.00284\dot{8}\dot{9}$$

---

[2] In MS. 67 Peirce describes how "to transform an integer from decimal or sextal to secundal expression." The rule follows.

"Establish a column for decimal expressions and a parallel column for secundal expressions. Let a be, at any stage, the last expression in the decimal column and β any in the secundal column. Write the expression to be transformed at the head of the decimal column, as the first a, and perform the operation Φ.

The operation Φ consists of the following steps. Remove the last figure of a and put the equivalent secundal expression in column B as a β with its last figure as far to the left of the fractional point as was the figure removed from a. In place of the removed figure of a put 0 and divide the resulting a by two to make a new a upon which to perform the operation Φ.

Repeat the operation Φ until a becomes 0.

Then the sum of the Φs is the expression desired.

Examples: Transform 1893 into secundals

A	B
189|3	11
189 0	
94|5	101
94 0	
47|0	0
47 0	
23|5	101
23 0	
11|5	101
11 0	
5|5	101
5 0	
2|5	101
2 0	
1|0	0
1 0	
|5	101
0	
0	11101100101

Transform 1025 into secundals

102|5	101
102 0	
51|0	0
51 0	
25|5	101
25 0	
12|5	101
12 0	
6|0	
6 0	
3|0	0
3 0	
1|5	101
10	
|5	101
1	1000000001 "

Peirce also tells how "to transform an integer from secundal to decimal expression." The rule runs:

"Establish two parallel columns, one of which, A itself, consists in a series of parallel columns for secundal expressions and mixed expressions, while the other B will contain only decimal expressions. [Peirce writes "This is a stupid performance."] Write the given secundal expression in A each successive figure under the preceding one. Perform operation Ψ.

Operation Ψ consists in transferring the number in the lowest line of column A to column B and then doubling the number in every other line, using Arabic figures, and at the same time bringing [it] down to the next lower line.

Repeat operation Ψ until column A is exhausted. Add the numbers in column B and the sum is the desired expression.

Example: Transform 11101100101 to decimals

```
     1
     1 2                                                    0
     1 2 4                                                  4
     0 2 4 8                                                0
     1 0 4 8 16                                             0
     1 2 0 8 16 32                                         32
     0 2 4 0 16 32 64                                      64
     0 0 4 8  0 32 64 128                                   0
     1 0 0 8 16  0 64 128 256                             256
     0 2 0 0 16 32  0 128 256 512                         512
     1 0 4 0  0 32 64   0 256 512 1024                   1024
                                                        ─────
                                                         1893 "
```

I will now calculate the reciprocal of the same number in the last two
ways.

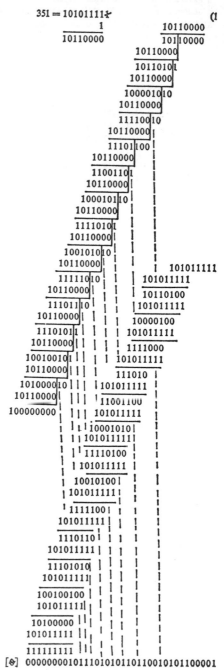

CHAPTER THE SIXTH. Evolution

To extract the Square Root of a given number,

1st, Move the bar through an even number of places to the right or left, so as to make the modified number > 4 and < 100.

Then the 1st approximation will be 4, and its square will be 4.

2nd, Go through the following Staple Operation repeatedly until the square of the last approximation is as near the modified number as you care to have it:

i. Under the square of the approximation last obtained write that approximation itself, beginning at such a place that when added to its square it shall give a sum less than the modified number but as little less as possible.

ii. Let $n - 1$ be the number of [the] place by which the last number extends to the right of the last 1 of the number above it. Affix to the last number n 0s and a 1.

iii. Add the last two numbers, and the sum will be the square of the next approximation, which approximation will be found by adding to the last a 1 in the nth place after its last 1.

3rd, When the Staple Operation has given a close enough result, move the bar back in the opposite direction and through half as many places as in the 1st operation.

Example. Find the square root of 7 or 11. Modified number 411

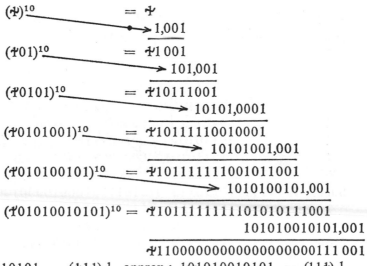

$(4)^{10}$ = 4

1,001

$(401)^{10}$ = 41 001

101,001

$(40101)^{10}$ = 410111001

10101,0001

$(40101001)^{10}$ = 410111110010001

10101001,001

$(4010100101)^{10}$ = 410111111001011001

1010100101,001

$(401010010101)^{10}$ = 4101111111101010111001

101010010101,001

411000000000000000000111 001

[401010010101 = (411)$\frac{1}{10}$ approx.; 101010010101 = (114)$\frac{1}{10}$ approx.]

[Find the square root of 2 or 10 as given below; also the square root of
the square root of 2 or 10 as given below.]

$\sqrt{2} = \sqrt{10}$

  ϯ   ϯ

01   1,001
1   101,01
01   1011,001
01   101101,001
000001   10110101,0000001
001   10110101000001,0001
1   10110101000001001,01
Sum so far   ϯ1111111111111111011011100101101001

Copy   { 10110101000001001,01
from ×   0110111001010110100
1   1010100000100110
1   10110101000000100111,01
001   101101011000001001111,0001
Sum   111111001001000111010011000001
1   101101010000001001111001,01
001   10110101010000100111100111,0001
1   10110101010000010011111001001,01
Sum   1111111111111101001100000100010000101001

Copy   { 10110101000001001111001101001,01
from ϲ   11010011000000100000000010100010
001   10110101000000100111100011001,0001
1   1011010100000010011100100100101,01
1   1011010100000010011110010001001,01
1   10110101000000100111100110011001,1,
1   1011010100000010011110010010011,
1   1011010100000010011110010011001
1   10110101000001001110011001100
001   101101010000010011110011001001
Sum   11111111111110110001010111010001000010001
1   10110101000001001111001100
1   10110101000001001111100110
01   10110101000001001111001

$\sqrt{10} = $ ϯ 011010100000100111100110011001111111110011101
[Errors: in second sum, one zero; in fourth, two zeros]

$\sqrt{\sqrt{}}10$

   ᛭   ᛭

  001   1,0001

    1   1001,01

  000001   10011,0000001

    1   10011000001,01

    1   100110000011,01

Sum   ᛭0110101000001010001 10001

Too much by 0000001   000100101010011 0000001

Sub 0000001   1001100000111

                       11100000111111

  $\sqrt{\sqrt{}}10$ = ᛭0011000001101111111

9

MISCELLANEOUS NOTES

A. [A TELEGRAPHIC CODE]   (parts of 1575 and 1361)

1. The principal part of a code for telegraphing consists of a classification of ideas. This is so no matter what the plan of it may be.

This work is about the most difficult task that can be set to a logician, and no other man is fit to undertake it. It is a problem upon which I have been constantly at work for more than forty years; and I probably know more about it than any other living wight.

2. The parts of the work are about as follows:

i. The machinery or *spelling* of the significant units.

ii. The distribution of kinds of meaning among them (to which your idea relates) or the *accidence*.

iii. The construction of the *vocabulary*.

iv. The manner of using the code, or the *syntax*.

3. The provision for secrecy is so very readily applied that this condition may as well be insisted upon.

Plan for the machinery of the Code

The telegraphic signs have to be considered; and when a mistake is suspected, the reader should consider what telegraphic mistake is likely to have occurred.

The international telegraphic alphabet, then, must be considered first.

Characters of the International Telegraphic Code

One mark	Four marks	Five marks
· E	· · · · H	· · · · · 5
– T	· · · – V	· · · · – 4
Two marks	· · – · F	· · · – – 3
· · I	· · – – Not used = UT	· · – – – 2
· – A	· – · · L	· – – – – 1
– · N	· – · – Not used = RT	– · · · · 6
– – M	· – – · P	– – · · · 7
Three marks	· – – – J	– – – · · 8
· · · S	– · · · B	– – – – · 9
· · – U	– · · – X	– – – – – 0
· – · R	– · – · C	**Six marks**
· – – W	– · – – Y	· · · · · · Period
– · · D	– – · · Z	· – · – · – Comma
– · – K	– – · – Q	– – · · – – !
– – · G	– – – · Not used = TG	· · – – · · ?
– – – O	– – – – Not used = TO	

I would propose to spell every code-word with four four-mark characters. Since there are 16 of these, there would be 16^4, or 65536 code-words. These, skillfully used, would be sufficient.

The Cable company would receive and send merely the dots and dashes, every dot being written 0 and every dash 1.

Each code-word would thus appear as a number in the binary notation of arithmetic. But the user of the code would only need to understand this in case he was going to employ a secret cipher.

The code dictionary would consist of 1024 pages with 64 code-words and their explanations on each page.

In order to make a secret cipher, it should be agreed between the correspondents, that the sender after getting his code-words should treat them as numbers and perform a certain arithmetical operation on each and that the receiver should perform the inverse operation. The *binary system is excessively easily and rapidly worked.*

If only one arithmetical operation were performed, the decipherer into whose hands the dispatch might fall, would only have to find out which one of the possible 209227898879999 operations this was. But since the operation might change with every word of the dispatch, with a different kind of change from one dispatch to the next, the decipherer would be up a tree.

It is an important fact that 65537 (one more than the number of code-words) is a *prime number*, that is, is exactly divisible by no whole number, while 65536 itself is exactly divisible by no odd number.

If, then, the result of any arithmetical operation had more than sixteen figures, all the figures to the left of the right hand sixteen should be cut off and being written under the others in the extreme right hand places should be subtracted from them.

If in performing the inverse operation one had to subtract a greater number from a smaller one, it would only be necessary to add certain figures to the left of the smaller, every figure so added being also added to the figure sixteen places to the right.

One very simple concealing operation then would be to add to the number corresponding to a word any number less than 65537.

It would also be permissible to multiply by any of those numbers, since (65537 being prime) no two different numbers multiplied by the same number (and brought down to 16 figures in the above manner) could produce the same 16-figure result.

Moreover, owing to 65536 being divisible by no odd number, it would be permissible to raise the number corresponding to a word by any of the 32767 odd powers whose exponents are less than 65537, and no ambiguity could arise.

Moreover all the first 65536 powers of any odd prime number (or at any rate of a great many such numbers) would be all different. The result of this would be that the code dictionary could give for every word a *logarithm* and *antilogarithm* of that word, by means of which it would be very easy to perform calculations otherwise tedious.

As an example, I will calculate a few powers of 3. Since 3 is written 11, to multiply by 3 we have only to increase each figure by the one next to the right of it.

Exponent	Power
0	0000,0000,0000,0001
1	0000,0000,0000,0011
2 = 10	0000,0000,0000,1001
3 = 11	0000,0000,0001,1011
4 = 100	0000,0000,0101,0001
5 = 101	0000,0000,1111,0011
6 = 110	0000,0010,1101,1001
7 = 111	0000,1000,1000,1011
8 = 1000	0001,1001,1010,0001
9 = 1001	0100,1100,1110,0011

$$1110,0110,1010,1001$$

Here the result is reduced to bring it into 16 figures.
That is, we subtract twice 65537.

$$\begin{array}{r} 10,1011,0011,1111,1011 \\ 10 \\ \hline 1011,0011,1111,1001 \end{array}$$

Again a similar reduction.

$$\begin{array}{r} 10,0001,1011,1110,1011 \\ 10 \\ \hline 0001,1011,1110,1001 \end{array}$$

I will calculate a few successive powers of 257

Exponent	Power
1 ————————————————	1 0000 0001

$$\begin{array}{r} 1\ 0000\ 0001 \\ \hline 1\ 0000\ 0010\ 0000\ 0001 \\ 1 \end{array}$$

2 = 10 ——— ———————————	0000 0010 0000 0000

$$\begin{array}{r} 10\ 0000\ 0000 \\ \hline 10\ 0000\ 0010\ 0000\ 0000 \\ 10 \end{array}$$

3 = 11 —————————————	0000 0001 1111 1110

$$\begin{array}{r} 1\ 1111\ 1110 \\ \hline 1111\ 1111\ 1111\ 1110 \\ 1 \end{array}$$

4 = 100 ——————————	1111 1111 1111 1101

$$\begin{array}{r} 1111\ 1111\ 1111\ 1101 \\ \hline 1\ 0000\ 0000\ 1111\ 1100\ 1111\ 1101 \\ 1\ 0000\ 0000 \end{array}$$

5 = 101 ——— ——————	1111 1011 1111 1101

$$\begin{array}{r} 1111\ 1011\ 1111\ 1101 \\ \hline 1111\ 1100\ 1111\ 1000\ 1111\ 1101 \end{array}$$

$$\begin{array}{r} 1111\ 1100 \\ \hline \end{array}$$

$$6 = 110 \ \text{——————————————} \ \overline{1111\ 1000\ 0000\ 0001}$$

1111 1000 0000 0001

$$\overline{1111\ 1000\ 1111\ 1001\ 0000\ 0001}$$

$$\begin{array}{r} 1111\ 1000 \\ \hline \end{array}$$

$$7 = 111 \ \text{——————————————} \ \overline{1111\ 1000\ 0000\ 1001}$$

1111 1000 0000 1001

$$\overline{1111\ 1001\ 0000\ 0001\ 0000\ 1001}$$

$$\begin{array}{r} 1111\ 1001 \\ \hline \end{array}$$

$$8 = 1000 \ \text{——————————————} \ \overline{0000\ 0000\ 0001\ 0000}$$

0001 0000

$$\overline{0001\ 0000\ 0001\ 0000}$$

$$9 = 1001 \ \text{——————————————} \ \overline{0001\ 0000\ 0001\ 0000}$$

1 0000 0001 0000

$$\overline{1\ 0000\ 0010\ 0000\ 0001\ 0000}$$

$$\begin{array}{r} 1\ 0000 \\ \hline \end{array}$$

$$10 = 1010 \ \text{——————————————} \ \overline{0010\ 0000\ 0000\ 0000}$$

10 0000 0000 0000

$$\overline{10\ 0000\ 0010\ 0000\ 0000\ 0000}$$

$$\begin{array}{r} 10\ 0000 \\ \hline \end{array}$$

$$11 = 1011 \ \text{——————————————} \ \overline{0001\ 1111\ 1110\ 0000}$$

1 1111 1110 0000

$$\overline{1\ 1111\ 1111\ 1111\ 1110\ 0000}$$

$$\begin{array}{r} 1\ 1111 \\ \hline \end{array}$$

$$12 = 1100 \ \text{——————————————} \ 1111\ 1111\ 1100\ 0001$$

B. [NOTE ON A THEOREM IN FERMAT][1] (236)

P.S. The following may amuse you. Fermat says that the area of a right triangle whose legs and hypotheneuse are whole numbers cannot be a square; and gives as the reason that if two squares had their sum and difference both squares, it would follow that there was another pair of squares of which the same was true, the sum of the second pair being less than that of the first. On this M. Cantor remarks "Er hat [auch] den Beweis jener Unmöglichkeit in räthselhafter Kürze angedeutet, dessen Schluss allein ganz klar und verständlich ist." This seems to me rather obtuse. Let M^2 and N^2 be such a pair of squares and assume that their sum is as small as that of any such pair. Then if they had any common divisor, division would give another pair of squares having the same property and a smaller sum, contrary to hypothesis. We may therefore assume they are relatively prime. As such both are not even. Nor can both be odd, since the form of an odd square is 1 + multiple of 8 and that of an even square a multiple of 4. Hence the larger is odd; the smaller, even. Let $M^2 > N^2$ and write

$$N^2 = 2^x n^2$$

where n is an odd number. Then the hypothesis is that

$$M^2 + 2^x n^2 = s^2$$
$$M^2 - 2^x n^2 = t^2$$

Then s and t are both odd; their sum and difference are even; and the halves of sum and difference are integers. Since the sum of $\frac{1}{2}(s+t)$ and $\frac{1}{2}(s-t)$ is s which is odd, it follows that one of the two, $\frac{1}{2}(s+t)$ and $\frac{1}{2}(s-t)$, is odd and the other even. Let u be the odd one and $2^y v$, where v is an odd number, be the even one. Or

---

[1] This manuscript is a postscript to a letter which has as yet not been identified.

$\frac{1}{2}(s \pm t) = u$

$\frac{1}{2}(s \mp t) = 2^y v.$

Now had u and v a common divisor, it would divide both s and t. But if s and t, being odd, had a common divisor it, would divide both $2M^2$ and $2^{x+1}n^2$, and therefore M^2 and N^2 which are relatively prime.

The equations give

$$M^2 = u^2 + 4^y v^2$$

Hence if M and either u or v had a common divisor it would divide both u and v. Hence M, u, v are relatively prime.

The equations also give

$$n^2 = 2^{-x+y+1} uv$$

and since n, u, v are all odd $-x+y+1 = 0$ and

$$n^2 = uv$$

Of course u and v are squares.

The other equation gives

$$u^2 = (M + 2^y v)(M - 2^y v)$$

and since M and v are odd numbers relatively prime, it follows that $M + 2^y v$ and $M - 2^y v$ are relatively prime, and are therefore squares, their product being a square. We may, therefore, write

$$M + 2^y v = p^2$$
$$M - 2^y v = q^2$$

Hence $u = pq$

and p and q being relatively prime are both squares.

$$2^{y-1} v = \frac{p+q}{2} \cdot \frac{p-q}{2}$$

whence

$$N^2 = 2^{y-1} uv = \frac{p+q}{2} \cdot \frac{p-q}{2} \cdot p \cdot q$$

If $\frac{p+q}{2}$ and $\frac{p-q}{2}$ had a common divisor, it would divide both p and q which are relatively prime. If either $\frac{p+q}{2}$ and $\frac{p-q}{2}$ and either p or q had a common divisor, it would divide both p and q. Hence $\frac{p+q}{2}, \frac{p-q}{2}$, p, q are relatively prime and since their product is a square all are squares.

(Of course the even one is $\frac{p-q}{2}$.)

Hence $\frac{p+q}{2}$ and $\frac{p-q}{2}$ are two squares whose sum and difference are both squares. Their sum is p. Now

$$p = \sqrt{M + 2^y v} = \sqrt{\sqrt{\tfrac{1}{2}(s^2 + t^2)} + \tfrac{1}{2}(s \mp t)}$$

$$= \sqrt{s}\sqrt{\sqrt{\frac{1 + \left(\frac{t}{s}\right)^2}{2}} + \frac{1 \mp \frac{t}{s}}{2}}$$

Hence $p < \sqrt{2s}$ and *a fortiori* $p < s^2$. Hence it is impossible that two squares should have their sum and difference both squares.

But if the right triangle whose legs and hypotheneuse are a, b, h, had its area, $\tfrac{1}{2}ab$ a square, h^2 and $4(\tfrac{1}{2}ab)$ would be two squares whose sum and difference were both squares.

$$h^2 + 4(\tfrac{1}{2}ab) = (a+b)^2$$
$$h^2 - 4(\tfrac{1}{2}ab) = (a-b)^2$$

Hence there is no such triangle. It seems to be quite clear that that is what Fermat had in mind.

If $N = 0$, the proof breaks down.

C. A COMPUTER'S DEVICE   (213)

In dealing with the problem of three moments, and elsewhere, powers of numbers of the form $P+Q\sqrt{N}$ occur. These satisfy the difference equation

$$u_{x+2}+(P^2-Q^2N)u_x = 2Pu_{x+1}.$$

By taking out $(P^2-Q^2N)^{\pm x}$ as a factor from u_x, the quotient satisfies the equation

$$v_{x+2}+v_x = 2P'v_{x+1}$$

which otherwise written is

$$v_{x-2}+v_x = 2P'v_{x-1}$$

The solution of this, dropping the accent, is

$$v_x = C_1(P+\sqrt{P^2-1})^x + C_2(P-\sqrt{P^2-1})^x.$$

But obviously

$$(P+\sqrt{P^2-1})(P-\sqrt{P^2-1}) = 1$$

Separating the square factor of P^2-1, we return to the form

$$P+Q\sqrt{N} = \frac{1}{P-Q\sqrt{N}}$$

Specimens of such numbers are

$$3+2\sqrt{2}$$
$$2+\sqrt{3}$$
$$9+4\sqrt{5}$$
$$5+2\sqrt{6}$$
$$8+3\sqrt{7}$$
$$3+\sqrt{8}$$
$$19+6\sqrt{10}$$
$$10+3\sqrt{11}$$
$$7+2\sqrt{12}$$
$$649+180\sqrt{13}$$

Of course all their powers possess the same property.

$$(P+Q\sqrt{N})^2 = 2P(P+Q\sqrt{N})-1$$
$$(P+Q\sqrt{N})^3 = (4P^2-1)(P+Q\sqrt{N})-2 \qquad\qquad \text{etc.}$$

A Device of Computation

Suppose we have a series of numbers such that

$$u_{x+2} = au_{x+1} + bu_x$$

where a and b are rational. Then

$$E^2 - aE = b$$

$$E = \frac{a}{2} \pm \sqrt{\frac{a^2}{4} + b}$$

$$u_x = C_1\left(\frac{a}{2} + \sqrt{\frac{a^2}{4} + b}\right)^x + C_2\left(\frac{a}{2} - \sqrt{\frac{a^2}{2} + b}\right)^x$$

$$= C_1 b^{\frac{1}{2}x}\left(\frac{a}{2\sqrt{b}} + \sqrt{\frac{a^2}{4b} + 1}\right)^x + C_2 b^{\frac{1}{2}x}\left(\frac{a}{2\sqrt{b}} + \sqrt{\frac{a^2}{4b} + 1}\right)^{-x}$$

If three rational numbers, P, Q, N are such that

$$P^2 - Q^2 N = 1,$$

then $(P + Q\sqrt{N})(P - Q\sqrt{N}) = 1$. For any given P, there is one largest possible Q and corresponding N. We write these Q' and N'. We have two functions of which the cosine and sine are special cases, which we may term the P-clos and P-slin, defined by the formulae,

$$\text{clos}_P x = \frac{(P + Q'\sqrt{N'})^x + (P + Q'\sqrt{N'})^{-x}}{2}$$

$$\text{slin}_P x = \frac{(P + Q'\sqrt{N'})^x - (P + Q'\sqrt{N'})^{-x}}{2\sqrt{N'}}$$

For the cosine and sine P, Q, N are not rational but $P = 1 - \frac{1}{2!} + \frac{1}{4!} +$ etc. $Q = 1 - \frac{1}{3!} + \frac{1}{5!} - \frac{1}{7!} +$ etc. $N = -1$. We shall always have

$$u_x = CR^x \text{Clos}_P \frac{(x - x_0)}{T}$$

For we have $\text{Clos}_P 1 = P$ $\text{Slin}_P 1 = Q'$ $\text{Clos } 0 = 1$ $\text{Slin } 0 = 0$

Now since in general $\dfrac{aA + bB}{2} = \dfrac{a+b}{2} \cdot \dfrac{A+B}{2} + \dfrac{a-b}{2} \cdot \dfrac{A-B}{2}$

$$\text{Clos } (x+y) = \text{Clos } x \cdot \text{Clos } y + N \text{ Slin } x \cdot \text{Slin } y$$
$$\text{Slin } (x+y) = \text{Slin } x \text{ Clos } y + \text{Clos } x \cdot \text{Slin } y$$
$$\text{Clos } (x+2) = P \text{ Clos } (x+1) + NQ' \text{ Slin } (x+1)$$
$$\text{Slin } (x+2) = Q' \text{ Clos } (x+1) + P \text{ Slin } (x+1)$$

D. NOTES OF A COMPUTOR[1] (213)

NO. 1

The first thing the computor must do is to decide upon this system of numerical notation. Now, as to the principle of "places," that a figure put one "place" further is multiplied by an integer, nothing could be more admirable. But the plan of taking for that integer a multiple of five is indisputably barbaric in the extreme, downright troglodytical. For it ought, as its prime requisite, to be an integer by which it is easy directly to divide with extreme precision anything directly measurable with precision, such as an angle and such as a weight. Now everybody knows that an angle cannot generally be geometrically divided by any number except a power of two; and everybody accustomed to weigh with precision knows that the only simple method of dividing a mass of powder by an integer is to put the whole upon one pan of an equal armed balance, and then by successive approximations, transfer such a part of it to the other pan as will balance the remainder. It is true that with a balance one of whose arms was four times the length of the other one could divide a mass of powder by five; but then the only technically precise way of testing such a balance would depend upon the facility with which multiplications and divisions by two can be performed.

The reasons of the economic kind, of which I have, thus far, given but two examples, appear to me to be conclusive; but all that I feel warranted in positively asserting by what has thus far been shown is that they are very strong.

I now come to a reason which ought, I think, to appeal still more strongly to the minds of mathematicians as such. It is founded on the principle that when an idea is introduced into mathematical procedure, it ought to be carried out as far as it will go and not be mixed up with any heterogeneous idea that conflicts with it. I will give an example or two to illus-

[1] *The Century Dictionary* gives this spelling as an alternate for computer.

trate my [meaning]. If, for example, then, there be good reason for counting by tens and powers of ten, I hold it to be bad mathematical procedure to do as the French do and from eighty to [a] hundred to count by twenties, or to do as the English sometimes do, to count by "long hundreds" or by "dozens" and "gross." Such procedures not only offend the esthetic sense of mathematicians but conflict with the character of the procedure which renders mathematics efficient by relieving the mind through the application of uniform general rules, which is the very life-blood of mathematical method. So, to give still another illustration, when it came to be perceived that a "tenth," a "hundredth," etc. are merely powers of ten that have negative exponents, it was a violation of good mathematical method to introduce the decimal point between the place of coefficients of ten to zero power and the places of coefficients of ten to negative powers, although the reason for doing so was *in itself* a good one, that the places to the left of it are places of whole numbers while those to the right are places of fractions. For though that was true enough in itself, it did not harmonize with the more important [design for procedure] and for the purposes of the class of computations that are facilitated by the decimal system, since zero is no more positive than it is negative. Instead of inserting that point, they should have put some mark on the place of the coefficients of ten to the zero power, itself;[2] and thus certain general exceptions for the place of the decimal point became inevitable, such as that 100. is the square of 10. while .001 is *not* the square of .01. The remarkable facility of the differential calculus is due to Leibniz's mind having been eminently one of those to whom such hybrids between different kinds of ideas were offensive.

---

[2] This is precisely what Peirce did at one time in the development of his secundal arithmetic. He used the symbol ⌣, 1 ⌣0⌣, for example, meaning 2; 1 ⌣1⌣ meaning 3.

E. A NEW RULE FOR DIVISION IN ARITHMETIC[1]

The ordinary process of long division is rather difficult, owing to the necessity of guessing at the successive figures which form the divisor. In case the repeating decimal expressing the *exact* quotient is required, the following method will be found convenient.

RULE FOR DIVISION

First, Treat the divisor as follows: —

If its last figure is a 0, strike this off, and treat what is left as the divisor.

If its last figure is a 5, multiply the whole by 2, and treat the product as the divisor.

If its last figure is an even number, multiply the whole by 5, and treat the product as a divisor.

Repeat this treatment until these precepts cease to be applicable. Call the result the *prepared divisor.*

Second, From the prepared divisor cut off the last figure; and, if this be a 9, change it to a 1, or, if it be a 1, change it to a 9: otherwise keep it unchanged. Call this figure the *extraneous multiplier.*

Multiply the extraneous multiplier into the divisor thus truncated, and increase the product by 1, unless the extraneous multiplier be 7, when increase the product by 5. Call the result the *current multiplier.*

Third, Multiply together the extraneous multiplier and all the multipliers used in the process of obtaining the prepared divisor. Use the product to multiply the dividend, calling the result the *prepared dividend.*

Fourth, From the prepared dividend cut off the last figure, multiply this by the current multiplier, and add the product to the truncated

[1] Reprinted from *Science* 2, 46 (Dec. 21, 1883).

dividend. Call the sum the *modified dividend,* and treat this in the same way. Continue this process until a modified dividend is reached which equals the original prepared dividend or some previous modified dividend; so that, were the process continued, the same figures would recur.

Fifth, Consider the series of last figures which have been successively cut off from the prepared dividend and from the modified dividends as constituting a number, the figure first cut off being in the units' place, the next in the tens' place, and so on. Call this the *first infinite number,* because its left-hand portion consists of a series of figures repeating itself indefinitely toward the left. Imagine another infinite number, identical with the first in the repeating part of the latter, but differing from this in that the same series is repeated uninterruptedly and indefinitely toward the right, into the decimal places.

Subtract the first infinite number from the second, and shift the decimal point as many places to the left as there were zeros dropped in the process of obtaining the prepared divisor.

The result is the quotient sought.

Examples

1. The following is taken at random. Divide 1883 by 365.

First, The divisor, since it ends in 5, must be multiplied by 2, giving 730. Dropping the 0, we have 73 for the prepared divisor.

Second, The last figure of the prepared divisor being 3, this is the extraneous multiplier. Multiplying the truncated divisor, 7, by the extraneous multiplier, 3, and adding 1, we have 22 for the current multiplier.

Third, The dividend, 1883, has now to be multiplied by the product of 3, the extraneous multiplier, and 2, the multiplier used in preparing the divisor. The product, 11298, is the prepared dividend.

Fourth, From the prepared dividend, 11298, we cut off the last figure, 8, and multiply this by the current multiplier, 22. The product, 176, is added to the truncated dividend, 1129, and gives 1305 for the first modified divisor. The whole operation is shown thus: —

```
            1 8 8 3
                  6
          ---------
          1 1 2 9|8
            1 7 6
          ---------
          1 3 0|5
          1 1 0
          ---------
          2|4 0

          8 8
          |9 0
        -------
        1 9|8
        1 7 6
        -------
        1 9|5
      1 1 0
      -------
      1 2|9
    1 9 8
    -------
    2|1 0
  2 2
  -------
  2 4
```

We stop at this point because 24 was a previous modified dividend, written under the form 240 above. Our two infinite numbers (which need not in practice be written down) are, with their difference, —

$$10,958,904,058$$
$$10,958,904,109.5890410958904$$
$$51.5890410958904$$

Hence the quotient sought is 5.158904109.

Example 2. Find the reciprocal of 333667.
The whole work is here given: —

```
    3 3 3 6 6|7                                   |7
                                        1 6 3 4 9 6|9
    2 3 3 5 6 7                         2 1 0 2 1 0 3
                                        -------------
                                        2 2 6 5 5 9|9
                                        2 1 0 2 1 0 3
                                        -------------
                                        2 3 2 8 6 6|2
                                        4 6 7 1 3 4
                                        -------------
                                        7 0 0 0 0 0
```

Answer, .000002997.

Example 3. Find the reciprocal of 41.

    Solution. —   4|1 |9
                3 7|9   3 3|$\overline{3}$
                                    1 1 1
                                  1 4|$\overline{4}$
                                  1 4 8
                                  1 6|$\overline{2}$
                                  7 4
Answer, .0̇243̇9.   9̇ 0̇

                                               C. S. Peirce.

F. NOTE ON A SERIES OF NUMBERS (68)

The series herein described appears interesting; but since my regular occupations do not permit me to develop its properties, I note such of them as I have remarked, in hopes that somebody else may be moved to make a systematic inquiry into them.

The series is that whose first two dozen members are
2.3.3.4.5.5.4.5.7.8.7.7.8.7.5.6.9.11.10.11.13.12.9.9
If p be the ordinal place of a number in the series, I will denote the number by Np.

If $p = 2^n + m$, where 2^n is the highest power of 2 which does not exceed p, I will speak of the *reflexion* of p, meaning $Rp = \dfrac{m + \frac{1}{2}}{2^n}$. Then, as long as p is neither a power of two nor one less than such a power, Np is the sum of the two Ns earlier in the series, the reflexions of whose ps are next larger and next smaller than Rp; namely, Np' and Np'', where $Rp' = \dfrac{m}{2^n}$, $Rp'' = \dfrac{m+1}{2^n}$. Thus, suppose $p = 17$, or if ... the figures are to be interpreted as written in the secundal (instead of decimal) notation, $p = 10001$. Then $Rp = .00011$ (the first significant figure being carried to the end and the fractional point inserted where it had been). This lies between $Rp' = .0001$ and $Rp'' = .001$, (which we get by subtracting and adding 1 in the last place.) Hence, $p' = 1000$, $p'' = 100$; (carrying the last unit to where the point has been, this being removed). Now $N1000 = 5$, $N100 = 4$; and accordingly $N10001 = 5 + 4 = 9$. If $p = 18 = 10010$, $Rp = .00101$; $Rp' = .001$, $Rp'' = .0011$; $p' = 100$, $p'' = 1001$. But $N100 = 4$, $N1001 = 7$. Whence $N18 = N10010 = 4 + 7 = 11$.

The definition of the series is completed by adding that $N(2^{n+1} - 1) = N2^n = n + 2$; and in accordance with this, $N0 = 1$.

From this definition it follows that if 2^n be the largest power of 2, not greater than p, then *every rational fraction whose value lies between 0 and 1 is expressed in its lowest terms by* $N(p - 2^m)/Np$, *where there is but one value which p can take to express the given fraction.* This is too obvious to require proof. The sequence of values of the fractions is that of the values of Rp.

An easy way of writing down the series will be to write in the lth line of a first column the number $l + 1$, l varying from 1 toward ∞. Then make a second column beginning with the second line, the number in this second line being the same that is in the same line of the first column; and to get the number to be written in successive lines, add each time the number in the first column that stands on the line unoccupied in this second column. Next, go to the third line; and start two more columns by writing the numbers already in that line in reversed order; and to fill up the columns add for each new figure of the first the number in the last column that stands in the last line unoccupied in this column and in the second of the new columns add always the number in the second column from the last (that is, the first) in this same line. Next form four more columns, beginning in the fourth line and repeating in reverse order the numbers already in that line, to start these new columns. To fill them up, use for the constant difference of the first of them the number in the last column of [the] last line that will remain unoccupied in the new column; for the constant difference of the second column the number in the same line of the second from the last of the completed columns, and so on. Thus we form the following table:

```
2
3. 3
4. 5. 5. 4
5. 7. 8. 7. 7. 8. 7. 5
6. 9.11.10.11.13.12. 9. 9.12. 13.11.10. 11. 9. 6
7.11.14.13.15.18.17.13.14.19. 21.18.17. 19.16.11.11. 16. 19. 17. 18. 21. 19. 14. 13. 17. 18. 15. 13. 14. 11. 7
8.13.17.16.19.23.22.17.19.26. 29.25.24. 27.23.16.17. 25. 30. 27. 29. 34. 31. 23. 22. 29. 31. 26. 23. 25. 20.13.1?
9.15.20.19.23.28.27.21.24.33. 37.32.31. 35.30.21.23. 34. 41. 37. 40. 47. 43. 32. 31. 41. 44. 37. 33. 36. 29.19.2?
10.17.23.22.27.33.32.25.29.40. 45.39.38. 43.37.26.29. 43. 52. 47. 51. 60. 55. 41. 40. 53. 57. 48. 43. 47. 38.25.2?
11.19.26.25.31.38.37.29.34.47. 53.46.45. 51.44.31.35. 52. 63. 57. 62. 73. 67. 50. 49. 65. 70. 59. 53. 58. 47.31.3?
12.21.29.28.35.43.42.33.39.54. 61.53.52. 59.51.36.41. 61. 74. 67. 73. 86. 79. 59. 58. 77. 83. 70. 63. 69. 56.37.4?
13.23.32.31.39.48.47.37.44.61. 69.60.59. 67.58.41.47. 70. 85. 77. 84. 99. 91. 68. 67. 89. 96. 81. 73. 80. 65.43.4?
14.25.35.34.43.53.52.41.49.68. 77.67.66. 75.65.46.53. 79. 96. 87. 95.112.103. 77. 76.101.109. 92. 83. 91. 74.49.5?
15.27.38.37.47.58.57.45.54.75. 85.74.73. 83.72.51.59. 88.107. 97.106.125.115. 86. 85.113.122.103. 93.102. 83.55.6?
16.29.41.40.51.63.62.49.59.82. 93.81.80. 91.79.56.65. 97.118.107.117.138.127. 95. 94.125.135.114.103.113. 92.61.6?
17.31.44.43.55.68.67.53.64.89.101.88.87. 99.86.61.71.106.129.117.128.151.139.104.103.147.148.125.113.124.101.67.7?
18.33.47.46.59.73.72.57.69.96.109.95.94.107.93.66.77.115.140.127.139.164.151.113.112.169.161.136.123.135.110.73.8?
```

I give a considerable number of values, because the inspection of the table will furnish a person with a choice of fractions approximating to any given value. If, however, the value of a single term should be wanted, it may be calculated as follows. First, take the reflexion of p, or R. It is, then, necessary (or desirable) to calculate a certain number MR, being, in fact, the numerator of the fraction of which Np is the denominator. In order to find this, we have the formulæ

$$M(2^m - 1) = m$$
$$M1^u0^z R = [u(z-1)+1] . MR + u.M1^1R$$

Here, 1^u0^zR denotes a number expressed by expressing R in the secundal notation and prefixing (or affixing) z zeros and outside of them u units. It will be convenient to have the lower values of MR before one's eyes, in making the calculation.

R	1	10	11	100	101	110	111	1000	1001	1010	1011	1100	1101	1110	1111
MR	1	1	2	1	3	2	3	1	2	3	5	3	5	3	4

R	10000	10001	10010	10011	10100	10101	10110	10111	11001	11010	11011	11100	11101	11110	11111
MR	1	5	4	7	3	8	5	7	7	5	8	3	7	4	5

Np is the sum of MRp and $M(1 - Rp)$. For example, required the value of $N65594$. This is given on the last line of our table, where its value appears as 203. The calculation proceeds as follows:

$$p = 65594 = 10000000000111010$$
$$Rp = .00000000001110101$$
$$M.00000000001110101 = M\,1110101$$
$$= M \quad\;\; 101 \Big\} = \Big\{ \begin{matrix} 3 \\ 15 \end{matrix}$$
$$+3M \quad 1101 $$
$$= 18$$

```
3. 26. 31.  29. 22. 23. 31. 34. 29. 27. 30. 25. 17. 16. 23. 27. 24. 25. 29. 26. 19. 17. 22. 23. 19. 16. 17. 13. 8
6. 41. 49.  46. 35. 37. 50. 55. 47. 44. 49. 41. 28. 27. 39. 46. 41. 43. 50. 45. 33. 30. 39. 41. 34. 29. 31. 24.15
9. 56. 67.  63. 48. 51. 69. 76. 65. 61. 68. 57. 39. 38. 55. 65. 58. 61. 71. 64. 47. 43. 56. 59. 49. 42. 45. 35.22
2. 71. 85.  80. 61. 65. 88. 97. 83. 78. 87. 73. 50. 49. 71. 84. 75. 79. 92. 83. 61. 56. 73. 77. 64. 55. 59. 46.29
5. 86.103.  97. 74. 79.107.118.101. 95.106. 89. 61. 60. 87.103. 92. 97.113.102. 75. 69. 90. 95. 79. 68. 73. 57.36
8.101. 121. [114]. 87. 94.126.139.119.112.125.105. 72. 71.103.122 109.115.134.121. 89. 82.107.113. 94. 81. 87. 68.43
1.116. 139. 131. 100.108.145.160.137.129.144.121. 83. 82.119.141.126.133.155.140.103. 95.124.131.109. 94.101. 79.50
4.131. 157. 148. 113.122.164.181.155.146.163.137. 94. 93.135.160.143.151.176.159.117.108.141.149.124.107.115. 90.57
7.146. 175. 165. 126.136.183.202.173.163.182.153.105.104.151.179.160.169.197.178.131.121.158.167.139.120.129.101.64
0.161. 193. 182. 139.150.202.223.191.180.201.169.116.115.167.198.177.187.218.197.145.134.175.185.154.133.143.112.71
3.176.[211]. 199. 152.164.221.244.209.197.220.185.127.126.183.217.194.205.239.216.159.147.192.203.169.146.157.123.78
```

$$M.11111111110001011 = M\,11111111110001011$$

$$= \left.\begin{array}{l} 21\,M\,1011 \\ + 10\,M\,11011 \end{array}\right\} = \left\{\begin{array}{l} 105 \\ 80 \end{array}\right.$$

$$= \overline{185}$$

$$Mp = MRp + M(1 - Rp) = 18 + 185 = 203.$$

My attention was first called to these series in an endeavor to make it clear that the conception of quantity, so far as it concerns mathematics, is merely that of serial order. This my pupils seemed to understand in some sort, as far as whole numbers were concerned; yet they could not disabuse themselves of the notion that the arithmetic of fractions assumed some unanalyzable so-much-ness. In order to show them that it was not so, I had to produce a definition of the order of succession of fractions, and demonstrate the arithmetic from that. The arithmetic of whole numbers was already developed. Namely, the system of whole numbers had been defined as a collection of objects, connected by a relation G, such, 1st, that for any integer, x, there was just one integer Gx, which is not x. 2nd, that there [are] never two integers, x and y, such that Gx and Gy are the same; and there is just one integer, 0, such that there is no integer, x, giving $Gx = 0$; and 3rd, that no integer exists which could be supposed nonexistent (whether alone or along with others) and still leave the first and second conditions satisfied. Addition had been defined by the formulæ, $0 + 0 = 0$ and $Gx + y = x + Gy = G(x + y)$. Multiplication had been defined by the formulæ $0 \cdot 0 = 0$ and $(Gx) \cdot y = xy + y$; $x \cdot (Gy) = y + x \cdot y$. I now define rational fractions, as follows:

1st, $\dfrac{M \mid P}{N + Q}$ is intermediate between $\dfrac{M}{N}$ and $\dfrac{P}{Q}$;

2nd, $\dfrac{1}{1} = 1$;

3rd, $\dfrac{x}{z} + \dfrac{y}{z} = \dfrac{x + y}{z}$;

4th, $\dfrac{u}{v} \cdot \dfrac{x}{y} = \dfrac{ux}{vy}$.

Of course, it had to be proved that the last clause was consistent with the arithmetic of integers. From the first clause it followed that $\dfrac{M + M}{N + N}$ equals $\dfrac{M}{N}$ and hence $\dfrac{xM}{xN}$; so that $\dfrac{M}{N} + \dfrac{P}{Q} = \dfrac{MQ + NP}{NQ}$.

Another way of defining the relations of fractions would be as follows: First write

$$\tfrac{0}{1} < \tfrac{1}{1} < \tfrac{2}{1} < \tfrac{3}{1} < \text{ etc.}$$

Now insert the fractions of denominator 2; then those of denominator 3; and generally those of any denominator only after having inserted all those of lower denominator (in the same limits of value). In thus inserting the fractions of any denominator, N, follow this rule:

1st, Do not insert any fraction until all fractions of the same denominator and lower numerators have been inserted.

2nd, Begin at the extreme left of the row and make the insertions in every $(n-1)$th space between a sign and a fraction.

3rd, When a fraction is inserted in a space bounded on the left by a fraction, the sign $=$ is to be inserted to the left of the new fraction; but when the space is bounded on the left by a sign, this sign is to be *repeated* to the right of the new fraction.

Following this rule, I get the following lines, in each of which I put commas to show where the next insertions are to be made:

$\tfrac{0}{1}, <, \tfrac{1}{1}, <, \tfrac{2}{1}, <, \tfrac{3}{1}, <, \tfrac{4}{1}$

$\tfrac{0}{1}=, \tfrac{0}{2}<, \tfrac{1}{2}<, \tfrac{1}{1}=, \tfrac{2}{2}<, \tfrac{3}{2}<, \tfrac{2}{1}=, \tfrac{4}{2}<, \tfrac{5}{2}<, \tfrac{3}{1}$

$\tfrac{0}{1}=\tfrac{0}{3}, =\tfrac{0}{2}<, \tfrac{1}{3}<\tfrac{1}{2}, <\tfrac{2}{3}<, \tfrac{1}{1}=\tfrac{3}{3}, =\tfrac{2}{2}<, \tfrac{4}{3}<\tfrac{3}{2}, \tfrac{5}{3}<, \tfrac{2}{1}$

$\tfrac{0}{1}=\tfrac{0}{3}=, \tfrac{0}{4}=\tfrac{0}{2}<, \tfrac{1}{4}<\tfrac{1}{3}<, \tfrac{1}{2}=\tfrac{2}{4}<, \tfrac{2}{3}<\tfrac{3}{4}<, \tfrac{1}{1}=\tfrac{3}{3}=, \tfrac{4}{4}=\tfrac{2}{2}<, \tfrac{5}{4}<\tfrac{4}{3}<, \tfrac{3}{2}$

$\tfrac{0}{1}=\tfrac{0}{3}=\tfrac{0}{5}, =\tfrac{0}{4}=\tfrac{0}{2}<, \tfrac{1}{5}<\tfrac{1}{4}<\tfrac{1}{3}, <\tfrac{2}{5}<\tfrac{1}{2}=, \tfrac{2}{4}<\tfrac{3}{5}<\tfrac{2}{3}, <\tfrac{3}{4}<\tfrac{4}{5}<, \tfrac{1}{1}=\tfrac{3}{3}=\tfrac{5}{5},$

$\tfrac{0}{1}=\tfrac{0}{3}=\tfrac{0}{5}=, \tfrac{0}{6}=\tfrac{0}{4}=\tfrac{0}{2}<, \tfrac{1}{6}<\tfrac{1}{5}<\tfrac{1}{4}<, \tfrac{1}{3}=\tfrac{2}{6}<\tfrac{2}{5}<, \tfrac{1}{2}=\tfrac{3}{6}=\tfrac{2}{4}<, \tfrac{3}{5}<\tfrac{2}{3}=\tfrac{4}{6}=,$

$\tfrac{0}{1}=\tfrac{0}{3}=\tfrac{0}{5}=\tfrac{0}{7}, =\tfrac{0}{6}=\tfrac{0}{4}=\tfrac{0}{2}<, \tfrac{1}{7}<\tfrac{1}{6}<\tfrac{1}{5}<\tfrac{1}{4}, <\tfrac{2}{7}<\tfrac{1}{3}=\tfrac{2}{6}<, \tfrac{2}{5}<\tfrac{3}{7}<\tfrac{1}{2}=\tfrac{3}{6};$

$\tfrac{0}{1}=\tfrac{0}{3}=\tfrac{0}{5}=\tfrac{0}{7}=, \tfrac{0}{8}=\tfrac{0}{6}=\tfrac{0}{4}=\tfrac{0}{2}<, \tfrac{1}{8}<\tfrac{1}{7}<\tfrac{1}{6}<\tfrac{1}{5}<, \tfrac{1}{4}=\tfrac{2}{8}<\tfrac{2}{7}<\tfrac{1}{3}=, \tfrac{2}{6}<\tfrac{3}{8}<\tfrac{2}{5}$

In concluding I give a single specimen of the formulæ relating to the Ms:

$$N2^n \cdot N(2^m+l) = N(2^n+2^m+l) + N(2^{2m+1}+2^{m+1}-l-1),$$

where $l < 2^m < 2^n$.

G. TEACHING NUMERATION   (part of 179)

It is only of late years that we have been in a condition to appreciate
the tremendous importance of the earliest lessons a child gets in counting.
It had already been recognized that numerals are not learned by children
in the same involuntary way in which they seem to learn the other parts
of speech. They have to be taught numbers; and it is almost indispensable to their future facility with arithmetic that they could be taught in
a scientific manner, so as not to burden their minds with fantastic notions.

It was Napoleon Bonaparte who first remarked the great differences
between men in respect to visualizing imagination. "There are some,"
he said, "who form a picture of everything. These men, no matter what
knowledge, courage, or other fine qualities they may possess, are unfit
to command." I have, for many years, collected data upon this subject.
I find these unfortunates to be extremely numerous, not often of masculine
and analytic intellect, always liable to self-deceptions. Owing to the
metaphorical use by all the world of phrases literally importing vision
to express the action of the imagination, it is easy to overlook the great
differences among mankind in respect to visualization. This test is this:
request the person under examination while he is seated with you quietly
in a well-lighted room to imagine a red vase; then when he has complied
with the request, inquire in precisely what part of the room he saw the
vase. If he does not visualize, he will be unable to answer this question,
if he is trained to accuracy. If he does visualize, he will say, "I saw it
under that chair, near the forward lefthand leg," or will give unhesitatingly
some other answer equally definite. With such a man, imagination almost amounts to hallucination; and intellectual imagination is slow, difficult, and hampered by clothing which it is the very purpose of thought
to strip off.

There is evidence that education does something for the cure of this hallucinatory imagination; at any rate, children are more subject to it than grown persons. Still, we cannot hope by any training totally to extinguish it in those to whom it is natural.

But there are others, who without localizing the objects of their imagination, still cannot think of an abstract number without the accompaniment of colors and of shapes which have no intrinsic connection with the number. These persons get into the habit of thinking of each number in connection with constant fantastic shapes. Galton, in his *Inquiries into Human Faculty* (Macmillan, 1883, ...) has given many examples of this.

If the teacher cannot prevent the formation of associations so unfavorable to arithmetical facility, as in many cases he certainly cannot, he can at least do something to give them the least disadvantageous peculiarities. To this end, it is desirable that children should receive their first lessons in number from an instructor conversant with the dangers of these phantasms.

There can be little harm in the association with a number of the Arabic figure, or figures, which express it. Such an association is, of course, requisite; but it is somewhat disadvantageous to be unable to shake it off. The number which we write as 137 is in the binary system of notation written 10001001. There are probably few persons who will not instinctively think of the former as the real number, and the latter as a mode of expressing it, and who can without difficulty think of 137 as a mode of expression of 10001001. But, for several reasons, it will be best to encourage the association with a number of the Arabic expression of it.

There is no better diagrammatic presentation of a number than a row of dots, all alike. For this reason, the usual abacus with round beads on wires is to be commended. The beads should be spherical, or somewhat flattened, in the direction of the length of the wire, so that their form may attract as little attention as possible. They should all be of one color, so as to avoid insignificant associations of color with number.

We must not fail, in teaching numbers, to show the child, at once, how numbers can serve his immediate wishes. The school-room clock should strike; and he must count the strokes to know when he will be free. He should count all stairs he goes up. In school recess playthings should be counted out to him; and the same number required of him. This is to teach the ethical side of arithmetic.

Many children will learn the names of numbers, and even apply those names pretty accurately, without having the slightest idea of what a number is. This should not discourage the teacher. Such children learn by first acquiring the use of a word, or phrase, and then, long after, getting some glimmer of what it means. If it were not for this, formulas would not have the vogue they have — How many of those who talk of the law of supply and demand have any idea what that law is, further than that it regulates prices by the relation between wants and stocks of goods?

The way to teach a child what numbers mean is to teach him to count. It is by studying the counting process that the philosopher must learn what the essence of number is.

In counting, the child should begin by arranging his pack of cards in regular order, and then laying down a card upon each object of the collection to be counted. In this way, he will count articles of furniture, flower-pots, plates, books etc.

Pay no attention to the ordinary names of numbers above nine. The child will learn those for himself. But in learning arithmetic the strict systematic character of numeration must be made prominent. Therefore, call ten, *onety*; eleven, onety-one; twelve, onety-two; thirteen, onety-three; twenty, twoty, etc. […].

Dear Risteen

The following method of division is good. Required the repeating decimal equal to $\frac{1}{367}$. I open Crelle at 367. Looking down the last column, I find 99 at 97 and $367 \times 297 = 108999$. Then I take 109 as multiplier

$$109 \times 297 = 32373. \text{ Set down 373 and carry 32}$$
$$109 \times 373 = 40657 \text{ and carrying 32 we have } 40689$$
$$109 \times 689 = 75101. \text{ Set down 689 and carry 40}$$

and so proceed, setting down numbers as follows:

```
 59296   13952   43055   40003   44799   15369   40657
43600104531   7085   10355   92323   48396   75101  32[373297]
 65940054495912806539509509536784741144414 1689      373297
```

Having got so far I keep doubling all I have got thus:

```
0108991825613079019073569482288 8 8 2 8 3 3 78746594
0217983651226158038147138964577 6 5 6 6 7|57493188
0435967302452316076294277929155 5 3 1 3 3|5 14986376
0871934604904632152588555858310 6 2 6|7 0 29972752
1743869209809264305177111716621 2 5|3 4 0 59945504
3487738419618528610354223433242 5|0 6 8 1 19891008
6975476839237057220708446866485|0 1 3 6 2 39782016
                               |.0 0 2 7 2 4 79564032
```

This is the decimal reading up from the last line. I prove it by noting that the last half is the arithmetical complement of the first half. It is also useful to check by adding successive numbers thus:

```
00544959128065395095367847411444141689373297
05994550408719346049046321525885558583106267
```

Also by subtracting successive numbers. In both ways we should get another portion of the decimal.

Very truly
C. S. Peirce

Dear Risteen

To extract a root proceed as follows. Required 5th root of 2. It evidently a little exceeds 1.1 for

$(1.1)^5 = 1.61051$

$$
\begin{array}{r}
\underline{2} \\
3.61051 \\
\underline{5} \\
18.05255 \\
0.38949 \\
\hline
18.44204 \\
17.66306 \\
\hline
.7789800 \\
.7065224 \\
\hline
.0724576 \\
.7065224 \\
.0180536 \\
\end{array}
$$

$$
\begin{array}{l}
1.0441 \\
\underline{.10441} \\
1.14851 \quad \ldots \quad \text{2}^{nd}\text{ approximation} \\
1.148698 \quad \ldots \quad \text{true answer}
\end{array}
$$

Yours faithfully
C. S. Peirce

P.S. Take any fraction whose period expressed in decimals has an even number of figures say $\frac{2}{13} = .\dot{1}5384\dot{6}$

$$
\begin{array}{r}
153 \\
\underline{846} \\
999 \\
\end{array}
$$

If a prime is the sum of three squares so is its square

$11 = 1 + 1 + 9$
$121 = 4 + 36 + 81$

APPENDICES

APPENDICES

A. PLAN OF THE PRIMARY ARITHMETIC (180)

I

The first ten numbers and their succession to be taught. (The Arabic figures to be shown but not insisted on.)

Their use in counting.

Exercises in counting objects in the room, with the use of the "Number Cards."

Counting various figures.

II

Higher numeration, with the Arabic figures.

False names to be used first, with a view of keeping irregularities of language in the background till the Arabic system is understood.

Then the usual names to be introduced.

III

Exercises in counting considerable numbers, up to a thousand with rapidity and accuracy.

IV

Counting by tens.

V

Counting by fives.

VI

Counting by twos.

VII

Counting by nines.

VIII

Counting by eights.

IX

Counting by fours.

X

Counting by sixes.

XI

Counting by threes.

XII

Counting by sevens.

In all these lessons the number-cards are to be used at first. Afterwards, coffee beans. The drill is to be carried so far that given any number under ten, the pupil immediately proceeds from that with perfect fluency, adding successive 1s, 2s, 3s, 4s, 5s, 6s, 7s, 8s, 9s, 10s, etc. up to 101. This drill is the foundation of all facility in arithmetic. Competition and prizes.

XIII

Sums in addition of two numbers done in the head, and expressed concretely.

XIV

Adding columns. These are gradually lengthened until fifty figures. Minute attention to all the details of the methods.

XV

Simple subtraction.

XVI

Subtraction taught with the abacus.

XVII

Multiplication.

B. C. S. PEIRCE'S ARITHMETICS (1546)

Conspectus of Copy and Notes 1893 May 21

1. Notes on the teaching as hitherto done.
A. Arithmetics now, or of late, used in American Schools.
  a. Primary Arithmetics.
    (1) Robinson's Progressive Primary A. (1st of a 6-book Series or 2nd of 7 books.)
    (2) Robinson's New Primary A. (1st of a 5-book Series or 2nd of 7 books.)
    (3) Robinson's First Lessons in Mental and Written A. On the Objective Method. (In what series not stated.)
    (4) Ray's New Primary A. (1st of 4-book Series.)
    (5) Greenleaf's First Lessons in Numbers. (1st of 3-book Series.)
    (6) Wentworth's Primary Arithmetic. (1st of 3-book Series.)
    (7) The Franklin Primary Arithmetic. (1st of 3-book Series.)
  β. Intermediate Arithmetics.
    (8) Robinson's Progressive Intellectual, on the Inductive Plan. (2nd of 6-book sequel to (1) or 3rd of 7.)
    (9) Sheldon's Elementary Arithmetic. (1st of 2-book Series.)
    (10) White's New Elementary Arithmetic. (1st of 2-book Series.)
    (11) Ray's New Elementary A. (1st of 2-book Series.)
    (12) Rickoff's First Lessons in A. (1st of 2-book Series.)
    (13) Cruttenden's Objective or Synthetic A. 1869. (1st of 2-book Series.)
    (14) Ray's New Intellectual A. (2nd of 4-book Series.)
    (15) Quackenbos's Elementary A. (2nd of 4-book Series.)
    (16) Robinson's Elements of A. (2nd of 4-book Series.)
    (17) Robinson's Rudiments of Written Arithmetic. (3rd of 6-book Series.)

(18) Robinson's New Rudiments of Arithmetic. (3rd of 5-book Series.)

(19) Franklin Elementary Arithmetic. (2nd of 3-book Series.)

(20) Greenleaf's Brief Course in A. (2nd of 3-book Series.)

(21) Wentworth's Grammar School A. (2nd of 3-book Series.)

(22) Robinson's Junior Class A. (4th of 6-book Series.)

(23) Ray's New Practical A. (3rd of 4-book Series.)

(24) Sanford's Common School A. (3rd of 4-book Series.)

(25) Robinson's New Practical A. (4th of 5-book Series.)

γ. Advanced Arithmetics.

(26) Franklin Higher A. (3rd of 3 books. But probably intended as 3rd of 4.)

(27) Sheldon's Complete A. (2nd of 2-book Series.)

(28) White's Complete A. (2nd of 2-book Series.)

(29) Davies and Peck Complete A. (2nd of 2-book Series.)

(30) Olney's Practical A. (2nd of 2-book Series. Probably originally 2nd of 3 books.)

(31) Rickoff Numbers Applied. A complete Arithmetic. (2nd of 2 books.)

(32) Loomis's Normal A. 1866. (2nd of 2 books.)

(33) Ficklin's National A. (2nd of 2 books.)

(34) Wentworth and Hill Practical A. (3rd of 3-book Series.)

(35) Wentworth and Hill High School A. (Same revised.)

(36) Greenleaf's Complete A. (3rd of 3 books.)

(37) Ray's New Higher A. (4th of 4-book Series.)

(38) Sanford's Analytical A. 1872. (4th of 4-book Series.)

(39) Dean's High School A. 1874.

(40) Mann and Chase. Arithmetic. 1850.

δ. Other books in use in American Schools.

(41) Renck's Practical Examples.

(42) Robinson's Arithmetical Examples.

B. Other Modern Arithmetics.

(43) Brook-Smith's Arithmetic.

(44) Orton's Lightening Calculator.

C. Old Arithmetics, not ancient.

a. In possession of C.S.P.

(45) Cuthbert Tonstall. De Arte Supputandi. 4to Paris 1538. The 3rd or 4th Ed. of this admirable book.

(46) Giovanni Sfortunati. Nuovo Lume. 1544. The book dates from 1490. This author is hardly known to the historians.

(47) Gemma Frisius. Arithmeticæ practicæ methodus, facilis. Paris 1549. Beautiful print. First ed.: 1540.

(48) Orontius Finaeus. De Arithmetica Practica. 4to Paris 1555. The Privilege is dated 1553. The author's preface 1555 January. He died the following October. This is the author's revision of 4 books of his protomathesis published in 1532.

(49) Christopher Clarius. Epitome Arithmeticae Practicae. Corrected by author. Rome. 1585. Not sufficiently known to historians.

(50) Robert Recorde. Grounde of Artes. With Dr. Dee's additions and Mellis's supplement 1668. This celebrated and important book was first published 1543.

(51) T. Hylles. Arte of Vulgar Arithmeticke. 1600. Described by DeMorgan.

(52) Gio. Battista Zuchetta. Prima parte della Arimmetica folio. 1600. Not in DeMorgan (except the name Zuchetta), Peacock, Cantor.

(53) Cataldi. The first two of 4 volumes of "Practica Arithmetica" folio 1602, 1606. The 4th part only is mentioned by De-Morgan. [Moritz] Cantor gives some information. A remarkable work.

(54) Antonio Pace. Scorta de' mercanti. 1628. Totally unknown to historians.

(55) Gio. Giacomo Pierantonio da Cravegna. Diversi Operationi d'aritmetica. 1653. The name "Pierantonio" alone known to DeMorgan.

(56) Cocker's Decimal Arithmetic. Perused, corrected, and published by John Hawkins. 4th Ed. 1713. This is *not* the original and most celebrated Cocker's Arithmetic, but was first published 1685. DeMorgan shows that both books were really written by Hawkins.

β. Not in C.S.P.'s possession.

(57) Leonardo of Pisa. Ed. by Boncompagni.

(58) Jordanus Nemorarius.

(59) Nicholas Oresme.

(60) The Treviso Arithmetic, 1478.

(61) Bamberger Rechenbuch. 1483.

(62) Luca Paciulo. Summa de arithmetica. 1489.

(63) Nicolas Chuquet. Triparty en la science des nombres 1880.

C. ROUGH LIST OF WORKS CONSULTED FOR ARITHMETIC
BY C. S. PEIRCE   (170)

DeMorgan.   Arithmetical Books. London 1847.

Peacock.   Article *Arithmetic* in Encyc. Metropolitana.[1]

Thirion.   Histoire de l'arithmétique. Not dated. 1886?

Cantor.   Geschichte der Mathematik.

Libri.   Histoire des sciences mathématiques.

Gow.   History of Greek Mathematics.

Eisenlohr.   Ein mathematisches Handbuch der alten Aegypter.

Euclid.   Elements Books VII, VIII, IX, X.

Boethius.   Arithmetica. Musica.

Margarita Philosophica.

Tonstall.   De Arte supputandi. (My ed. 1538)

Orontius Finaeus.   De Arithmetica practica. (My 2nd Ed. 1555)

Recorde.   Ground of Artes.

Gemma Frisius.   Arithmeticae Practicae Methodus Facilis. (My ed. 1549)

---

[1]   On another list of Peirce's old arithmetics he writes "Peacock, Geo. Arithmetic, 4ᵗᵒ. A most valuable work and difficult to obtain separate. I was about 5 years hunting for mine. The plate referred to is wanting." Peirce's copy is now in the Houghton Library. The author is identified in Peirce's hand on the title page written in another hand as the "Very Reverend George Peacock, Dean of Ely Cathedral." Under the date "1849" written at the bottom of the page Peirce inserted the observation: "this date, which was in the book when I bought it, indicates that its former possessor was pretty careless about the *history of the history* of arithmetic. For it appeared in 1825 and 1826. See De Morgan's Notes on Arithmetical Books, p. 91. It is a most extraordinary performance, and has marvelously few errors." This Arithmetic by Peacock appeared in the *Encyclopedia Metropolitana* with which Peirce was very familiar. Peirce, himself, planned a scientific dictionary called "Summa Scientiae; or Summary of Human Knowledge" (see 1176). Of the 1500 pages in the projected work, 250 pages were to be distributed in the mathematics section as follows: History (25), Synopsis of Pure Mathematics (100), Tables (25), Rigid Dynamics (25), Hydrodynamics (15), Thermodynamics (10), Kinetical theory of bodies (5), Thermotics, etc. (5), Optics (5), Electricity and Magnetism (10), Mathematical psychics (5), Mathematical economics (5), Probabilities (10), Miscellaneous (5).

Christopher Clavius.   Epitomae Arithmeticae 1585.

Cataldi.   Practica Arithmetica. (I have only the first two volumes of this important work: 1602, 1606.)

Th. Hylles.   Vulgar Arithmeticke 1600.

Giov. Sfortunati.   Nuovo Lume. 1544 (First Ed. 1516?)

Gio. Batt. Zuchetta.   Aritmetica 1600 (I have only 1st vol. 400 page folio.)

Antonio Pace.   Scorta de' Mercanti 1628.

Gio. Giacomo Pierantonio.   Diverse Operationi d'aritmetica 1653.

Hawkins.   Cocker's Arithmetick.

Horace Mann and Pliny E. Chase.   Arithmetic 1850.

W. G. Peck.   Complete Arithmetic (Barnes) 1877.

Ficklin.   National Arithmetic. (Barnes) 1881 (considerable success)

Sanford.   Common School Arithmetic (Lippincott) 1872.

Sanford.   Analytical Arithmetic (Lippincott) 1870.

Orton.   Lightning Calculator 1871. (Many useful dodges)

White, E. E.   New Complete Arithmetic (Van Antwerp Bragg and Co.) 1883.

Cruttenden.   The Objective or Synthetic Arithmetic. 1st Course 1869.

Robinson.   Arithmetical Examples. 1864 (pretty good)

Quackenbos.   Elementary Arithmetic 1863.

Reuck.   Practical Examples in Arithmetic 1854 (poor).

Dean, Philotus.   High School Arithmetic 1874.

Olney.   Practical Arithmetic (Sheldon) 1879.

Wentworth and Hill.   Practical Arithmetic 1881 (The *best.*).

Brook-Smith.   Arithmetic (Macmillan) 6th Ed. 1881.

Rickoff.   Numbers Applied (Appleton) 1886 Good.

Loomis, S. L.   Normal Arithmetic 1858. Some merit. Has an alphabetical index with references to statistical information. But very little of it.

HIGHER ARITHMETIC

Schröder

Gauss.   Disquisitiones arithmeticae

Legendre.   Théorie des nombres

Dirichlet.   Zahlentheorie

CABBALA

Mahan.   Palmond.

WEIGHTS AND MEASURES

Petrie.   Article Weights and Measures in Encyc. Brit.

——.   Inductive Metrology.

Paucton.   Métrologie 1780.

Böckh.   Métrologische Untersuchungen 1838.

Fenner von Fennerberg.   Untersuchungen 1859.

Lepsius.   Die Länenmasse der Alten 1884.

Nissen.   Grieschische und römische Metrologie 1886.

Hultsch.   Grieschische und römische Metrologie 2nd ed.

Aurès.   Métrologie égyptienne 1880.

Brandis.   Das Münz-, Mass- und Gewichtswesen in Vord Crasien 1866.

Queipo.   Systemes métriques. 4 vols.

A book of Ms. copied by me from many books.

Kupfer.   Travaux de la commission russe. 2 vols.

Chisholm.   Weighing and Measuring 1877.

Noel.   Natural Weights and Measures.

Report on Weights and Measures 1857.

Warden of Standards Reports.

Publications of commission internationale.

Petrie.   Pyramids and Temples of Gizeh.

Smyth.   Our inheritance in the Great Pyramid.

Description of the City of Canton.

Barnard.   Metric System.

Scriptons metrologici.

Kelly   Cambist.

Tate.   Cambist Last Ed.

Jackson.   Metrology.

Browne.   Handbook.

Woolhouse.   Money Weights and Measures.

Clarke.   Measures Weights and Money.

Nelkenbreche.   Tasehenbuch.

Base du Système métrique.

Bleibtren.   Handbuch.

Lemale.   Monnaies Poids Mesures.

Zuan Manenti.   Tariffa 1534.

Zuan Mariani.   Tariffa perpetua 1564.

Many private official letters.

D. AXIOMS OF NUMBER (40)

The following is a complete list of the assumptions of arithmetic. They may be considered as constituting a definition of positive, discrete number. From them, every proposition of the theory of numbers may be deduced by formal logic.

I

Whatever is greater than, is other than.

II

"Greater than" is a transitive relative; that is, whatever is greater than something greater than, is greater than.

III

Whatever is greater than a number is a number.

IV

Number is a system of simple quantity; that is to say, every number is related to every other either as greater or less.

V

There is no maximum number; every number is less than a number.

VI

Unity is the minimum number.

VII

Number increases by discrete steps. Whatever is greater than a number is greater than some number without being greater than an intermediate number greater than that.

VIII

Number is singly infinite; that is, any number can be reached by successive minimum steps. More precisely, if every number greater than but not greater than a number greater than another is in any transitive relation to that other, then every number greater than another is in the same transitive relation to that other.

IX

In any counting, every object of the lot counted is counted off by a number.

X

No number, in any counting, counts off anything counted off by any other number in the same counting.

XI

No object in any counting is counted off by any number that counts off any other object in the same counting.

XII

In any counting, every number counting off an object is less than every number that does not count off an object.

XIII

The lot counted being finite, there is a final number in every counting of it.

XIV

In any counting, the final number of the count counts off an object.

XV

In any counting, the final number of the count is greater than any other number that counts off an object.

DEFINITIONS OF ADDITION AND MULTIPLICATION

The sum of two numbers n_1 and n_2 (whether these be the same or different) is the final number of a count of a lot of objects, consisting of two mutually exclusive lots, of countings of which n_1 and n_2 are the final numbers respectively.

The product of a number n_1 by a number m is the final number of a count of a lot of objects that consists of mutually exclusive lots, the final number of a count of each of which being n_1, while the final number of the count of these final numbers, considered as a lot of objects, is m_2.[1]

---

[1] In Peircian representation 3×2 would be given as follows:

$$n_1$$
$$m$$

There are 3 sets of 2 rays each and $m_2 = 6$.

E. PROOF OF THE FUNDAMENTAL PROPOSITION OF ARITHMETIC (47)

The proposition is that the order of sequence in which the things of any collection are counted makes no difference in the result, provided there be any order of counting in which the count can be completed.

I wish to use this language. Suppose there is a class of ordered pairs such that PQ is one of them (QP may, or may not, belong to the class). Then, supposing λ signifies this class of pairs, I say that P is λ of Q and Q is λ'd by P.

Suppose a collection of things, say the As is such that whatever class of ordered pairs λ may signify, the following conclusion shall hold. Namely, if every A is λ of an A, and if no A is λ'd by more than one A, then every A is λ'd by an A. If that necessarily follows, I term the collection of As *finite*. That is the sense in which I use the word *finite*.

I begin with the following lemma. Every collection of things the count of which can be completed by counting them in a suitable order of suc cession is finite. For suppose there be a collection of which this is not true, and call it the As. Then there is some relative, λ, such that while every A is λ of an A, and no two As λ of the same A, there is some A not λ'd by any A. Remove this A which is not λ'd by any A. Then, the same thing will be true. Namely, 1st, every A is still λ of an A, for no A λ'd by an A has been removed; 2nd, no two As are λ of the same A; and third there is an A not λ'd by any A, namely, that A which was λ'd by the removed A, and by no other A. Now if we consider the terminated counting of the collection, and lower by one every cardinal number higher than that which in the counting was called against the removed A, we see that after this A has been removed, the counting of the collection can still be terminated; only it is terminated by a number less by one than before. It follows by a Fermatian inference that if there be a collection not finite the count of which can by a suitable arrangement be terminated by any number n, then the same is true of some collection the count of which can be terminated by any lower number. Then there must be some collection whose count can be terminated by 1 which is not finite. But if this unit, say A, is λ to an A, which can only be itself, it is λ'd by an A; and so it is finite; and thus the original supposition is reduced to absurdity, and the lemma is proved.

The whole difficulty of the main proposition will be found to be contained in this lemma (which another proposed proof virtually takes for granted). For let the As, which have been counted in two ways, be ranged in a row, with the number which was called against each in the first count written above it, and that which was called against it in the second count written below it, and let the terminating number of the second count (if either) be the greatest. Let the cardinal numbers from 1 up to the highest number of the second count be called the as. Then, as they stand written above and below the As, every a is under an a, but no two as are under the same a (for no number occurs twice in the upper line). Consequently, the number of as being finite (since a count of them is terminable), every a is above an a, or in other words every a, including the greatest, is found in the upper line and was used in the first count.

I may mention that I have written off this proof without running over it in my mind; for the principles of logic showed me that a "syllogism of transposed quantity" must be used, and that for that purpose, the lemma was required; and further that this lemma could only be proved by Fermatian inference.[1] Of course, such a proposition has only a logical interest.

---

[1] Recall the Hottentot illustration for DeMorgan's syllogism of transposed quantity. See Volume IV, 3.

F. NOTES ON NUMERICAL NOTATION (52)

All mathematicians are great admirers of what they call "elegance." By this they seem to mean a style of exposition in which, a fertile form of representing certain mathematical objects having been found, all possible use is made of that form before introducing any point foreign to the idea of that one. The quality is not only pleasing but usually facilitates the development of a mathematical subject to a certain point. But pushed too far, its practical inconveniences may become extreme. Thus, no notation for integers could exceed in elegance that by a row of marks equal in their multiplicity to the integer represented; and I suppose the whole Theory of Numbers could be elegantly developed from this germ, in view of the perspicuous forms of representing addition, multiplication, and involution, to which this system naturally lends itself. But however prettily some general propositions might be so demonstrable, such a mode of representation would be the worst conceivable for the computation of individual numbers; and moreover it would only represent a count and not any system of subdivision. The Roman system show[s] about the best accommodation of the method to practical purposes.

For a computor's purposes a very promising idea has been applied to the notation of numbers for over a millenium, although as yet inelegantly, inconsistently, and stupidly. It consists in, firstly, establishing a row of places, in each of which the same numerical character would have a special value. This part of the idea is at least of double the antiquity of the rest, and was, of itself, of incontestable utility; and this utility was immensely augmented by the second part of the idea, which was to endow every place that was next to another on a certain side of it (say, on its left) with the power of making any numerical character standing in it, denote in every case a number greater by one and the same multiplier than it would have denoted had it occupied the other place.

But the awkward stupidity and incapacity for discerning a simple regularity which has been displayed especially by the earlier of modern mathematicians is most striking. Even to this twentieth century men put a point between the places where the base has negative exponents and that where its exponent is zero; as if zero were more positive than negative, instead of marking the place of the zero power itself.

As soon as the waning, as well as the waxing, exponents of the base of numeration come to be employed, it becomes urgent to inquire what number is most suitable to serve as that base. To thoroughly unmathematical minds, to whom alone all questions concerning numeration seem hitherto to have been referred, the question will naturally take the shape, "Into what number of equal parts is it easiest to separate a length of space or time or bending?" And, of course, the answer will be in each case, "Two!"

A person who looks upon numbers as expressions of weighing and measurements, will be in the constant habit of roughly estimating how much labour a given task of weighing or measuring would demand by the number of numerical places that are required to be exact. Therefore, in order to render such estimates as accurate as it is in their nature to be, such a person would prefer not to use as base of numeration a greater number than two. Several analogous advantages would accrue from the use of this same base.

A somewhat different sort of consideration presents itself in a large and varied class of operations of which chemical analysis is an instance. For precise weighings the only instrument ordinarily to be seriously proposed is an equal-armed balance; and expedition is always important, not seldom imperative. Now the most rapid weighing with an equal-armed balance is one with weights each just one half the one last tried, until one has almost reached the limit of accuracy; and even then, so far as time is valued, the method of bisection ought to be continued until the limits of oscillation give the mean inclination of the beam. In every research that is based upon a hope that there are realities that are expressible, to some considerable degree of approximation, at any rate, in terms of general conceptions within the range of human understanding, and that this is true of the particular subject of the inquiry, so that there is some finite chance of a human conjecture's approximating to an expression of an element of the reality, and so being either quite or almost what we call a "*truth*"; what to aim at doing, so as to attain to that approximate truth through the smallest number of guesses, each of which will have to be subjected to a test, which will be more and more laborious as the approximation becomes closer, is at each new testing to bisect the probabilities.

One can see, almost instinctively, that this would be the case; and owing to the complication[s] that arise in considering other modes of partition, I will here drop this consideration, only mentioning that if, every time there were 3 chances of the truth being in one alternative, against two chances in the other, one would by such a mode of partition, in ten repetitions and testings only, on the average, have separated the possibilities into about 733 parts, one would by bisections with the same labour have infallibly separated them in 1024 parts, or a good deal more than half as many again.

I pass over other advantages of two as the base of numeration because I suppose the reader to be already impatient for the examination of its inconveniences. I will, therefore, hasten to that inquiry. Only, for the purposes of that inquiry, a somewhat closer acquaintance with the properties of different bases of numeration must be gained; and the subject is of sufficient importance to warrant our giving as much time and attention to it as may be requisite for forming an intelligent opinion about it.

To begin with, I will give a table of a few of the lowest numbers as they might be represented in the primitive and most elegant system, in the *secundal* numeration (that is, with two as the base of numeration), both graphically and orally and in the decimal system, graphically, in our present oral system, and in a more rational oral system ....

If you were to ask me how many different objects could be distinguished by the answers, yes or no, to twenty questions, I should reply that their possible multitude would be two to the twentieth power. Thereupon, you might very likely ask "How much is 2^{20}?" And if I were to reply, 1048576 you might say "Now I know; before you only replied by telling me that it was the solution of a problem in arithmetic." Yet how can you be said to know the multitude any better when you are told that it is 1048576 than when you are told that it is 2^{20}? Why should $10^6 + 4.10^4 + 8.10^3 + 5.10^2 + 7.10 + 6$ express the essence of the number rather than 2^{20}? One expression is in the decimal system of numeration, the other in the secundal system.

The answer to this question is that the decimal system of expressing multitudes is the system that is familiar to us; and whenever we ask *what* a thing is what we desire is that its relation to familiar ideas should be set forth.

The decimal system of numeration is by far the commonest among all the races of mankind. The reason for this is commonly and doubtless rightly said to be that the fingers are the most convenient instruments for counting and that men have ten fingers. If that be the true explanation, the decimal system is a monument to human stupidity. For in that way, the ten fingers will only count to ten. There are five on each hand. Now if in counting at one we put down, *l*, the little finger of the right hand, at two, *r*, the ring-finger, at three *m*, the middle finger, at four *f*, the fore-finger, at five *t*, the thumb, still of the right hand, at six *L*, the little finger of the left hand, at seven *Ll*, both little fingers (*L* for 6 and *l* for 1), at eight *Lr*, the right little finger for 6 and the left ring-finger for 2, etc., we could count to 35 upon the fingers. This sextal system would have the great advantage that every prime number except 2 and 3 (or as we should express it, except r and m) would use either l or t. Thus every number on division by 5 would leave the same remainder as the sum of the values of its figures. Thus 1000 would appear written (as if an indefinite number of hands were used) as *fmff*. The sum of the figures is 15 or *rm*; and the sum of these again is t.

The remainder after division by 7 (or ll) would be the same as that of the sum of the figures in odd places less those in even places. Thus, in the case of 1000, $m+f = ll$ and $f+f = lr$, $ll - lr = -l$ showing that 1001 is divisible by 7.

The remainder after division by 11 (or lt) would be the same as that of the number resulting from removing any figures of the original number and adding a half of them one place further to the right, or adding their triple two places to the right. Thus 1000, or *fmff*, twice subjected to the former process gives

$$\begin{array}{l} f\,m\,f\,|\,f \\ \underline{\quad r\,l\ \ t} \\ \underline{\ \ r\,r\,|\,m} \\ \underline{\ \ l\ l} \\ \ \ l\,f = 10 \end{array}$$

Subjected to the other process, it gives

$$\begin{array}{l} f\,m\,|\,f\,f \\ \underline{\quad l\,m} \\ \underline{\ m|\,o\,l} \\ \ \ l\ m \\ \overline{\ \ l\,f} - 10 \end{array}$$

Of course, $1000 = 11 \times 90 + 10$.

H. REASONING POWERS OF MEN IN DIFFERENT AGES (1121)

... I should not wonder if the power of thought of the future historian of reasoning were to enable him signally to improve upon my attempt to state the elements of the excellence of a reasoning.

I should not wonder if that same historian were able to begin some estimate of the power of reasoning even of prehistoric man. For my part, I detect only considerable ability in social and even in artistic lines without being able to form any idea of the brightness of his reasonings. His counting in tens, as he seems to have done everywhere, as soon as he had once really grasped the idea of numeration (which clearly implies its endlessness) was certainly a stupidity. For after he had counted up to five on the fingers of one hand, the natural suggestion to a mind not densely stupid would have been to make each finger of the other hand count for six. He would thus have naturally been led to make six, instead of ten, the base of his numeration. It really seems as if the angel who created Man, intended this suggestion, so obtrusive was it. Had six taken the place in numeration that ten has actually taken division by 3 would have been performed as easily as divisions by 5 now are, that is by doubling the number and showing the decimal point one place to the right. Now we naturally, that is, in the absence of any special influence tending to increase the frequency of divisions by any particular number, should have 1013 occasions to divide by 3, for every 642 occasions to divide by 5; so that there would have been a marked superiority of convenience in this respect in a sextal over a decimal system of arithmetic. Moreover, the multiplication table would have been only about one third as hard to learn as it is, since in place of containing 13 easy products (those of which 2 and 5 are factors) and 15 harder products (where only 3, 4, 6, 7, 8, 9 are factors), it would have contained but 7 easy products, and only 3 hard ones (namely, $4 \times 4 = 24$, $4 \times 5 = 32$, and $5 \times 5 = 41$).

Now, it is true that today, this is no advantage at all, since it is a beneficial exercise of children's memories and morals to learn the multiplication-table. But the history of arithmetic shows that multiplication and division were, down to about two centuries ago, regarded by serious men as really serious difficulties; and as long as this was the case the facilitation of these operations would have made a great difference in daily affairs by preventing ordinary people from being victimized by experts in special branches of accounts. It is true that it would have been necessary to write more than five figures for every four that are now written. For example, the number 21, 848,743 which is written with 8 figures would in sextal notation be written 2100543331 in 10 figures. But this doubtful disadvantage in dealings with enormous numbers, — such dealings being usually extremely expensive, since the average cost of avoiding a small proportionate error is inversely proportional to the square of its ratio to the quantity it affects, so that making three more figures right multi-plies the expense by a million, — this disadvantage, I say, if it be at all appreciable, is small compared to a considerable increase in the promp-titude with which a number may be divided by three, since the latter will be a need perhaps of almost every grown person once a week on the average, while the need of dealing with millions occurs to hardly one man in a million in any given week, and that man will be a trained accountant or computer, who will not be conscious of difficulties which would bring the average citizen to a full stop. The choice of the decimal instead of the sextal numeration was therefore, without speaking of its awkward division of the circle, a misfortune from which the race bids fair to suffer to the end of time. Of course, if 2 had been adopted as the base of nu-meration one might have counted on the fingers up to 1023, and there would have been *no* multiplication table, and scarce a possibility of committing any mistake of ciphering. But instead of writing "A.D. 1910 Dec. 31," we should have to write "A.D. 11101110110 Dec. 11111," which would, perhaps, be mincing numbers a little too small. Division by 3 would [be] quite as easy as division by 11 now is. To find the remainder after division by three, count the ones in the 1st, 3rd, 5th, etc. places beginning at the right hand, and from the sum subtract one for every one in the 2nd, 4th, 6th, etc. place; the result will be the place sought. To find the remainder after division by five, add the 1st, 3rd, 5th, etc. pairs of figures, and subtract from them the other pairs. Thus, to find the remainder after dividing 110110 by five, we add 10 and 11, or two and three, and from the sum we subtract 01, or one. The remainder is 4, which is correct since the original number was fifty-four. The remainder after division by seven is obtainable just as, in decimal arithmetic, the remainder after division by 999 might be obtained. Namely, separate the secundal expression of the dividend into periods of three figures each (beginning of course with the coefficients [of the] three lowest powers of two), write these periods under one another as separate numbers; and add them. If the sum exceeds seven treat it in the same way, and the first sum less than seven will be the remainder in question. Take for example as dividend the number of the year above 11101110110. The adoption of decimal numeration was therefore a misfortune and a fault. It is, of course, easy to see how it came about. Before speech was fully developed, while men communicated their thoughts in large part by gestures, but when society had reached the stage when business was conducted, and men, with insufficient speech-facilities, had to show numbers by their fingers, in the absence of any previous understanding, had to give each finger the value of a unit. Then, ten being the number of fingers, necessarily became for the time being the base of numeration. This was the expedient of the moment. By neglect to consider the tremendous problem of the future, it was allowed to grow into a permanent institution; and day by day, year by year, generation by generation, a difficulty of changing it [as] the base grew up until it seems to have become an impossibility. A makeshift expedient, a mere jury-mast, was inconsiderately allowed to stand until it grew into an ineradicable inconvenience. This is what has happened and is still happening. The same thing is still happening to the injury of individuals and of communities continually. It is a defect in man's reasoning instinct which can now only be remedied by some company who by avoiding this fault drives the rest of us to ruin and establishes itself on the ground we are too indolent to retain. It is a lesson in logic that will make the fortune of the community that first corrects it, while it is as certain to destroy us as a stone left to itself is to fall with accelerated speed. We see the error repeated every day in one field or another. Men do not foresee the inevitable future magnitude of problems of small beginnings.

I need not say that the most remarkable relic of the reasoning of prehistoric man is speech. It is curious what difficulties writers have made in accounting for this phenomenon. It is ridiculous to say, as many have said that men have lost the power of originating language. They are, of course, less ready at inventing roots now-a-days, that new roots are so seldom needed than they were when it used to be frequently needful to practise such invention. But in spite of that roots are invented today and so are syntaxes.

To begin my defence of this statement, which has been so often, so flatly and so warmly contradicted in advance of its assertion, by considering the question of roots, I maintain that they are today created and adopted whenever seriously needed, in precisely the same manner that they always were. Namely, two persons fall into a habit of using some articulated sound to express some very [...].

I do not intend to dwell on this subject or any other, except so far as I can make it aid in the briefest possible survey of the reasoning powers of men in different ages. I cannot see that men's present powers are not fully adequate to producing all the languages that exist within the time of Man's existence. Yet it seems to me that Hyatt's hypothesis that the course of the development and decline of the different races of animals parallels that of individual animals, quite independently of any specific evidence in its favor, is an exceedingly plausible one...

I. SECUNDAL COMPUTATION (53)

All people who really *count*, and do not merely recognize the characters of small collections, count by tens. Some of them sometimes reckon, besides, by dozens, by scores, by sixties, etc. But every people that count at all, be they Indo-European, or Shemitic, or Hamitic, or Chinese, or Turanian, or Dravidian, or Malay, or Polynesian, or Australian, or Papuan, or Caucasian, or Basque, or Bantu, or Nubian, or American speakers, chiefly count in tens. It seems as if they must have done so from the time they ceased to be apes. For this system is not only the most universal character of mankind, but it is also the one that is most marked by lack of thought. It is supposed to have grown up from the habit of counting on the fingers. But a person of any intelligence who proposed to count upon his fingers would have seen that it was much better to count by sixes than by tens, not merely because the things one has to count much oftener are grouped in threes or in multiples of threes than in fives or multiples of fives, but also because having counted up to five on fingers of one hand, an intelligent person would have seen that by calling each finger of the other hand a half-dozen, and then each toe of one foot as half a dozen of half dozens, and each toe of the other foot as half a dozen dozens, he would be able by showing only a single finger or toe of any one limb, to reckon up to within one of a gross. Will man never rise above his thralldom to apehood?

Mathematics is not listed, along with music, architecture, and the rest, among the fine arts. Nor ought it to, — since feeling is not what it aims to produce. Yet there is one esthetic quality that all mathematicians unite in extolling, because its beauty is due to its economy. They call it "elegance," meaning that pleasurable quality which results when, driven to use a novel principle, we make that principle do us all of the service that it is naturally adapted to rendering, and so escape resort to a lot of devices unrelated to one another, to further a purpose that one of them, by itself, could more simply accomplish, without any such intermeddling. In short, elegance — mathematical elegance, at any rate, — might be defined as the beauty of full utilization. As such, it belongs to the same general category as the beauty of holiness; that is, it is one of those kinds of beauty that spring from deeper and more vital sources than any need of mere contemplative pleasure. So perhaps, the most elegant woman is not so much the most esthetically adorned as she is that woman who, as long as she must appear in the world, contrives the most successfully so to appear as to command that particular shade of pleasurable regard that a lady of her personal qualities and her standing entitles her to expect.

Let us, however, confine ourselves here to mathematical elegance, and in order to acquaint ourselves with its *issues*, i.e. with the nature of the practical effects that can result from it, let us study it in the simplest of all its applications, which is the application of it to the notation of numbers.

The series of whole numbers, — "*integers*," mathematicians call them, — is endless: a person who really knew how to count at all, whether by keeping tally or otherwise, would never, in doing so, reach a number beyond which he could not count, — unless he fell asleep, or otherwise encountered some obstacle entirely extraneous to the nature of the series of integers itself. Therefore, since nobody can commit to memory the meanings of purely arbitrary characters in any such vast multitude as, say, a million, it follows that, unless one contents oneself with keeping tally, — that is to say, with having a simple figure to mean *one*, with or without a few others to denote, each of them, a collection of a fixed amount, — he will find it utterly impossibly to invent a system of notation adequate to expressing every integer, unless he resorts to some device whereby one or more of his figures shall denote an endless series of different integers, according to the different ways in which it is joined to other signs.

We may be confident, then, that almost as early as civilization anywhere reached the stage at which men dealt accurately with numbers reaching into the millions, they must have made use of the same general principle that we apply in our system of decimal places: I mean the principle of so expressing numbers in writing that, in interpreting what has been written, the only thing that has to be counted is a series whose single members express the *exponents*, or numbers of times in which a *fixed number*, — the so-called *base*, — is to be understood to be multiplied into itself.

The reader ought [to] feel that an apology is due to him for the apparent irrelevancy of introducing any statement about the course of history in discussing the issues of mathematical elegance. For this is a pure question of mathematics; and mathematics has nothing whatever to do with the truth or falsity of any statement of fact. A mathematician may happen to share in the general preference for statements that accord with facts over such as conflict with them; but he will not be a bit the better mathematician on that account. There are two reasons for his being on his guard against too strong a preference of that sort. The stronger of the two is that in more than one way it may lead him into mathematical error, which it is his special business to avoid. The other reason is that the study of mathematics being (as it would seem) the most completely, and (beyond question) the most narrowly, engrossing of all pure scientific pursuits, and at the same time affording far less than any other occupation, — one might almost say none at all, — of training in the ascertainment and estimation of evidences of matters of fact, it results that great mathematicians are found to be, *other things being equal*, inferior to the average of men in judging of the truth in matters of fact. Yet their known profundity leads most men to defer to the judgments of eminent mathematicians more than they would defer to those of other men. This, it is true, is the fault of those who are so deferential, and is no fault of the sincere mathematicians. But it is a second reason why the mathematician should be upon his guard against too passionate a love for truth of fact.

Perhaps the reader is puzzled to know just what is meant by "truth of fact," as distinguished from other truth. There are three "modes" of reality. There is that which really can be or may be, of which the distinguishing mark is that while it either can be in any given way or else can be otherwise, without any third way, but always either in the given way or else not so, yet on the other hand, nothing prevents *both* these things being true; viz: that it can be *so*, and at the same time *can* be otherwise. Thus, I *can* raise my arm, and yet I *can* refrain from raising it. That is the very essence of that which merely *can be*. Contrast this with another "mode" of reality that of the *would be*. It is never true that that which *would be* agreeable at the same time *would be* disagreeable. *Would-bes* differ therein from *can-bes*. Moreover, while I either *can* raise my arm or else *can* go without raising it, it is not necessarily true that a given state of things either *would be* agreeable or *would be* disagreeable; since it might depend upon other circumstances whether it pleased me or not.

J.   TRANSFORMATIONS OF CARDS   (1535)

Let N be the number of cards in the pack. Suppose them numbered from 0 up to $N-1$.

If dealt out into P packs numbered from zero up to $P-1$, and if the cards in each pack are numbered from zero up,

Let n_0 be the original position of a card

$\quad p_0$ be the pack it comes in

$\quad q_0$ be its position in the pack

$\quad n_0 = Pq_0 + p_0 \qquad\qquad p_0 \equiv n_0 \;(\mathrm{mod}\; P)$

or if $R\!\begin{smallmatrix}x\\[-2pt]\\[-6pt]y\end{smallmatrix}$ denotes the remainder after division of x by y.

$Q\dfrac{x}{y}$ the quotient after division of x by y so that

$$x = yQ\frac{x}{y} + R\frac{x}{y}$$

$$R\frac{n_0}{P} = p_0 \qquad\qquad Q\frac{n_0}{P} = q_0$$

$$n_0 = Pq_0 + p_0 \qquad\qquad p_0 \equiv n_0 \;(\mathrm{mod}\; P)$$

Let the packs so laid down be taken up in the order

$$0 \quad L \quad 2L \quad 3L \quad \text{etc. (mod } P)$$

Let the position of a card in the new order be n_1

Then first suppose N divisible by P. There are $\dfrac{N}{P}$ cards in a pile. For the first $\dfrac{N}{P}$ cards $n_0 = Pn_1$

so that for $n_1 = \dfrac{N}{P} - 1 \qquad\qquad n_0 = N - P$

For the next card $n_1 = \dfrac{N}{P} \qquad\qquad n_0 = L$ instead of N

That is the modulus is such that

$$N \equiv L$$

or the modulus is $N-L$ and we have in general

$$n_0 \equiv Pn_1 \ (\mathrm{mod} \ N - L)$$

$$n_0 = R\frac{Pn_1}{N - L}$$

If N is not divisible by P let the maximum number of cards in a pack

be $Q = Q\dfrac{N}{P} + 1$

Take $N' = QP$

n'_1 so that $n_0 = R\dfrac{Pn'_1}{N' - L}$

and imaginary cards may be conceived to be inverted so as to make

$$N' = N \qquad n'_1 = n_1$$

We shall return to this.

Suppose the dealing out and taking up to be repeated then we shall have

$$n_1 = R\frac{P_2 n_2}{N - L_2} \ \text{or rather}$$

$$n_0 = R\frac{PR\dfrac{P_2 n_2}{N - L_2}}{N - L}$$

or $\qquad n_1 \equiv P_2 n_2 \ (\mathrm{mod} \ N - L_2)$

$$Pn_1 \equiv PP_2 n_2 \ (\mathrm{mod} \ N - L_2)$$

K.   [AN ARITHMETIC PROBLEM]   (L 217)

Editor Illustrated American:

Divide any number by 1234. Then, the ultimate sum of digits of the dividend is equal to that of the quotient and remainder.

Thus: 1234) 314159 (254 $2+5+4=11$

             2468 $7+2+3=12$

              6735   23

              6170

              5659

              4936

              723          $3+1+4+1+5+9=23$

The reason is obvious; and the same thing is true of 19 and many other numbers.

Divide any number by 53. Then the ultimate sum of digits of [the] quotient subtracted from the remainder equals that of the dividend.

       53) 1891 (35

          159         $36-35=1$

          301

          265         $1+8+9+1=19$ $1+9=10$ $1+0=1$

          36

                                                        P.

L. LETTER TO E. S. HOLDEN (L 200)
January 1901.

My dear Holden:

I am going to send you the Arithmetic papers I found, although on looking them over I see that the principal piece has not yet turned up. My Arithmetic was to [be] a Two-Book Arithmetic. On the advanced book I had not done much, and very likely the papers I send include all I ever did. But my labor was expended mainly on the primary book. I had a final copy of a great part of it, 50 pages of MS at least (for I find a mem. to the effect that that amount was finished on a certain date). It was all in dialogue between a mother Lydia and two children, Benjamin and Eulalie. An incredible amount of effort had been put upon it. I shall make a new search for it, but not just now, and must eventually find it. All the papers I now send belonging to the primary arithmetic are rejected matter. Nevertheless, they show what I was trying to do, and how I proposed to accomplish it. So you will be able to form a judgment of it.

Counting beans and things is to be practised first up to a thousand.

Addition was taught by teaching children to count up to a hundred or near a hundred by *tens*, by *fives*, by *twos*, by *nines*, by *eights*, by *fours*, by *threes*, by *sevens*, by *sixes*, beginning with any number.

In order to enliven this task, the principal aid was to be a pack of a hundred cards, numbered from 1 up to 100. There might be a zero card beside, but that is not necessary. These cards are to be arranged in regular order from back to face of the pack and then being turned face down are to be dealt out one by one, turning up each one, into N packs.

Then the children are to learn, first, to say off the numbers in each pile forwards and backwards, and then to say at once what is the mth number in the nth pile, and also where is any given number to be found.

This is a long job and requires to be enlivened and varied in every possible way; since it must never disgust the child nor fatigue it.

But when it is once done, the child not only has very little more to learn in addition, but also little to learn in multiplication and has laid a solid foundation for a computer.

If two such packs are taken in regular order as above and one of them is dealt into 3 piles, except the last card which begins a new heap and the first card of the second pack is put where that last would have been placed, — and if then the middle pile is taken up and the first is placed at the back of it and the third at the back of that, — and the pack is dealt anew into 3 piles, except that the last card is made the second of the new heap, and the top one of the other pack put where it would have gone — and this is continued over and over again a hundred times, the result will be that all the cards of the first pack will be in the new heap, in the order shown in column B of Table 1. [See end of letter.]

The arrangement of the pack in the hand will be that of the Ds in Table II.

If a card marked zero is added to the pack in hand and it be cut and dealt out into any number of piles and these be taken up so that if M is the number of piles and the last card is laid on the mth pile, then the first pile to be taken up is the mth and after taking up the nth pile (whatever n may be) the next to take up is the $(n+m)^{th}$ or $(n+m-M)^{th}$. And each pile is to be placed with its face to the back of the pile last taken up. Finally the pack is to be so cut as to bring the zero card to the face of the pack. Then the other pack can be so cut that if in either pack the pth card has the value q, in the other pack the qth card will have the value p.

It follows that the arrangement can be used as an aid in multiplication. For taking out the Ds corresponding to the two quantities to be multiplied considered as Cs and adding (neglecting the hundreds place) and taking the B of the sum regarded as an A, this B will give the product when the appropriate multiple of 101 is added to it. For example:

Find 2 × 3   Find 5 × 7   Find 2 × 6   Find 11 × 12
C   D   C   D   C   D   C   D
2   80   5   47   2   80   11   28
3   52   7   12   6   81   12   10
A = $\overline{32}$ B = 6   A = $\overline{59}$ B = 35   A = $\overline{61}$ B = 12   A = $\overline{38}$ B = 31
Answer 6   Answer 35   Answer 12   But the last fig-
                                       ures of 11 and 12
                                       show that
                                       product ends
                                       in   2
                                       Hence add $\overline{101}$
                                       Answer: $\overline{132}$

Find 98 × 99   Find 7 × 49   Find 365 × 24
                                                     303

C   D   C   D   C   D
98   2   7   12   62   16
99   30   49   73   24   39
A = $\overline{32}$ B = 6   A = $\overline{85}$ B = 40   A = $\overline{55}$ B
But 98 × 99   Product ends in   3   74
ends in   2   Add   303   404
                 $\overline{606}$ Answer: $\overline{343}$ $\overline{101}$
And since $\overline{612}$ 62 × 24   1488
nearly 10000   909   303 × 24   7272
Answer: $\overline{9702}$ Answer: $\overline{8760}$

Find 49×49		Find 7×2401	
C	D	C	D
49	73	7	12
49	73	$2401 = 78$	95
$A = \overline{46}$ B $= 78$		$A = \overline{7}$ B $= 41$	
Product ends in 1			606
Add	303	But 0 in	$\overline{647}$
	$\overline{381}$	10s place $\therefore$	1616
But near 2500	202	Answer	$\overline{16807}$
Answer:	$\overline{2401}$		

Many other things can be done with the pack calculated to stimulate the children to cipher. The book *must* be made positively agreeable to them.

The greatest pains to be taken with all minutiae as the papers herewith indicate.

There are a vast number of little dodges for the advanced arithmetic. For example required $\sqrt[5]{2}$. Here is how I do it. $u_{n+5} = u_n + 5u_{n+1} + 10u_{n+2} + 10u_{n+3} + 5u_{n+4}$

$$
\begin{array}{l}
0 \\
0 \\
0 \\
0 \\
1 \\
5 \\
35 \\
235 \\
1580 \\
10626 \\
71460 \\
480570 \\
3231845
\end{array}
$$

$\sqrt[5]{2}$ is about $1\dfrac{71460}{480570} = 1.14869842$

$\sqrt[5]{2}$ is about $1\dfrac{480570}{323845} = 1.14869835$

Numbers can by themselves express nothing but serial order. Hence it must be possible to arrange the rational fractions in their order of values without doing more than count the places. The rule is as follows:

1st Write

$$\tfrac{0}{1} < \tfrac{1}{1} < \tfrac{2}{1} < \tfrac{3}{1} < \tfrac{4}{1} < \text{etc.}$$

and $\quad \tfrac{1}{0} > \tfrac{1}{1} > \tfrac{1}{2} > \tfrac{1}{3} > \tfrac{1}{4} > \text{etc.}$

2nd Having written all the fractions of $\left\{\begin{array}{l}\text{denominators}\\\text{numerators}\end{array}\right\}$ less than N with a sign between each successive two, start from just before the fraction with $\left\{\begin{array}{l}\text{numerator}\\\text{denominator}\end{array}\right\}$ zero and mark every $(N-1)$th interval between a fraction and a sign.

3rd Insert the fractions of $\left\{\begin{array}{l}\text{denominator}\\\text{numerator}\end{array}\right\}$ N in those places putting after each fraction the same sign that immediately precedes it, if it is a sign that immediately precedes it. But if it immediately follows a fraction write $=$ immediately before it. Thus:

Mark every place

$$\tfrac{0}{1}| < |\tfrac{1}{1}| < |\tfrac{2}{1}| < |\tfrac{3}{1}| < |\tfrac{4}{1}|$$

$$\tfrac{1}{0}| > |\tfrac{1}{1}| > |\tfrac{1}{2}| > |\tfrac{1}{3}| > |\tfrac{1}{4}| > |\tfrac{1}{5}|$$

Insert the 2s thus

$$\tfrac{0}{1} = \tfrac{0}{2} < \tfrac{1}{2} < \tfrac{1}{1} = \tfrac{2}{2} < \tfrac{3}{2} < \tfrac{2}{1} = \tfrac{4}{2} < \tfrac{5}{2} < \tfrac{3}{1} = \tfrac{6}{2} < \tfrac{7}{2} < \tfrac{4}{1}$$

$$\tfrac{1}{0} = \tfrac{2}{0} > \tfrac{2}{1} > \tfrac{1}{1} = \tfrac{2}{2} > \tfrac{2}{3} > \tfrac{1}{2} = \tfrac{2}{4} > \tfrac{2}{5} > \tfrac{1}{3} = \tfrac{2}{6} > \tfrac{2}{7} > \tfrac{1}{4} = \tfrac{2}{8} > \tfrac{2}{9}$$

Mark every 2nd place

$$\tfrac{0}{1} = |\tfrac{0}{2}| < |\tfrac{1}{2}| < |\tfrac{1}{1} = |\tfrac{2}{2}| < |\tfrac{3}{2}| < |\tfrac{2}{1} = |\tfrac{4}{2}| < |\tfrac{5}{2}| < |\tfrac{3}{1} = |\tfrac{6}{2}| < |\tfrac{7}{2}| < |$$

$$\tfrac{1}{0} = |\tfrac{2}{0}| > |\tfrac{2}{1}| > |\tfrac{1}{1} = |\tfrac{2}{2}| > |\tfrac{2}{3}| > |\tfrac{1}{2} = |\tfrac{2}{4}| > |\tfrac{2}{5}| > |\tfrac{1}{3} = |\tfrac{2}{6}| > |\tfrac{2}{7}| > |$$

Insert the 3s thus:

$$\tfrac{0}{1} = \tfrac{0}{3} = \tfrac{0}{2} < \tfrac{1}{3} < \tfrac{1}{2} < \tfrac{2}{3} < \tfrac{1}{1} = \tfrac{3}{3} = \tfrac{2}{2} < \tfrac{4}{3} < \tfrac{3}{2} < \tfrac{5}{3} < \tfrac{2}{1} = \tfrac{6}{3} = \tfrac{4}{2} < \tfrac{7}{3} < \tfrac{5}{2} < \tfrac{8}{3} <$$

Mark every 3rd place thus

$$\tfrac{0}{1} = \tfrac{0}{3}| = \tfrac{0}{2} < |\tfrac{1}{3} < \tfrac{1}{2}| < \tfrac{2}{3} < |\tfrac{1}{1} = \tfrac{3}{3}| = \tfrac{2}{2} < |\tfrac{4}{3} < \tfrac{3}{2}| < \tfrac{5}{3} < |\tfrac{2}{1} = \tfrac{6}{3}| = \tfrac{4}{2} < |\tfrac{7}{3} < \tfrac{5}{2}| < |$$

Insert the 4s thus:

$$\tfrac{0}{1} = \tfrac{0}{3} = \tfrac{0}{4} = \tfrac{0}{2} < \tfrac{1}{4} < \tfrac{1}{3} < \tfrac{1}{2} = \tfrac{2}{4} < \tfrac{2}{3} < \tfrac{3}{4} < \tfrac{1}{1} = \tfrac{3}{3} = \tfrac{4}{4} = \tfrac{2}{2} < \tfrac{5}{4} < \tfrac{4}{3} < \tfrac{3}{2} = \tfrac{6}{4} < \tfrac{5}{3} < \tfrac{7}{4} <$$

Mark every 4th place

$$\tfrac{0}{1} = \tfrac{0}{3} = |\tfrac{0}{4} = \tfrac{0}{2} < |\tfrac{1}{4} < \tfrac{1}{3} < |\tfrac{1}{2} = \tfrac{2}{4} < |\tfrac{2}{3} < \tfrac{3}{4} < |\tfrac{1}{1} = \tfrac{3}{3} = |\tfrac{4}{4} = \tfrac{2}{2} < |\tfrac{5}{4} < \tfrac{4}{3} < |\tfrac{3}{2} = \tfrac{6}{4} < |\tfrac{5}{3}$$

Insert the 5s thus

$$\tfrac{0}{1} = \tfrac{0}{3} = \tfrac{0}{5} = \tfrac{0}{4} = \tfrac{0}{2} < \tfrac{1}{5} < \tfrac{1}{4} < \tfrac{1}{3} < \tfrac{2}{5} < \tfrac{1}{2} = \tfrac{2}{4} < \tfrac{3}{5} < \tfrac{2}{3} < \tfrac{3}{4} < \tfrac{4}{5} < \tfrac{1}{1} = \tfrac{3}{3} = \tfrac{5}{5} = \tfrac{4}{4} =$$

$$\tfrac{2}{2} < \tfrac{6}{5} < \tfrac{5}{4}$$

Mark every 5th place

$$\tfrac{0}{1} = \tfrac{0}{3} = \tfrac{0}{5}| = \tfrac{0}{4} = \tfrac{0}{2} < |\tfrac{1}{5} < \tfrac{1}{4} < \tfrac{1}{3}| < \tfrac{2}{5} < \tfrac{1}{2} = |\tfrac{2}{4} < \tfrac{3}{5} < \tfrac{2}{3}| < \tfrac{3}{4} < \tfrac{4}{5} < |\tfrac{1}{1} = \tfrac{3}{3} = \tfrac{5}{5}|$$

$$= \tfrac{4}{4} = \tfrac{2}{2} < |\tfrac{6}{5} < \tfrac{5}{4}$$

Insert the 6s thus

$$\tfrac{0}{1} = \tfrac{0}{3} = \tfrac{0}{5} = \tfrac{0}{6} = \tfrac{0}{4} = \tfrac{0}{2} < \tfrac{1}{6} < \tfrac{1}{5} < \tfrac{1}{4} < \tfrac{1}{3} = \tfrac{2}{6} < \tfrac{2}{5} < \tfrac{1}{2} = \tfrac{3}{6} = \tfrac{2}{4} < \tfrac{3}{5} < \tfrac{2}{3} = \tfrac{4}{6} < \tfrac{3}{4} < \tfrac{4}{5} <$$

$$\tfrac{5}{6} < \tfrac{1}{1} = \tfrac{3}{3} = \tfrac{5}{5} = \tfrac{6}{6} = \tfrac{4}{4}$$

We see that owing to the great number of signs of equality near fractions of low denomination the values of rational fractions are thinly scattered in those neighborhoods.

A practical rule about fractional values suggested by the above is that the fraction $\dfrac{A+B}{C+D}$ is always intermediate in value between $\dfrac{A}{C}$ and $\dfrac{B}{D}$.

In fact, from this the whole theory of rational numbers can be deduced. To begin with, since $\dfrac{A+A}{C+C}$ is intermediate between $\dfrac{A}{C}$ and $\dfrac{A}{C}$ it is equal to them.

Which is the greatest $\dfrac{27}{109}$ or $\dfrac{28}{113}$? We have the sequence

$$\frac{27}{109} \quad \frac{28}{113} \quad \frac{1}{4}$$

But $\frac{1}{4} = \frac{28}{112}$. Hence we have the sequence

$$\frac{0}{1} \quad \frac{28}{113} \quad \frac{1}{4} = \frac{28}{112}$$

$$\therefore \frac{27}{109} < \frac{28}{113}$$

Very faithfully
C. S. Peirce

I have made a glowing eulogium of your classic little Life of Herschel, if the Post will only print it.

Table 1

A	B	A	B	A	B	A	B	A	B	A	B	A	B	A	B	A	B	A	B
		61	12	71	73	81	99	91	72	1	34	11	89	21	28	31	2	41	29
52	100	62	36	72	17	82	95	92	14	2	1	12	65	22	84	32	6	42	87
53	98	63	7	73	51	53	83	93	42	3	3	13	94	23	50	33	18	43	59
54	92	64	21	74	52	84	47	94	25	4	9	14	80	24	49	34	54	44	76
55	74	65	63	75	55	85	40	95	75	5	27	15	38	25	46	35	61	45	26
56	20	66	88	76	64	86	19	96	23	6	81	16	13	26	37	36	82	46	78
57	60	67	62	77	91	87	57	97	69	7	41	17	39	27	10	37	44	47	32
58	79	68	85	78	71	88	70	98	5	8	22	18	16	28	30	38	31	48	96
59	35	69	53	79	11	89	8	99	15	9	66	19	48	29	90	39	93	49	86
60	4	70	58	80	33	90	24	0	45	10	97	20	43	30	68	40	77	50	56
																		51	67

Table 2

C	D	C	D	C	D	C	D	C	D	C	D	C	D	C	D	C	D	C	D
1	51	11	28	21	13	31	87	41	56	51	22	61	84	71	27	81	53	91	26
2	80	12	10	22	57	32	96	42	42	52	23	62	16	72	40	82	85	92	3
3	52	13	65	23	45	33	29	43	69	53	18	63	14	73	20	83	32	93	88
4	9	14	41	24	39	34	50	44	86	54	83	64	25	74	4	84	71	94	62
5	47	15	48	25	43	35	8	45	49	55	24	65	61	75	44	85	17	95	31
6	81	16	67	26	94	36	11	46	74	56	99	66	58	76	93	86	98	96	97
7	12	17	21	27	54	37	75	47	33	57	36	67	100	77	89	87	91	97	59
8	38	18	82	28	70	38	64	48	68	58	19	68	79	78	95	88	15	98	2
9	53	19	35	29	90	39	66	49	73	59	92	69	46	79	7	89	60	99	30
10	76	20	5	30	77	40	34	50	72	60	6	70	37	80	63	90	78	100	1

M. "MAGIC SQUARES" FROM INTERLEAF OF THE CENTURY DICTIONARY[1]

1	15	12	6
8	10	13	3
14	4	7	9
11	5	2	16

1	12	15	6
8	13	10	3
14	7	4	9
11	2	5	16

A better even-numbered Magic Square

$a+e$	$b+f$	$c+g$	$d+h$
$d+g$	$c+h$	$b+e$	$a+f$
$b+h$	$a+g$	$d+f$	$c+e$
$c+f$	$d+e$	$a+h$	$b+g$

Let a, b, c, and d be 0, 4, 8, 12

Let e, f, g, h be 1, 2, 3, 4.

We thus got 576 magic squares, which number is doubled by turning over an axis.

If we take $a+b = c+d = 12$

$$e+g = f+h = 5$$

we get a square with many interesting properties

1	14	8	11
12	7	13	2
15	4	10	5
6	9	3	16

---

[1] Peirce's copy of the interleaved *Century Dictionary*, which was sent to him for his corrections and commentary before final publication in 1889, is to be found in the Charles S. Peirce Manuscript Collection at Houghton Library.

The sum of any four numbers in one line, or in one quarter of the square, or at the corners of a parallelogram concentric with the square equals 34.

1	16	11	6
13	4	7	10
8	9	14	3
12	5	2	15

N. "MATHEMATICS" FROM INTERLEAF OF THE CENTURY DICTIONARY

The traditional definition of mathematics as the science of quantity was put forth and adopted at a time when three words had utterly different meanings from those they now bear. These three words are *mathematics, science,* and *quantity*. By *mathematics* was then meant what were called Geometry, Arithmetic, Astronomy, and Music. The geometry meant metrical geometry. The arithmetic excluded what we now so call (then called *logistic*) and was a wordy business since well forgotten. The astronomy assumed the Ptolemaic system and sought only to correct the periods. The music related to tones given by strings of different length etc. These four branches related to measures, or ratios, and what was then meant by mathematics was supposed to give a comprehension of ratios. The real nature of mathematics has only come to be understood by mathematicians during the last half century. B. Peirce in 1870 first gave the definition now substantially approved by all competent persons. Mathematics is the science which draws necessary conclusions. There is no other necessary inference than mathematical inference. Some (as Dedekind) make mathematics a branch of logic. But mathematics is synthetic of inferences, logic analytic.

Mathematics may be divided according to the degree of complexity of its hypotheses. (No more natural division has hitherto been clearly made out.)

Mathematics of logic (two grades of value only: truth and falsehood)

Mathematics of finite collections

Mathematics of integers (theory of numbers)

Mathematics of irrational quantity (theory of functions)

Higher quite undeveloped forms of mathematics

Mathematics of continuity (topology or geometrical topic or topical geometry).

INDEX OF NAMES

INDEX OF SUBJECTS